The Canterbury Papers

THE CANTERBURY PAPERS
Essays on Religion and Society

Edited by Dan Cohn-Sherbok

Bellew Publishing
London
1990

First published in Great Britain in 1990 by
Bellew Publishing Company Limited
7 Southampton Place, London WC1A 2DR

Copyright © The Centre for the Study of Religion and Society 1990

British Library Cataloguing in Publication Data
The Canterbury papers.
  1. Religion. Social aspects
  I. Cohn – Sherbok, Dan
  291.17

  ISBN 0 947792 44 9 (cased)
  ISBN 0 947792 49 X (limp)

Phototypeset by Input Typesetting Ltd, London
Printed by Billings & Sons Ltd

For Victor de Waal who inspired the project.

Acknowledgements

I would like to thank the Centre for the Study of Religion and Society at the University of Kent at Canterbury for giving permission for the contributions to The Pamphlet Library to be brought together in this volume. Thanks are due as well to the individual contributors.

'Old Laws and New Religions' by Brian Wilson was first published in German in J Neumann and M Fischer (eds) *Toleranz und Repression: Zur Lage religiöser Minderheiten in modernen Gesellschaft* (Frankfurt am Main: Campus Verlag, 1987), reproduced here in English with the Publisher's permission.

Contents

Foreword

Throughout the world Canterbury is known as a place of Christian pilgrimage. From the time of Thomas à Becket the devout have followed the steps of Chaucer's pilgrims to this seat of Christendom. Yet what is little recognized is that Canterbury has recently become a focus of theological reflection about religion and society. In this medieval city scholars, clergy, and townspeople gather together to explore the interconnections between religious faith and social institutions and structures.

Through the initiative of the University of Kent at Canterbury and the Dean and Chapter of Canterbury Cathedral, a Centre for the Study of Religion and Society was established in the city in 1978. In the years that have passed since its foundation, the Centre has engaged in two major spheres of activity. First, it has held lectures at the University where distinguished scholars have presented original studies in their respective disciplines. In a small setting the audience – composed of teachers at the University, students, and members of the local community – have engaged in a common quest for understanding.

Second, the Centre has published these lectures as individual pamphlets. This series, known as 'The Pamphlet Library' has attracted widespread acclaim in the United Kingdom and beyond. For example, in reviewing the series, Professor Anthony Dyson of Manchester University has praised the educational character of the various contributions. 'These are learned and lively pamphlets by specialists,' he writes, 'successfully introducing key subjects. They are particularly recommended for students and as discussion group material.' Again, Professor Stewart Sutherland of Kings College, London, has emphasized the importance of this new venture: 'Religion and society are interwoven; a series of pamphlets to explore specific aspects of this is very welcome indeed. The quality of pamphlets already published gives every encouragement for the future of the series.'

The contributors to this series have been carefully chosen: they are all leading experts in their various fields, and each study is an original contribution breaking new ground. Taken together The Pamphlet Library constitutes a new development in the exploration of religion in the modern world. Filled with illuminating insights over a wide range of subjects, it constitutes an excellent introduction to the study of modern religion and contemporary society.

This book brings together the studies that have appeared in this series. As such, we hope it will give rise to the sort of lively discussions that have taken place in Canterbury. Each of the contributors advances views familiar within his or her own field. The level of the argument is pitched quite high, but in no case does it presuppose specialist knowledge of the disciplines concerned. The interested reader should be able not only to keep up with the discussion, but also to join in.

The Canterbury Papers are intended as much for teaching purposes as for general reading. They ask fundamental questions about a variety of important topics: religion and the media, Marxism and liberal theology, the Church and social problems, Christianity and religious pluralism, liberation theology and Utopia, the new religious movements, religion and political conflict. Christianity in communist countries, the concept of sanctuary, and faith after the Holocaust. Throughout the authors pose bold and challenging solutions. Only in a place like Canterbury, where the University and Cathedral support one another, could such a project of exploration have taken place. It is hoped that teachers, students and general readers elsewhere will find the essays presented in this volume as stimulating as they were when they were originally delivered.

Dan Cohn-Sherbok
Director of the Centre for
the Study of Religion and Society
University of Kent at Canterbury, 1990

Chapter 1
Religious Broadcasting Today
Robert Runcie

Archbishops of Canterbury have been involved with broadcasting since its early days. There was a famous occasion in 1923 when John Reith invited Archbishop Randall Davidson and his wife to dinner. Seeking to convince the Archbishop of the power of radio, Reith succeeded in surreptitiously switching on the wireless while they ate, and the Davidsons were amazed to hear the music of Schubert suddenly burst forth. Davidson was indeed impressed, and Mrs Davidson is said to have asked whether the windows had to be left open so the waves could reach the set.

My own interest in religious broadcasting also goes back a long time: I was for six years Chairman of the Central Religious Advisory Committee which, on behalf of the churches advises the BBC and IBA on their religious output. Today, however, I cannot claim much expertise, since one of the sadnesses of being an Archbishop is that other demands cut down the amount of time I have either to listen or to view. So I write today less as a specialist than as somebody following a dictum of Clive James that, although only a few may write it down, we are all TV and radio critics.

What I should like to do is to start by looking at some general questions concerning the presentation of religion in the media.

Knowing that the leading authority on the history of broadcasting religion, Dr Kenneth Wolfe, is one of the contributors to this volume, I will avoid trying to offer an historical analysis. But one point that must strike anybody looking back is the high significance attached to such broadcasting in the early days, and the enormous expectations it aroused. Although it was but a tiny proportion of the BBC's total output, Reith commented in 1930, 'I have been more anxious about the general religious policy of the BBC in matters great and small than about anything else.'

Broadcasters have a far wider audience than any parish clergyman, and have opportunities for communication that he can only dream about. Nonetheless, I want to take as a starting-point the clear but often forgotten fact that the rise of religious broadcasting in this country has coincided with a decline in church attendance, in the numbers holding basic Christian beliefs and in the influence of organized religion. So the question to ask is, 'What are the challenges which face those who work in religious broadcasting?' In large measure they are inherent in the nature of broadcasting and religion.

The debate about how far mass communication affects people's beliefs and actions, both consciously and unconsciously, is long-established and, I suspect, inconclusive. The questions arise most sharply in the area of violence on television, but they apply far more widely as well.

At one end of the spectrum are views which so emphasize the manipulative force of mass communication as to place it in an almost unique position as a determinant of human thought and action. I would wish to be sceptical about such thinking on the basis both of theological principle and personal observation. Indeed I understand that some research indicates that, on the contrary, people only receive what they want to receive, what builds on existing values. Experience suggests that we screen out or flatly reject contradictory ideas.

However, can we really say that 'mass communication is unpersuasive?' The entire independent broadcasting system, in this country and world-wide, survives solely on advertising revenue, because it offers a persuasive medium. Bob Geldof says he was converted to the plight of starving Ethiopians by BBC's 9 O'Clock News.

I personally suspect that the impact of what is broadcast operates most enduringly on what I would call a person's world-view. By this I mean that part-expressed, part-assumed collection of opinions, observations, axioms and question-marks by which we all try to make sense of the reality that confronts us.

Let me quote a very personal example. My postbag testifies to the fact that many who write to me already have a clear picture of what they expect from this Archbishop and, usually, of where he is going wrong. Very often this is based on what they have gleaned from the broadcasting media, which has given world coverage to certain dominant images: the pictures of me officiating at the Royal Wedding, of me embracing the Pope, and of me battling with Mrs Thatcher. Descartes said '*Cogito ergo sum*' and a cynic suggested that this should now be replaced by 'I appear on television therefore I am'. Perhaps that goes too far, but we might say, 'what appears on television is what matters about me'.

But I don't just mean what has been broadcast by or about me directly. I think every reference, from discussions in soap operas to caricatures in *Spitting Image*, plays its part in building up an artificial memory – a collection of events and experiences which never actually happened directly to the viewer or listener, but which he shared in vicariously, and can recall because they appeared in the broadcast media.

Naturally, I think especially here about television because images undoubtedly have a potency to act on more than just the rational level. In all broadcasting, there is a plethora of decisions to be made about what material to select and how to present it, and all those decisions play their part in influencing the message that is received and incorporated into a person's world-view. So we need to ask what message is conveyed in this way about the place of religion and its values.

Broadcasting has a vast and undifferentiated audience. So the broadcaster's first aim must naturally be to catch our interest and hold it. This inevitably puts a premium on certain aspects of human experience which do this most successfully, and they are not necessarily aspects which are most applicable or helpful to religion.

Television, for example, needs pictures, and preferably pictures which catch attention. Furthermore, television and radio both need a certain flow of words and images. Programmes must move on to some concluding point. Radio is a marvellous medium for many things but not for silence. And yet at the heart of religious experience silence is very often the moment of revelation. Such experiences are private, profound and without words – they do not make easy broadcasting.

By its very nature, broadcasting must be interested in movement, excitement, tension and drama; the instant response and the immediate comment. Dr Colin Morris has commented that 'we often know when television is showing us real life because nothing much is happening.' Yet the Church's ministry at its best is grounded in 'real life' – it depends on constant, patient, unpublicized pastoral care and support. No news or current events programme can measure the amount of such care, but we must question any judgement on the Church which does not reflect it. When we come to drama or fantasy this applies even more strongly, and Simone Weil hit the point precisely when she said:

'Nothing is so beautiful, nothing is so continually fresh and surprising. . . . as the good; no desert is so dreary, monotonous and boring as evil. But with fantasy, it is the other way round. Fictional good is boring and flat, while fictional evil is varied, intriguing, attractive and full of charm.'

Broadcasting also thrives on conflict and contradiction. A deferential 'what do you think about this, Archbishop' is less striking than 'I think the Archbishop is talking nonsense' – especially if the latter is said by a clergyman. The effect of this is to place the emphasis on competing opinions, with a strong hint that the only values that really matter are tolerance and open-mindedness, and that truth is not to be found in one opinion rather than another. This can be a challenge to religious bigotry and closed-mindedness but it can also work against any suggestion that there might be *one* approach to truth to which a viewer or listener might commit his life. Information and images flow with such relentless rapidity that the viewer turns voyeur – suspending judgement on the significance of all he sees.

Kierkegaard has a story which illustrates this well. He tells of a circus owner. On one occasion the circus caught fire and the proprietor alerted one of his staff to go into the centre of the ring and tell the audience to move. So the man went into the arena and did this. But nobody moved. He went back to the proprietor and said, 'I have given them the message but they are all sitting still and nobody has moved.' The proprietor replied, 'For goodness sake go back. You can see for yourself that the tent is blazing and the people will be killed.' So back he went to the centre of the ring: 'Will you please leave because the tent is well alight and you are going to be killed!' But still nobody moved – because the proprietor had made a critical error of judgement. The man he had selected was the clown. People know what to expect of the clown, and it is not a serious communication, let alone one which demands a decision on a matter of life and death. This is not the clown's fault or his design but it is inherent in his relationship with his audience. We should do well to remember this when we consider the way in which the media presents religion and how far those who speak for religion have to conform to its demands.

So far I have spoken at a theoretical level about the limitations of broadcasting in handling religion. Let me now turn to more specific comments on the institutional structure of broadcasting. A working party set up by the Church of England Committee for Communications gave the following evidence to the Home Office Enquiry on Financing the BBC – which is known as the Peacock Committee:

'Public Service Broadcasting is more than a matter of high standards. It has to do with comprehensiveness – not the comprehensiveness of doing everything that other companies do, nor that of attending to so-called "minority groups", but a comprehensiveness derived from taking seriously all aspects of any human person. Public Service Broadcasting recognizes the universal desire to be entertained, but it also has regard to other equally universal desires: to be honestly informed and enabled to think for oneself; to extend one's interests and capabilities; to be credited with some degree of responsibility for other people and for a local community; to find authentic opportunities for engaging the aesthetic and spiritual sides of one's nature. It is its balanced attention to the wholeness of a human being that gives Public Service Broadcasting its essentially moral purpose.'

The Peacock Committee was speaking to the BBC. However, the Church of England evidence continued: 'The IBA has managed to maintain a broadly similar balance, so it cannot be claimed that advertising-revenue precludes the concept of Public Service Broadcasting. But reliance upon advertisers, especially when the supply from that source is limited, offers no positive motive to pursue a public service policy, whereas the receipt of the licence fee lays a distinctive obligation to do so. It is the BBC's reputation in this respect that has been the major stimulus to its competitors to emulate its example and this will continue to be the case as long as the BBC accepts the distinctiveness of its role as the guardian of balance and "wholeness". If, however, the BBC abandons or is robbed of this distinctiveness, either by having to compete for the same source of revenue (advertising) or by trying to imitate what other broadcasting companies are doing, then it will have become simply another commercial enterprise among many, and the question must arise whether we need such a BBC at all. I think that is a fair definition of where broadcasting stands today.'

So religious broadcasting does not need to be defended as pandering to the esoteric hobby of a significant minority. It is essential to a balanced diet of broadcasting which takes seriously every aspect of human activity. And opinion polls, personal experience and the response to religious broadcasts themselves all show that some kind of interest in religion is far more widespread than the comparatively small number of its active participants. It therefore needs emphasizing repeatedly that religious broadcasting needs and should have the same resources as other sectors. And the corollary is that the same rigorous professional standards should be demanded from it.

But what is a religious programme? There are programmes of worship, programmes with a format which looks more like entertainment, such as *Highway* (IBA) and *Songs of Praise* (BBC), and there are documentary and current affairs programmes which explore people's beliefs and discuss current issues in the churches and the world. While faith influences and colours every aspect of life, I recognize the institutional need for religious departments with their own distinctive ground.

In practice the lines can become blurred: whether the influence of Cardinal Sin in the Philippines is dealt with under religious affairs or current affairs must be largely a matter of chance. Both are valid. I find it more helpful to map out the field of religious broadcasting in terms of certain questions. What is religious faith today? How is it expressed in worship or prayer? And what are its consequences for individuals and for society – what are people of faith doing, and how does the world appear through their eyes? If our broadcasting is holding a balance between those questions, it is fulfilling its task as a public service.

It is generally agreed that worship is the hardest thing to get right in broadcasting. Worship is of course both a solitary and a communal activity and the communal aspect in particular has received increasing emphasis in the churches in recent years.

Broadcast worship has historically been communal: the audience is in ones and twos, mutely watching or listening to the communal devotions of a congregation somewhere else. The television set becomes a chancel arch, beyond which other people make their motions on the viewer's behalf but without the viewer's involvement.

But this is the very type of worship the churches have been reacting against, and the idea of thousands passively half-present at a Eucharist strikes us as seriously impoverished. So I welcome the determination of BBC's *This is the Day* to encourage viewers to participate and feel part of a worshipping community, however scattered. This does not mean I would rule out the broadcasting of church services, since they can be vivid testimonies to the continuing life of the Church. Radio is particularly evocative here, since the absence of images gives space for listeners to form and develop their own. But above all, I would wish to encourage variety and experiment based on an awareness of the inevitable limitations of broadcasting as a means of apprehending the holy and transcendent.

What else works? Hymn singing certainly. *Songs of Praise* (BBC 1), in its 25th year, is still the most popular religious programme on television with audiences of 8 million and more. *Highway* on ITV is a close competitor. Sometimes their combined audience, and they are usually transmitted at the same time, is 16 million – that's well over 25 percent of the population. And there are programmes on two other channels as alternatives.

These programmes are often maligned, perhaps as examples of lowest common denominator religion. But there is much theology in hymns – memorable and robust. Hymns are perhaps the last great remnant of a common culture, known in scraps to millions, and a corpus of English writing it is still pointful to quote from. This is something to cherish.

Furthermore, these programmes show believers at their best – enthusiastic and numerous in their singing, honest and human in their personal accounts of faith.

Although radio has given way, like the press, to television as the prime source of information to the general public, its output still needs to be recognized. Radio 4's *Today* programme has an audience which runs into millions. It includes a *Thought For The Day*, in the midst of the news of the day. Listeners to the *Sunday* programme outnumber the combined readership of *The Times*, the *Guardian* and all church papers put together.

All I have said so far concerns the existing situation in broadcasting. But what of the possible effect on religious broadcasting of the significant changes now forecast in our broadcasting structures?

Television, not only in England but in Europe, is faced with profound changes. New television technology has brought us Cable and Satellite Television. This has significant political and economic consequences. It enables broadcasters to break out of the national boundaries which so far have contained television systems. I have seen the direct effect of this myself in the West Indies, where round the clock Cable Television from American Channels bombards the islands. In these circumstances, religious programmes are dominated by frenetic televised evangelism from independent preachers who raise huge sums from their viewers to buy time.

If the US experience is repeated here, the mainstream churches will lose the 'balance diet' policy of public service broadcasting, and will be displaced by the Electronic Church. It seems reasonable to expect that soon domestic satellite receiving dishes will be so reduced in size and price as to bring them within the reach of most viewers. This could mean that the BBC and ITV, and national and local radio, would be hard put to survive, and religious broadcasting would comprise whatever those with the commitment and money chose to provide.

If we reach a point of deregulation where broadcasting is treated solely as a product like oil or gas, then we shall find ourselves in the market place where the consumer is King. What then is the price of religious broadcasting? It might be argued that the churches will get the religious broadcasting they deserve. I am glad to hear of meetings in Strasburg and Brussels where UNDA* and WACC† have been exploring the possibilities of a united church strategy towards the new technology.

That warning note is necessary but I would balance it with a sign of hope. Since its inception, local radio has provided great opportunities for church-people to become involved in learning the skills of broadcasting, obeying the constraints of the medium and of their station and making programmes which speak regularly to a considerable audience. Local radio has also long seen some of the healthiest examples of local ecumenical co-operation, where denominational differences are made secondary to the common task of communicating the gospel.

But local radio has also provided the most striking new example of religious broadcasting we have seen for some time and one which has, I think, taken professionals in both broadcasting and the churches by surprise. Over one million people joined in the Local Radio Lent Course *What on Earth is the Church For?* This included 32 denominations and 57 radio stations. Some of the written material was produced centrally but the broadcasting was overwhelmingly local, with a response which must be encouraging for radio stations and churches alike.

It should be clear from what I have said that I do not see religious

* UNDA: the title for the international Catholic association for radio and television
† WACC: World Association for Christian Communication

broadcasting as a medium for direct evangelism. Its rôle as part of a service offered to a pluralist society makes this inappropriate and, in any case, the ethos of the media makes it largely ineffective. What I look for is an honest presentation of how religion stands today and an exploration of the way in which a religious viewpoint can make sense of daily reality.

One example of a successful attempt to do this is a programme which has won critical acclaim. The drama *Shadowlands*, in the Everyman series on BBC1, told the story of C S Lewis's marriage to a woman slowly dying of cancer. It had dramatic merit as a story, but underlying it were profound comments on Christian responses to bereavement, suffering and grief. This sort of oblique presentation can be very powerful.

The American sociologist Peter Berger has painted a gloomy picture of our secularized world from which religion is excluded. But in his book *A Rumour of Angels* he identifies five 'signals of transcendence' – five aspects of human life which point beyond it. I offer them as possible material for the kind of oblique presentation I have described.

The first is the human propensity for order, the wish to believe that it is possible to make sense of our own lives and of the universe. For Christians this demands a religious frame of reference and there is power in the example of individuals living their lives and making sense of even the greatest difficulty in terms of such a frame of reference. Not so much arguing for it but assuming it and living in its light.

Berger's second signal relates to the experience of joy. Much of our religion is rightly serious but we need to learn the importance of celebration – not as something on the margin of normal human existence but at its centre.

A third point is hope even in the face of death: a wish to believe that there is a greater reality. This of all things is vindicated by religious belief. It is not the hope of unreality and escapism. It is the hope which leads to courage and resilience in the face of suffering and death.

The fourth signal involves the condemnation of evil. However much people may say moralities are relative, there is still a deeply-held feeling that some evils (Berger quotes Eichmann as an example) are crimes against humanity which cry out for judgement. It needs very careful handling, but the Christian prophetic voice on behalf of a righteous God needs to be heard in our society.

And finally there is the signal of humour and laughter. The Christian tradition has an honoured place for the fool who turns reality upside down by his laughter. This too is something we need in religious broadcasting if our presentation is not to take itself too seriously. Humour is, in itself, a safeguard against fantastic nonsense.

I think religious people often have a tendency to expect religious broadcasting to do what they cannot do themselves. My own expectations are more limited and seek to reflect the realities of society, the place of religion and the constraints of the media themselves and of broadcasting structures. But I remain convinced that there is an important task to be tackled. It concerns some of the deepest issues that touch the human spirit and the foundations on which people build their lives.

Chapter 2
Must the Media be Bad News for Religion?

Colin Seymour-Ure

The impetuous urge to blame the messenger for his bad news has an element of sense. For news is always to some degree shaped by the medium in which it is carried. Someone such as myself who studies media mainly in relation to politics finds messengers slain in all directions. Governments blame media when things go wrong; so do opposition parties. The press, typically, are blamed for parti- sanship and the broadcast media for trivializing politics. How far should we expect comparable complaints from people whose par- ticular concern is religion?*

News, to quote the journalist Claud Cockburn, does not just lie around like nuggets waiting for prospecting journalists to come along and pick them up. It is shaped, for example, by the nature of a medium (words? pictures? sound?), by the structure of a news organization (plentiful resources? interventionist proprietor?), and by the organization's beliefs about its audience (do they want nudes on page 3?). Fact and fiction, moreover, though logically distinct, are on the same continuum in mass media. Truth is to be measured in terms of the audience's existing degree of knowledge. Is the film *Gandhi* fiction for example? In one sense, obviously, it is: it involves gross over-simplification and imaginary dialogue; it is a form of historical novel. Equally, though, it involves real historical events: dates and places are correct, and to one ignorant of Gandhi's life it could be offered as 'factual'. Most news is like *Gandhi*. Even appar- ently clear facts such as sporting results dissolve into ambiguity. Was the crucial goal scorer offside? Was the lbw decision incorrect? Are defeats really moral victories? The notion of an 'event', too, is thoroughly artificial.

Shaped by such considerations, then, observation suggests that 'facts' are more likely to become news if they fit the frequency of a medium (e.g. the 24-hour cycle of a daily newspaper); are clear and unambiguous; reach a certain volume (runs scored, jewels stolen, villages flooded); are 'culturally proximate' (i.e. not about foreign-

* I take 'religion' to be a belief in the existence of a higher power deserving recog- nition as a guide to our behaviour on earth, and of reverence or worship; and a 'church' to be an organization for the expression of such a belief. Implicitly I talk of the Christian churches in Britain today.

ers); are unpredictable within a certain range of what is expected (what will be in the next Budget?); involve élite individuals, groups and nations (the Queen, the Cabinet, the USA); are unusual (man bites dog), negative (motorway holocaust), personalized (hunger strikers) or involve conflict (Northern Ireland). Much news, of course, meets several of these criteria; and a low score on one (e.g. 'cultural proximity') may be countered by a high one on another (e.g. numbers dead in an air crash).

How may Religion be expected to score? The answer must surely be, judged by its own standards, badly. To the churches, their news coverage must seem random, indiscriminate, malproportioned, superficial, sensational, erratic. 'Religion', distinct from 'churches', is a hopeless news subject. It concerns the boundaries of human understanding – our attempts to encompass the incomprehensible. It has no cycles and 'events' but inherent abstractions and ambiguities. But mass media cannot cope with the incomprehensible: inexplicable phenomena have to be given everyday names, such as 'flying saucers'. A *Monty Python* sketch absurdly pointed to the problem by showing a bishop and an atheist going 15 rounds to settle the question whether God exists. ('God exists by five falls to three.') For mass media, God has to be personalized, in the tradition of the benign bearded old gentleman 'up there'.

What mass media cover, clearly, are churches not religions. The tabloid press or *News at Ten* could do a good job on the Ten Commandments but would be flummoxed by *Revelations*. The list of conventional news values enables us to predict quite easily the sort of things that will make news. There are the great Christian Festivals reaching a certain 'volume' of participation at Christmas and Easter; ordinary people doing unexpected, extraordinary religious things, such as faith-healing and religious pop songs; puzzles like the Turin Shroud; or religious wars and massacres. Then the clergy comprise a kind of social élite, who attract attention not for the intrinsic interest of their actions but because those actions are done by clergy. Their distinction is marked for news media by the existence of a stereotype, epitomized in the dog collar. They will make news because they have done negative things, in terms of the stereotype. In 1896 the very first issue of the *Daily Mail*, the forerunner of today's popular press, contained an item entitled 'Curate's Divorce'. Priests on motorbikes, women priests, unfrocked vicars: these are the small change. Within the general group, bishops and archbishops, of course, are few and important enough to acquire an individual stamp beyond the stereotype; and for that reason, my guess is that they are as likely to attract attention irrelevant to their religious rôle as relevant to it. (Consider the publicity for Mrs Runcie, for instance).

In an absolute sense media coverage along such lines is 'bad news' for the churches simply because it does not coincide with what churches would like. No group in society, surely, is treated exactly as it would like. But news values do coincide more closely with the self-image of some groups than of others. The point can be demonstrated by a number of obvious contrasts. The police, for instance, receive news coverage which is generally favourable – not out of crude bias, but because media tend to favour 'law and order', equating the police interest and the public interest. Police work is often dramatic and exciting; and it is backed up by endlessly recycled forms of TV police series in which the goodies (always?) get their man. By contrast, 'criminals' generally get a bad press, carrying a weight of opprobrium in which the shades of grey between black and white are rarely acknowledged. In politics, the Prime Minister and Cabinet gain enormous advantage from actually doing something – government – which may not in itself involve much worth watching but which provides endless opportunity for travel (an excellent hook for news coverage) and fits the daily news cycle comfortably. (Indeed the Prime Minister's Public Relations Adviser has routine press conferences twice a day: once to fit the evening newspaper and TV cycle, and once for the morning papers.) The Opposition parties, in contrast, constantly have to manufacture the appearance of activity and forums of publicity. When Parliament rises in the summer, their major platform is removed. Parties not represented in Parliament have an even harder time. But among these too some fit news values better than others. The street politics of the National Front is easier to convey in a tabloid paper or on TV than is the complex ideology and rhetoric of the Workers' Revolutionary Party or the Revolutionary Communist Tendency. The SDP, without excess ideological baggage, but with well-known leaders and accomplished TV performers such as Shirley Williams, seemed to its enemies the very creation of the media. Business groups and management, again, enjoy special 'Business News' sections in the 'heavy' papers and tend to be identified with the national interest. Trades Unions, in contrast, attract attention mainly for negative activities such as strikes and are portrayed as pursuing selfish, sectional interests. Sport is exceptionally easy to portray in media; Science is exceptionally difficult. ('Explain the Atom Bomb to the housewife, Ronnie', was the editor's injunction to the *Daily Mirror* Science Correspondent in 1945). The Science Report in *The Times* has a little box round it which implicitly says, 'Look out, everybody. This is Science'. Science journalism is at constant risk from sensationalization ('miracle cures' for cancer).

Science, like religion, is at the boundaries of human understanding. Appropriately enough, then, religion sits on the same side of the fence. Not only in absolute terms but also comparatively, the churches are in my view among those groups most disadvantaged by prevailing news values.

When the churches do attract news, I have suggested that it is often linked to a stereotype of the clergy. The familiarity of a stereotype provides a reference point for stories that make news because they are 'unpredictable within a certain range of what is expected'. Yet is this stereotype a fair one? Some stereotypes have a factual basis rooted in popular experience. Most people have met a GP, a nurse and a dentist. Everyone has met so many schoolteachers that there are several schoolteacher stereotypes – dry-as-dust; sarcastic; jolly-hockey-sticks. For other stereotypes the basis is fictional, since most people have limited, if any, direct experience. The image is constructed by conjecture or superficial observation, aided sometimes by the existence of a uniform. How often do most people, even in these days of active police PR work, see a policeman without a helmet? Where uniforms are not worn in reality, the stereotype may incorporate them, to assist the process of assimilation. The stereotype scientist wears a white coat and the burglar a mask; the civil servant has a dull suit, the 'city' man still, perhaps, an umbrella and bowler hat; the student has long hair and scruffy jeans.

Some stereotypes, then, are true to life while others are not. Yet stereotypes serve indifferently as a basis for news. Some groups will therefore find stories picked out as news items because they fit a stereotype which is essentially fictional or false. For other groups, the selection of stories and the accuracy of the stereotype will coincide. In which category does the stereotype clergyman fall? My guess is that it is rooted in relatively distant or casual acquaintance, not unlike that of the citizen and the policeman; with the dog collar taking the place of the helmet. It is essentially a fictional stereotype. But whereas the stereotype policeman perhaps lacks certain real-world rough edges that might, if known, diminish his public reputation, the stereotype clergyman is unfairly attributed certain negative characteristics. Is he not typically passive, ineffectual, upper class, pompous, sanctimonious; a figure of fun? The last guise doubtless reflects his status as an authority figure. By being made a butt, whom people score off (like the 'Mr Plod' type of policeman), his implicit power is gently reduced.

Much poking fun nowadays takes place in TV comedy programmes, heirs to a long literary and stage tradition. These presumably reinforce the fictional stereotype which serves as the criterion for real-life stories in the news programmes and the press. In the press (the tabloid press, at least – which most people read) these perhaps have an extra edge. The tabloids' populist character seems to imply editorial belief that the aspiration to goodness entails hypocrisy. We are all human, and without sin we could not recognize good. Those, such as clergy, who set themselves up to be good and tell us how to behave must, in the nature of things, fall short of their aspirations. If they admit this, they simply underscore their hypocrisy with sanctimoniousness. This tabloid morality is epitomized in such words as 'saucy' ('What's in your saucy *Sun* today?') with their nuances of good-natured titillation and harmless naughtiness. Such papers are sceptical of preaching and piety for the preacher is a hypocrite and the pious are smug. The way to puncture them is by teasing and humour. An echo of the same attitude is found among TV audiences. An ITV survey in 1970, for example, found that the chief reason for switching off the religious programmes after the news on Sunday evening was that viewers did not like having religion 'crammed down their throats'.

In the presentation of factual information, or news, then, the churches and religion are subject to quite inappropriate criteria (judged from their own viewpoint); and these are applied by reference to a false stereotype without much basis in popular experience. Increasingly in the last twenty years the stereotype has been maintained through broadcast media and in the format of comedy series and light entertainment. But broadcasting naturally has much more – and more positive – to offer religion than that. In turning to it I am particularly conscious that it is a subject for the specialist, and one in which many clergy and laymen have a considerable experience which I entirely lack. My remarks are therefore intended essentially as the kind which ask questions rather than answer them.

The greatest potential of television, which it has scarcely yet begun to realize, is in destroying the tyranny of geography, or space. 'Assembly' used to mean coming together in one place. The development of communications technology of all kinds – rail, road and air as well as telegraph, telephone and radio – has increasingly reduced the need for people to come together in order to exchange information and share experience. When Parliament first met, its timetable was formed by the cycle of the seasons and the awkwardness of travel. To perform one's functions as an MP meant sojourning at Westminster. That is still of course true, as far as the rituals of voting and debates on the floor of the House are concerned. Increasingly, though, the work of a parliamentarian has become separated, by the diversity of communications technology, from the pinpoint location of Westminster. As many MPs may see the Prime Minister interviewed on *Panorama* as see her in the Commons. In communication terms, what is the difference?

The same disintegration of the *purposes* of assembly from its physical location must obviously affect religious practice. Churches and cathedrals were not built just as places of assembly. But how far today do churches (in the abstract sense) depend upon the regular ritual congregation of their members? In some ways television is clearly a boon. Sight and sound permit a more faithful representation of religious practice to the audience – especially the symbolic meanings of music and liturgy – then ever the printed word conveyed. Television, in other words, goes further than any previous medium in not just reporting services to an audience but enabling them to participate; so that even great occasions like the enthronement of an Archbishop or the visit of the Pope are accessible to all. Yet do these very opportunities threaten the integrity of congregations in the parishes?

The long run implications of such questions seem to me fundamental. More immediately, the conundrum in religious broadcasting is the 'slot'. It is, again, a problem over which politicians also agonize. How far should there be programmes for the committed, with labels saying 'This is Politics' (echoes of *The Times* Science Report?). How far, on the other hand, should 'politics' feature in programmes for the uncommitted (news, documentaries, plays, sports)? With politics, the broadcast authorities are neurotically and understandably obsessed with maintaining partisan balance. This is easiest done in the 'committed' programmes; the extreme case being the party political broadcasts that each party may do what it likes with. Most difficult, evidently, are the plays, in which questions of political balance get tangled up with questions of fact and fiction as well as artistic integrity. It is plays, usually, that cause the rows. More generally, however, politicians say that their subject is 'trivialized' by the TV medium.

In religion, I take it, the problem has a different emphasis. Nonetheless at root it is the same. The first part of the conundrum, just touched on, is 'slot' versus 'non-slot'; and there will presumably always be arguments about how many slots should be set aside, even though the days of back-to-back slots – i.e. times when only religious programmes were shown – are gone. (They are gone for party political broadcasts too). The second part of the conundrum is what sort of religious content may be expected in general (i.e. 'non-slot') programmes. This has been the subject of the earlier part of my essay. Here I would simply stress that, compared with newspapers, whose contents still consist mainly in reporting and commenting on news – events that have a real existence – TV has much more content at the fiction end of the fact/fiction continuum. Compared with the press there is a far greater fiction/show biz representation of religion on TV.

The third part of the conundrum is what to put in the slots. This again is a problem facing all specialist programme makers and not one in which I shall become embroiled. It quickly reduces to the claims of reassurance and orthodoxy against challenge and innovation. As the Annan Committee on the future of broadcasting commented in 1977, 'A Sunday panel of two reporters and a Bishop of advanced views answering phone-in questions is not likely to give much reassurance to the faithful'. To me the striking thing in this argument – indeed in the whole business of slots, is how very quickly and strongly the Church of England seems to have entrenched itself in the network of broadcast advisory committees, acquiring a more specific role in the determination of programme content than comparable advisory committees.

The problem of 'slots' versus 'non-slots' is also at the heart of the arguments about the future directions of television. Channel 4, as an avowedly minority channel, is almost bound to have a 'slots' approach. Britain at present leads the world, I believe, in taking up the idea of video-recording. This, too, means greater control of programming by the TV set user: he or she no longer watches what the broadcasters choose to show but puts on the programme he or she has chosen to hire. The biggest questionmarks, however, are in the future of satellite and cable broadcasting. Governments are going to have little control over satellite programmes: viewers will be able to pick up whatever is in range (provided they have a disk) and it might be, in our terms, a religious cowboy. Cable is a national matter. The Thatcher Government's White Paper excluded religious (and political) groups from the ownership of cable channels; but it was not opposed to religious channels as such, provided that they 'give an opportunity for a variety of views to be expressed'. How fast cable channels will develop is difficult to guess. The White Paper envisages ten or twelve pilot schemes, each covering about 100,000 homes and providing up to twenty-five channels. But the development is to be 'market-led' – in other words, financed from private capital – and it is therefore difficult to predict.

So how much of all this is 'bad news' for religion? My views, in summary, amount to this. Churches, because they have something to say about all aspects of life, are bound to be caught in a dilemma about how far to talk to the converted, to confirm and deepen their beliefs, understanding and experience, and how far to try and reach to the unbeliever. Wherever this balance is struck, a popular religion must be popularly comprehensible. It must therefore be capable of expression through the society's dominant media. For religious behaviour, like politics, has no existence independent of the media of communication through which it is conducted. Like election campaigns and political rhetoric, religious behaviour must inevitably change in response to changes in media technology. Media technology is socially determined, to be sure – the development of cable being the latest example; and churches may therefore help to shape media. But ultimately media are 'bigger' than social institutions: if these do not adapt to changes in media technology they atrophy and die.

In the twentieth century a major implication of media development is that physical proximity is decreasingly relevant to the idea of community. This is not to say that community itself is irrelevant: shared values may remain the same, but the sharing does not have to be done by means of simultaneous assembly in one place. The values expressed in the dominant British media are overwhelmingly individualist, materialist and acquisitive. How far these are really the values of the majority of the people, not just of those who control the media, is imponderable. How far, too, they reflect the values of the people rather than create them is another of the perennial conundrums of the student of media. How far, lastly, they are the values of the churches will obviously be a matter of opinion. I have suggested that no social group is portrayed in media quite as it would wish, and that the churches do worse, by this standard, than some other groups. But I am sure that any religion which loses touch with modern media sets out for oblivion.

Chapter 3
The Politics of Religion in Broadcasting

Kenneth Wolfe

In a 1931 *Punch* cartoon, an elegant lady interviewing her prospective maid asked if she was a member of the Church of England. 'My father goes to Chapel,' she answered, 'but personally, I'm Wireless.' From the beginning of public broadcasting by Reith's British Broadcasting Company in November 1922, the slogan of 'BBC' or 'Wireless' religion precisely focused an engaging tension between two institutions in British culture. By the time of this cartoon, the mainstream Protestant and the Roman Catholic churches had organized themselves so as to provide a powerful instrument of control over this fledgling broadcasting institution which – as Robert Runcie reminded the BBC 60th Anniversary congregation in St Paul's Cathedral in 1982 – had, in 1923, hoped to bring the wedding of Lady Elizabeth Bowes-Lyon and the Duke of York to the listening public through the wireless. As is now well known, the Chapter of Westminster Abbey refused for fear that men would be listening in public houses with their hats on! What it would have said about London Weekend Television's series 'Jesus, the Evidence', we can only guess. Then, as now, offence was quickly taken at those initiatives which provided a quite novel challenge to traditional styles and, moreover, which were undertaken independently on behalf of a public conceived not so much in terms of a congregation that could switch off metaphorically but rather of an audience that could do so literally.

The controversial and puzzling figure of Reith is central to any understanding of the foundations of broadcasting in the first half of the twentieth century. He had a strong, perhaps fanatical and certainly superstitious, religious commitment in which, however, his regard for institutional Christianity was painfully ambivalent. His biographer has clarified his urge to be recognized and approved, not the least by the palaces of Westminster and Lambeth.[1] He told Temple in 1930 that he was more concerned with the general religious policy of the Corporation than any other,[2] and wanted to do the right thing by both the churches and the Christian religion. Much later, when considering his successor, Reith hoped the next DG would be 'a Christian believer who should give the Christian religion a privileged place in the BBC's output'.[3] The emphasis is important; Reith believed in a species of non-institutional Christianity. Once away from the orbit of his father's Presbyterian totems, Reith had little time for regular congregational participation. He complained to the Dean of Canterbury how difficult it was for him to attend ordinary church services 'the fault is so often with the clergyman'.[4] For this reason he was attracted so strongly to HRL 'Dick' Sheppard of St Martin's-in-the-Fields who shared Reith's impatience with all things parsonic and who believed with Reith that broadcasting could reach those ears that the clergy could not. Not the least the rank and file half-churched, the lapsed, the non-churched and simply those who had become disenchanted. Reith believed that Sheppard and his padre sort were ideally suited to reach especially the disillusioned rank and file after that most catastrophic war. Broadcast Christianity was thus to be 'thoroughgoing, manly and optimistic'.[5] Unfortunately, there were not enough Sheppards to go round and in 1924, once the controversy over broadcasting actual church services had turned a more positive colour, it was clear to Reith that his small Sunday Committee would have to work much harder.

January 1924 was celebrated: St Martin's-in-the-Fields was chosen for the first broadcast service simply because neither St Paul's nor Westminster Abbey would entertain any broadcasting 'stunts' and because the Sunday Committee Chairman, Garbett, thought Southwark Cathedral services would be rather boring. A measure of Protestant flexibility (not open to the Roman Catholics) allowed the evolution of a liturgical hybrid which would surely be appreciated by the non-churched. It turned into a great success and was widely welcomed.

Roman Catholics, however, began to feel decidedly discriminated against, particularly as they wanted above all else the mass; they were not free to conjure their liturgical heritage for a wider and non-Catholic audience. When, in a Catholic service from Savoy Hill, a diligent priest prayed for the conversion of an England regarded as the 'dowry of Our Lady' much wrath broke loose from firmly endorsed Protestant institutions such as the Imperial Alliance for the Defence of Sunday, the Protestant Truth Society and the World's Evangelical Alliance. They were never to be silent and never quite satisfied with the BBC initiatives in religious utterance.

In the early years Reith was more or less satisfied with the quality of religious utterance from Savoy Hill; they comprised short studio talks during the Sunday concert interval. The BBC could, as it were, call all the tunes. Once the Corporation began combing the country for actual broadcast services Sunday by Sunday, the church leaderships each began to take Reith at his word and claimed their share of the privilege about which he had spoken; and in so doing translated it into protection. Most ecclesial scruples had been gradually overcome and by 1930 the idea of carrying the recital of both Christian creed and biblical narrative into millions of homes animated the visions of many a churchman who discovered undreamed-of evangelical sides to their natures. Broadcasting beguiled the vast majority into the belief that the very transmission of the churches' arcane language and ritual would lead to the revitalization of Christianity and in effect the life of the mainstream churches. They were not quite so ready to accept Reith's challenge to understand the peculiarities of this new medium, but instead, he believed, they regarded it merely as an extension of pulpit and stall. Broadcasting challenged the churches to give nothing less than the highest quality and to accept that the microphone turned recital into a new form of discourse which had a discipline of its own – as the BBC was discovering elsewhere in the output and especially in radio drama. If the churches recognized their new opportunity, Reith had said, 'there will not be room enough to hold their people.'[6] For their part the churches insisted upon their denominational allocations and in 1930, just as the Church of England was about to give the first formal ecclesial approval to Reith's religious policy, the Central Religious Advisory Committee (as the Sunday Committee had now become) strengthened its membership with chairman bishops from its counterpart committees in the regions. Nonconformists were no longer quite so happy to have the Free Church Federal Council represent them and wanted each Free Church to send its own man. The stage was set for the churches to have more of their own way and not the least on Sundays where the religious output was most heavily concentrated. Sunday broadcasting was to become the first major and continuing dispute between the Central Religious Advisory Committee (hereafter CRAC) and the broadcasting executive – which must be clearly distinguished from the BBC's Board of Governors[7] which represented the public.

Once straight church services were on the Sunday agenda, matters became so much more complex that Reith decided to engage a specialist. To all intents and purposes Sunday afternoon talks (designed to strengthen the faithful and hopefully the outsider) were educational, and so the educationalist now in charge of Schools broadcasting took religion under his wing. John Stobart, however, had little time for what he called the wrangles over 'unwanted theological lumber' in the churches and hoped to bring the influences of an educationalist, Basil Yeaxlee, to bear. He believed the BBC could do exceedingly abundantly in the service of an intelligent and well informed Christian culture, above all among the committed and baptized.

Reith was a firm, even fanatical, believer in the importance of the Sabbath, but had no time for the Lord's Day Observance Society which would continue to wield a baton against the BBC (later to be carried by Mrs Whitehouse).[8] Whilst the churches accepted that there would have to be other programmes on Sundays, two things bothered them: the timing of the broadcast service and the character of the rest of the Sunday output. Reith had invited advice from the churches and was thus never short of it! As increasing demands were made to lighten the now notorious Reithian Sunday, Reith could only comply; Geraldo's orchestra could play but not dance music. There could be no electronic organ and no saxophones. He didn't mind the devil having the best tunes; he simply did not care for their accompaniment! The churches agreed that Sunday broadcasting should above all be appropriate to the day and before long broadcasters and churchmen were at loggerheads over matters of taste and aesthetic convictions. One thing was sure, broadcasting Sunday services must not take place during the churches' normal office hours between 6.30 p.m. and 8.00 p.m. For two reasons: first, that the faithful would be enticed to listen at home and the churches would be emptied; second, that the rising stars of broadcast religion would not be heard by the committed: Soper, Weatherhead, McLeod, Flemming, J S Whale, Martindale and others who had a way with words at the microphone. It was a two-edged sword: broadcasting not only helped to inform and educate, but, as Reith had recognized, it highlighted a disparity between the wireless excellence both in speech and music and what actually happened on the ground. People began to write in and complain that although (as Sheppard had hoped) the relationship between the religious broadcaster and his audience was widening into a friendship,[9] one consequence was the disappointment felt when those who had been encouraged by broadcast services to return to their churches found the experience rather flat. For this reason Reith soon had many cathedrals permanently wired for the regular transmission of what even he regarded as one sublime and profoundly eloquent feature of British – or at any rate English – Christianity, namely Evensong. He preferred to sing Scottish Metrical Psalms, and was well aware that most Christians preferred to sing hymns: his experience in the trenches had taught him that. Increasingly as broadcasting developed, not the least in the field of religion (there had been a Daily Service since 1928), there were persistent calls from all sections to improve the BBC Sunday and attract people back from Radio Luxembourg; that meant increasing the output. The churches for their part had got an evening service and now wanted one in the morning and were faced with an unexpected dilemma: a broadcast service in the morning would ensure that more in the Sunday output was religiously appropriate but it would create a gap to be filled between the close of the service and the beginning of afternoon programmes and thus more secular material to desecrate the day. The provision of a second service ensured not only that programmes filled the whole day, but fuelled the indignation of increasing numbers who complained of the churches' monopoly over religious programmes and thought the Advisory Committee should more properly be called Christian instead of Religious.

From the outset Reith had maintained a policy of no open access and the Advisory Committee had quite predictably supported it. Systematically the Committee had allocated the lion's share of services etc. to the Church of England; the remainder of just under a half shared between the Free Churches, the Roman Catholics and the Church of Scotland. The Salvation Army were given special status along with the Society of Friends. Unitarians were banned along with Jehovah's Witnesses and any American imports of like kind. If the Corporation wanted to invite Jews it could, but the Committee made itself quite clear that it would offer no advice (and by that it meant criticism) if non-mainstream churches or groups were represented in what was then (by the mid-thirties) understood to be the Christian liturgical spaces in the output. The BBC, it was said, was offering worship to God and such programmes should not be controversial. For example, the Oxford Group Movement had some powerful friends as did the Christian Scientists whose famous American advocate, Lady Astor, organized a campaign to assert her Christian orthodoxy into the fifties. CRAC believed that Sunday broadcasting was not the place to engage in such debate; broadcast services, talks and lectures should commend, elucidate and support the recital of Christian certainty. Churchmen generally thought entertainments on Sunday were threatening and the so-called and disreputable 'Reithian Sunday' was as much their doing as his. CRAC wanted more or less Christian programmes; Reith wanted simply a different intellectual standard. The churches, however, wanted more: as the regions urged for their own autonomy, an alternative regional wavelength was provided but not, of course, during the time of broadcast Sunday services. CRAC wanted to retain this silence; the BBC wanted to offer a choice: why not put the religious service on the regional programme so that the national programme could carry material of wider national interest? Absolutely not, said CRAC defiantly.

The complexities of the CRAC's protective energy to keep Sunday sacred took little account of Reith's worries about drawing a licence fee from a public which turned in vast numbers to the continentals on Sundays. One other major contention added to his burdens: the clamour by myriad groups and individuals to relax the Christian mainstream monopoly or at least to provide an opportunity for some rapport between belief and unbelief on the air. In 1927 when the Anglicans were racked over the Prayer Book, Reith had thought such controversy appropriate for airing before the widest public. Controversial religious, political and ideological issues had been banned from the air by the Postmaster General who had bowed to pressure from the newspapers. When finally Reith effected release in 1928, it was hailed by radicals as an opportunity for Christians at last to engage in dialogue and argument with the growing lobby from the Julian Huxleys, Bertrand Russells and C E M Joads who thought that at least the Christians should be obliged to answer for their unchallenged assertions. Here, it was thought, was an unparallelled opportunity for the churches to respond to prevailing intellectual challenges from within Christianity itself and from the more or less popular expressions of dissent by those wanting to hear more than one side of the argument for Christian revelation. The Church leaderships were not at all convinced and said no. (They were to maintain their hold on the Postmaster General's prohibition well into the fifties.)

By 1933 the BBC output was expanded notably in the regions and overseas.[10] With the church pressing on all sides, Reith wanted a man of religion rather than education to negotiate the complex labyrinth of ecclesial and theological foliage which overgrew the pathways between the BBC and its audiences. Reith found in Frederick Iremonger (the eventual biographer of William Temple) a man after his own heart and one equally impatient with his fellow clergy. The churches now had their 'mole' inside the Corporation and no longer had grounds to complain that the BBC was acting above its station. But they did! Iremonger however could now exercise an influence upon the CRAC to face outwards to the churches in favour of protecting the Corporation which was, after all, doing unprecedented good for religion in general and Christianity (and the churches) in particular. But it was not so simple: CRAC kept its back to the churches and made sure the Corporation did most of its bidding. Before long Iremonger (and those who were to follow him) discovered that initiatives had to be rather more clandestine; as CRAC became more of a watchdog, Iremonger barked back more vigorously: standards must improve and the BBC must make its own choices. It became increasingly clear that there was now a substantial audience for religious services and for the increasing number of educationally-styled religious talks which Iremonger organized on Sundays. It looked as if broadcast talks could shed a great deal of light upon the arcane secrets of theology and biblical hermeneutics which for so long had been kept hidden by the clergy who broadly insisted that in any broadcast setting such matters were bound to undermine the faith of the average churchgoer. They may have been right. Lucky for them, the attempts to educate the rank and file churchgoer seemed not greatly successful. The clergy, by and large, discouraged any such initiatives and shielded their congregations from threatening new movements in theology which looked as if they might undermine security and Christian morale.

The Church of England clergy were not unaware that since 1921 baptisms had fallen (and would take an upturn only again in 1947).[11]

Iremonger increased the output still further and religious programmes began to be heard during weekdays in addition to the now well established Daily Service which had inspired three service books; the latter, *New Every Morning*, was sold by the thousands. A weekday evening service since 1931 produced a veritable star in W H Elliott, the rector of St Michael's Chester Square, an accomplished preacher who carefully managed to distil a Christian message which – on thin theological ice at the best of times – kept to the outer edges mixing the safe language of popular wisdom with Christian features recognizable by a vast audience which had acquired their fundamental pennant concepts from Sunday School. The trouble for Iremonger was that Archbishop Lang was overshadowed: Elliott seemed best to represent Anglican, even Christian, utterance to the majority and Lang complained that whilst he had slain his thousands, Elliott claimed ten thousands! As war clouds gathered in the late thirties, Elliott as a self-appointed radio chaplain concentrated his homilies upon raising public morale. His League of Prayer for Peace attracted vast thousands and convinced them that with sufficient prayer there would indeed be peace. It was a style of broadcast religion with which both the churches and the BBC were increasingly unhappy; they wanted rather more challenge as well as comfort. William Temple introducing notions of Christian sociology had set an agenda for broadcast religion concerned with relationships between church, community and state; all the more pertinent as the country expected conflict. In 1938 Reith and Iremonger left the Corporation and whilst the Governors were uneasy with the new Director General, their approval of the new Religion Director was enthusiastic: in James Welch of York they had an educationalist and theologian – and one singularly influenced by William Temple.

Religious policy, once the war had begun, underwent a profound shift in the political centre of gravity. Whereas the churches had – since 1922 – called most of the tunes, wartime censorship of all spoken words unequivocally subjected religious utterance to the authority of the BBC – now painfully on its guard against the Ministry of Information and rumours of Government control. The BBC's output was now packed into a single wavelength and religious talks had all the more to appeal to the general listener now that the churches had to forfeit some of their use of Sundays.

Welch believed the times were critical and demanded a more intelligent and systematic presentation of Christian theology to a country reputedly fighting for King, Country and Christian democracy. The BBC must take an initiative and lead the churches into areas where otherwise angels might fear to tread. It was not enough to have random sermons broadcast from churches up and down the land by clergy who queued up for their turn at the microphone. He wanted a sequential utterance which would delineate and clarify the Christianity in the culture at large and present the sharp relevance of Christian belief in the churches themselves in the face of the ideological tensions between Marxism in the East and fascism in the West. In broadcasting terms this meant not only sermons on Sundays and extra prayers for peace after the 9 o'clock news, but a systematic exposition of Christian creed for a nation fighting for a Christianity it hardly knew. As never before Welch believed the churches should bury their confessional differences in favour of a confident corporate utterance which, he believed, broadcasting could carry so ably – at least to people who anyway hardly understood the differences between the denominations and their creeds. It was a sublime expectation. A talented BBC producer helped devise the first of such programmes which put a hierarch of the Church of England in the hot seat and answered the common man's questions. The bishop was F A Cockin of Bristol and the producer Guy Burgess of the Talks Department – and later of Moscow!

There was one polarity in Christianity which Welch could not erase; indeed, he believed that above all the BBC had a vocation to carry utterance above the level of propaganda and give both sides of any Christian ideological conflict. It was not so easy. In 1940, a Congregational Minister from Birmingham preached a pacifist sermon and the reverberations juddered the churches' relation with the Corporation more than any issue before or since: pacifists were banned from the microphone. Most of these were clergy: they suffered – said the Board of Governors and the Minister of Information – from a 'civil disability'. And not only the clergy: the conductor of the Glasgow Orpheus Choir, Sir Hugh Roberton, was also a pacifist and was banned. When Vaughan Williams protested, the issue was raised in the House: did pacifism make a musician play flat? Churchill merely replied that the distinction was not worth pursuing; his endeavour was rather that they should play up! The struggle continued until the end of the war and Donald Soper, Charles Raven and other famous names were not to be heard at the microphone.

With the Corporation firmly in control of its affairs for fear of the Home Office looking over its shoulder it asked why, anyway, should the clergy or bishops be regarded as any more authoritative than any other competent person when expressing their views on political, economic or social affairs. The present Bishop of Liverpool in his Dimbleby Lecture has been at the centre of precisely this discussion. Did clerical orders cast opinions into something more than opinions. It was clearly one thing to have William Temple or Archbishop Lang addressing themselves to the authority of the Christian Scriptures. Was it not open to question that their remarks on rationing or unemployment or bombing were as competent? Temple guided this debate with characteristic skill and distinguished between ex cathedra utterance and his views as an individual.[12] The BBC Talks Controller, however, regarded the pacifism issue as the craggy tip of a dangerous iceberg. The clergy came under pressure to make sure it was clear that this or that was their opinion and that they gave proper and careful representation of opposite views. A concordat was finally reached between the Talks and Religion Departments which sought not to stifle but rather to discipline clergy into a religious utterance which would naturally speak to contemporary issues, but which would remain explicitly related to Christian belief to justify its place in the religious output.

These were heady and erudite areas and religion was under pressure not only to support the war effort but to be popular. With pacifists banned and religious talks under pressure to be clearly religious, Welch turned his creative interests away from the complexities of Christian dogma to the so-called historical Jesus. Val Gielgud had, by then, created effectively a new art as Head of Radio Drama. Welch saw an unequalled opportunity to dramatize the real-life figure at the centre of Christian theology. In the series *A Man Born to be King*, Dorothy L Sayers fought against fundamentalists and fanatics inside and outside the mainstream churches. Jesus impersonated on the radio, said an irate letter to the Director General, had caused Pearl Harbour and the fall of Singapore. Sayers the Christian apologist passionately believed in the inextricable relation of dogma to drama.[13] She was not a theologian and succumbed to a species of liberal scholarship in the hope of stringing together the Gospels and making a credible sequential history appropriate to the broadcasting medium. *The Man Born to be King*[14] was excellent radio and was heard by millions. It was incarnational theology writ large and thus potentially very controversial. Because, in the event, they were so very entertaining these plays did not, after all, upset the confidence of CRAC largely because a vast audience was confronted at home with the founder and root fact of Christianity. The cycle of plays nevertheless provoked questions about the 'how', 'why' and 'when' of biblical assertion and these were difficult to answer. The churches preferred to leave well alone and evoke the 1928 Postmaster General's ban on controversy. But the public for the Sayers's Cycle were asking real questions about the veracity and historicity of the New Testament documentation. In the fifties a similar dramatization was made on television, but not until the sixties were hermeneutic questions exposed on radio. In the seventies it was more strikingly and more popularly attempted (by Don Cupitt)[15] on BBC 1. As with Sayers and *Jesus the Evidence*, there was a measure of outrage, as there was for Dennis Potter's *Son of Man* in 1969.[16]

Welch struggled with two conflicting notions attached to broadcast religion: intelligibility and democracy. His approach to the clergy involved an unheard of challenge to submit to training in those special skills which would not merely attract an unseen audience but retain it. Well thought-out systematic and even popular Christian dogmatics were increasingly noticed by the Listener Research operation as appealing to very few indeed. Moreover, the Forces Programme (to foreshadow the Light Programme and Radios 1 and 2) was beginning to attract vast numbers from the national programme and, much to Reith's disappointment, the output was beginning an inexorable stratification into audiences and specially sculptured to meet class and education differences. It appeared to some simply as high- and low-brow standards in aesthetic judgement. It was perhaps inevitable: the power of the BBC to educate its Christian public – or the audience for religion – was being undermined by the churches and its middle management. The Third Programme was welcomed after the war because, e.g., the complexity of theology from Germany or the common ground between Bertrand Russell and Father Frederick Coppleston could be hidden away on a wavelength hardly listened to by the rank and file; and, moreover, not altogether encouraged by their clerical mentors. There was, however, Cathedral Evensong for some and the Daily Service or Sunday Half-Hour for others. On paying the licence fee, one newspaper wag put it: 'You pays for your hymnody and takes your chants.'

In 1946, the arrival of the Third Programme was accompanied by increased pressure on the Christian cartel in broadcasting and hopes that CRAC would allow debate and at least the questioning of Christian assertion on the air. The Religion Department urged, the Director General (Haley, eventually of *The Times*) urged, the Rationalist Press Association and a few radical Christians such as Bell, Oldham, Cockin, all urged CRAC to the view that Christian veracity was not finally secured by the fragile 1920s' protective coating which had construed rapport between believers and nonbelievers as controversial; and, moreover, regarded controversy as negative, even conspiratorial and no doubt designed to unchurch the faithful and probably unseat the power of CRAC as sole arbiter in matters of religion and the BBC. CRAC decided that a public utility in a Christian country could not expect the churches to perpetrate their own demise. Nevertheless, the Governors went ahead with modest innovations on their own.

So the Corporation and the churches parted company. Haley told the churches[17] that it was their business to make converts and it was the broadcaster's business to entertain, inform and educate. The churches could no longer expect to have the Corporation protect Christian interests in every branch of its output, particularly in drama – about which some were increasingly uneasy. The issue could persist and under Hugh Greene in the sixties provoke the

MRA to spawn the National Viewers and Listeners Association and its rather whiter than Whitehouse.[18]

In the post-war era, it was clear to the churches that broadcast religion must meet the demands of an ever-increasing low-brow audience on the Light Programme and, however democratically the Department was obliged to reflect the diversity of confessional and institutional religion, for their part the churches had to produce popular broadcast artefacts which above all would fashion a twentieth-century simplicity in religious utterance; it must prepare the ground for the evangelistic enterprise of local missions and perhaps even save some. Broadcasting innovations were kept firmly in check, much to the exasperation of the Religion Department. It had been preparing the churches to see that the arcane language and ritual of participant religious commitment could not be presented untreated to an audience unschooled, untutored and even uncaring of such matters. Broadcasting was preparatory to the churches' endeavour and in a culture increasingly distanced from Christian traditions, there was – as a notable Presbyterian put it – a danger of 'casting pearls before swine'. In the tradition of William Temple, religious broadcasters wanted to face the questions being asked by any within earshot of the churches' utterance however erudite or humble. The churches, for their part, reflected an increasing disparagement of dogma and creed in favour of Christian moral values at best or a species of simplistic Jesus worship at worst. Just when progress seemed to be made, evangelical Christianity was beguiled by techniques from across the Atlantic about to take Britain by storm. Billy Graham became a model for many who were deeply concerned by a secular Britain and a declining church.

By the mid-fifties, the traditions of religion in broadcasting were firmly set and, as television emerged, a competitive element revealed a St Andreas weakness in the foundations: commerce. Television stimulated the urge for democratic representation by the various churches and with the new ITA it was clear that if the BBC would not do the bidding then others would!

It is, of course, impossible to calculate with any precision the extent of the financial investment in Christianity by the Corporation during our period. It is easy to see that television costs far outstripped broadcasts on sound only; for example, the Harington TV series *Jesus of Nazareth* cost around £13,000 in 1955–6. Before that, Welch estimated that the churches were benefiting to the sum of £30,000 each year; after the war the RBD increased its staff around the country and in 1950 salaries alone amounted to this figure. The costs involved in making programmes and in particular in mounting outside broadcasts and notably in television were and remain astronomical.

It is often said that the wealth of the Christian churches lies in the legacy of Victorian and Edwardian church buildings and the vast investment in valuable land of which twentieth-century Christianity is now custodian. This enormous heritage was the fruit of substantial sacrifice, devotion and commitment by generations of Christians who believed they were laying foundations upon which others would build. The twentieth-century church has been not a little embarrassed and even scandalized by this rich legacy. Notwithstanding significant post-war investments in new church building, the unease remains: too much wealth is tied to obsolete buildings in which congregations have long since ceased to thrive. The twentieth-century church in Britain, it is said, remains the poorer for having to maintain so many buildings at such high costs when some might be rationalized in order to service the remainder more efficiently, perhaps with more real respect to the commitment of previous generations, no matter how old-fashioned former motivations may now seem.

At the outset of broadcasting in 1922 many churchmen felt precisely this unease very deeply, not the least in the light of the dreadful war recently ended. Nevertheless, as broadcasting developed, church-going began a seemingly inexorable decline which some began to think might only be reversed by the new technology of mass communication. Yet had the churches been sent the bill for the growing provision of religion in the BBC's budget year after year, sooner or later they would have curtailed the operation as an expense that simply could not be met. As it was, the mainstream churches believed that the BBC had a clear duty to the Christian majority who bought their licences.

Thus vast sums of broadcasting revenue were committed week by week to servicing the established and 'mainstream' churches. What is surprising is that the churches, in their zeal to evangelize through broadcasting, were seemingly blind to the foundations they were laying in a stereotyped utterance of oversimplified Christian belief prepared for a largely untutored audience. The Corporation was, in effect, obliged to finance a rapport with populism so small was the proportion spent upon debate. When radical investigations were eventually attempted on a regular basis, it had come too late, Roy McKay declared in 1964. Church leaders insisted that this public utility was their servant and that its incalculable funding must not be used to undermine the nominally faithful majority, no matter how intelligent the unbelieving minority. Perhaps the clergy who did most of the speaking in their protected times should have done more listening, not least on the air. Broadcast religion might then have equipped the committed man in the pew to be a match for his clerical mentors. Their congregations might have begun to understand Maurice Reckitt, Reinhold Niebuhr, William Temple, Charles Raven or John A T Robinson and all the others brought to the microphone to address the church as well as the general audience. The religious broadcasters consistently complained that the clergy as a whole did not help their flocks to listen to the leading minds who provided materials for the new grass-root dialogue between Christians and all manner of others. There was now a variety of emerging movements wherein truth, as Haley often reminded the RBD, was not only given but must be sought. The churches, he thought, were speaking but not being spoken to – just when it seemed crucial for religious broadcasting to become a channel for the many new and widely overheard conversations between all shades of opinion. What was heard instead was a publicly financed monologue. The CRAC was regionally and numerically a formidable institution and the BBC hierarchy frequently lamented that the members had little idea of the problems of broadcasting and that the interests which they were invariably deputed to protect were being financed beyond the wildest dreams of ecclesiastical accountants! CRAC advised the BBC as to what the churches expected of it; only rarely did it do the reverse. There were, of course, many notable exceptions and perhaps most eminently F A Cockin, the Bishop of Bristol.

Broadcast religion thus contributed with unimaginable financial resources to the dissemination of Christian dogma, creed and piety. Congregational Christian ritual and the language of the Bible were conceived for and received by individuals in their most familiar and homely environments with greater or lesser degrees of reverence which may have matched or even exceeded the intensity of response during physical presence in normal church worship. This was specially true for the housebound and hospitalized who valued broadcast religion very highly. But there were now great numbers, according to Silvey's department, whose only contact with religion was now at home.[19] The worship of the church, no matter how attractive and 'entertaining' it could be made to retain the casual listener, was, in a subtle way, being gradually de-sacralized; alongside the decline in churchgoing, religion came mainly as word and not as sight to see or ritual participation. Many churchmen were increasingly uneasy. Religion was slowly but inexorably being honed into an efficient verbal communiqué with a limited dogmatic content mostly riding safely inside a hymnodic Trojan Horse. Broadcast 'missions' did little to bring the lapsed back into congregational life, particularly as local churches tended to resent BBC interference. Christianity was being discreetly withdrawn from beneath its mysterious and numinous canopy. Liturgy and creed were less crucial than the speculative language of popular discourse: the poetry of religious aspiration had to be sacrificed for a supposed 'intelligentibility' that the churches, rather more than the broadcasters, broadly believed would bring forth fruit or at least fill out the warp and woof of the somewhat threadbare public knowledge of Christian belief. Notwithstanding, great numbers both at home and overseas continued to listen with pleasure, particularly the middle-aged and the middle classes: but they were mostly the converted, as Francis House later admitted. The churches' historic utterance at perhaps its most aesthetic was the regularly broadcast Evensong and Christmas Carols from King's College Cambridge. There was no attempt to conjure their traditions; to significant numbers listening they were and remain sublime. Evensong was fought for, then as now, by Christian and non-Christian alike. Sadly, as religious broadcasting sought greater credibility, it became increasingly considered elitist or anachronistic.

Popular Christianity however, during our period, had little time for aesthetic or historical language or even poetry unless set to good hymn tunes. Moreover, at the end of our period, the churches were soon to be enamoured of new evangelical techniques from across the Atlantic.

For all the creative ingenuity of the Directors of the RBD, the churches in general and CRAC in particular placed too much unsubstantial faith in the advantages of broadcasting for the restoration of faith and even the conversion of the nation. Early hesitations had given way to co-operation once the religious policy of the Corporation was consistently presented in service to the churches as 'not doing what they could best do themselves'. Successive Directors knew only too well that there was no serious or concerted effort by the majority of church leaders to take the consequences of broadcasting religion seriously enough to involve the theological colleges and the rising generation of clergy in the problems of religious utterance to a Light Programme audience which had effectively no background whatever in religious commitment, knowledge or insight.

They saw clearly that this was a culture increasingly confident in its rejection of inherited 'hand-me-down' credal formulas. To the disappointment of Iremonger, Welch, Grayston and House in turn, only a few church leaders regarded broadcasting as the most astonishing invitation of all time to twentieth-century Christianity to provide as best it could for the spirituality of a newly emerging technological and pluralist society. It was an offer to the churches to do for religion what the wireless had done so well for music: to co-operate in refining the latent faith of millions by exposing – as only radio could – excellence in the liturgical and scholarly heritage of a nominally Christian culture.

The history of religion in broadcasting policy might, of course, have been different; it might have been less paternalistic, even ecumenical; it might have been more imaginative, open-ended, self-critical and flexible. But at a critical period in the life of the British churches, they would not allow the Corporation, as Welch once put it, to 'strike out on its own and, instead of reflecting church life in general, make a clear bid to lead the religious life and thought of the nation'. With the arrival of a visual competitor in television all the more sharpened in the relation between the Corporation and the ITA, the beguiling power of radio was over and vast tracts of the population moved rapidly out of earshot. Television simply heightened the variations between the styles of the Christian denominations. By protesting their traditions almost at all costs in the post-war decade of reawakening rapport between so many new shades of contemporary thought, the churches forfeited their most golden opportunity to enhance the intellectual and aesthetic climate. However much BBC Christianity might be intelligent, cogent and even entertaining on the air, on the ground the churches made sure that Christian utterance was their affair and not the business, finally, of a state corporation, for all its indigenous and even benevolent commitment to a more or less Christian nation.

Chapter 4

Religious Vision and Political Reality

David Martin

I am not concerned with some miniature inquiry into the influence of religion on society. I am interested rather in the nature, rôle and impact of Christian social comment, particularly of recent years. I want to elucidate certain resistances built into social arrangements and processes which I think Christian social comment likely to encounter and also likely to misunderstand or ignore. However, I will also indicate in summary form how Christian social comment may vary in impact and direction according to different types of situation.

I have to begin by arguing that my problem takes the form it does because of the special nature of Christianity. The Christian religion has a positive relationship to society and embodies affirmations which have social implications, mostly of a very general kind. But it is not a religion, like Buddhism, where the monastery might siphon off the tension between religious ideals and social requirements. Equally it is not a religion like Islam that codifies its claim vis-à-vis society in a comprehensive system of law. The Buddhist tension with social requirements can be very high while that of Islam is fairly low. Christians, however, are placed in the special position of accepting society and of wanting the Kingdom of God to come on earth without any extensive legal specification.

Christians lack any blueprint for the right ordering of society. In so far as a complex system of law is required, it has to be taken from elsewhere and worked up within a Christian framework. Notoriously the new law offered by the New Testament, especially in the Sermon on the Mount, does not constitute a viable social system. Of course, it is always possible to return to the law of the Old Testament, and to legalism, but legalism is precisely what the New Testament claims to supercede.

This open texture of Christianity can be variously viewed from a sociological viewpoint. Talcott Parsons saw Christianity as part of a progressive process of social differentiation whereby the religious sphere and the social system became increasingly distinct. Dr John Hall argues on the contrary that Islam presents the most socially advanced of religions precisely because it presents so comprehensive a scheme of social regulation.

At any rate, the new law is vision rather than specification. One solution I have already alluded to is to call in a different system to fill up the gap between the City of God and the City of Man. Another solution is to proclaim an eschatological freedom. We are in the end-time and man may sin the more that grace may abound the more. The external prop of rules is no longer required. In the nature of things this antinomian anarchy will be adopted in times of revolutionary excitement and dissolution, but it cannot last. Yet another solution is to make an heroic attempt to see whether the Sermon on the Mount can be treated as the basis of a new law. This attempt is almost bound to lead to the formation of a small and probably exclusive sect. It will represent a social capsule of Christian revolution and from time to time certain reforms may be picked up from this capsule and applied more generally. A Comenius with his advanced schemes of educational reform was in part a late flowering of sectarian vision; the same is true of the Quaker Ebenezer Howard and his ideas for 'Garden Cities of Tomorrow'.

But more frequent, perhaps, than these various solutions is simply an amnesia about the nature of the Christian documents. This may arise because they are simply not read, as in much of medieval Christendom, or because they are given a particular kind of reading as in much of the history of Protestantism. Obviously I cannot go into the various Protestant readings of the New Testament, but one with which we are familiar complements, perhaps even helps create, the Pelagian apathy of the average sensual Englishman. This reading presents the New Testament as a series of *ad hoc* injunctions to behave well, even to be very, very good. Awkward and explosive charges secreted in the text can be defused and turned into bland exhortation or a manual of proverbial wisdom.

I am inclined to suppose that this kind of *ad hoc*, moralistic reading of the New Testament and of Christianity is likely to exercise a vigorous influence so long as religion and society are in a major way coextensive. This is not to say that religion and society will be folded one into the other without tension. There will be intermittent demands from prophets, saints and visionaries, who want to give up the security of profession and family. There will be assertions of the freedom of the spiritual arm, which will in part represent revivals of radically religious perspectives and, in part, derive from the temporal interests of ecclesiastical institutions and of the clerical caste. There will be certain discrete but radical extrapolations from the foundation documents which prove difficult to implement: to avoid usury; to embrace sister poverty without reserve; to establish the Peace of God; to outlaw the crossbow.

But in the main, ideal teachings will be applied only to the family, in the form of life-long loyalty, and that only in principle. The most characteristic operation of Christianity will be a vast network of charitable endeavour, especially schools, hospitals, orphanages and the like. The Church will offer ambulance work to a society which can be sacralized but not saved or transformed.

With the onset of the modern period, however, two crucial developments are to be observed. The first is the vast increase in the scope of personal option, which in particular erodes the force of the rules governing the family. So the limited enclave in which church law about the ideal character of relationships is supposed to operate collapses. The second development is that the Church (or churches) becomes increasingly marginal to the spheres of economics, politics and even social control. The Church moves out of the structure of semi-necessity governing each of these spheres and can adopt a stance of free-floating comment. This comment will simultaneously involve yet another reading of the foundation documents and some assimilation to the kind of viewpoint found in other marginal strata, adjacent to the clergy i.e. the intelligentsia and the service professions.

This re-reading and this alignment with the view of adjacent strata will vary a great deal according to the social situation of the Church (or churches) in different areas of the world. In some places the Church will not be particularly close to any intellectual stratum or service profession: it may be still aligned with a land-owning class or, indeed, with an exploited group. Nowadays there are, maybe, certain typical situations. One is where the Church has been loosed from old social alignments with military, legal, political, and other professional castes, and develops a distinctive social dynamic. That is the situation in much of contemporary Europe. Or it may be placed in a missionary situation, where it carries and represents the identity of groups excluded politically or economically, or where it is associated with new élites educated under its aegis.

Clearly, places still exist where the Church remains more 'integral' as, for example, when old social alignments are retained in parts of South America, though this exacts a well-known price in terms of massive alienation among large sections of the population. Again, the Church remains integral where it embodies and represents a frustrated national group; Poles, Lithuanians, or Croats. But in general there is a marginalization in Europe which combines with a missionary situation in many other cultures.

The reading that results combines various elements. There is a partial adoption of political possibilities previously restricted to the Free Churches. *Vis-à-vis* governments and the semi-determinate dynamics of power which govern the political sphere, the traditional churches have acquired the structural position as well as the perspective of the Free Churches. They have done so, however, while still retaining a more collectivist ethos from the organic relationships in which they were previously embedded. Moreover, this new free denominational status has been acquired at the same time as a new free interpretative style has become increasingly available. The old integrated condition, meaning some variety of establishment, or unity with the core institutions of a culture, can be reinterpreted as a Babylonish captivity into which the Church was inducted under Constantine, and from which she is now finally at liberty. This interpretative freedom can, under the impulses available from the New Testament criticism, be developed so as to remint the old symbols, and also to undermine the authoritative character of the previous modes of interpretation. The Christian vocabulary can be given new meanings, congruent with critical political ideologies. The new meanings will be devised in fora like the WCC where the marginalized Christians of Europe meet both with the new élites and the exploited groups of the Third World.

Now, I would wish to be careful here in that what is argued by those armed with this approach may be as viable as what is argued by any other socially critical pressure group of left or right. Certainly its proponents will have called upon experts to ensure that relevant empirical knowledge can be taken into account. It is not my object to assert that the political position taken by churches in their rôle as pressure groups are simply amateur essays in social comment fuelled by the old naive moralism. My aim is rather to indicate what seem to me the characteristics of much contemporary Christian comment, and, more importantly, to outline what I think are recalcitrant features of social reality. The motto inscribed over my enterprise is 'If way to the better there be, it exacts a full look at the worst'.

Ecclesiastical comment works initially as part of the high level of social rhetoric. At this level speakers of all kinds, secular and religious, simply invoke the great and good words, like liberty, democracy, peace and progress. The additional contribution of ecclesiastical spokesmen, or to make it wider, of comment with a religious provenance, is in the use of words like loving, sharing, caring, supportive, compassionate, generous and reconciling. These are not exclusively religious words but they have a natural habitat in the shared discourse of the Church and the service professions. Perhaps it is worth noticing that such words as 'loving' and 'reconciling' have a closer relationship to personal intentions and motives than abstract terms like democracy. All the great and good works, whether abstract or personal, which circulate constantly at this level of social rhetoric, have been worn quite smooth. They are not expected to carry much practical cutting edge, but people are, nevertheless, reassured by their presence. They provide an aura if not substance.

However, there are certain notions which hover ambiguously between the theological and the social vocabulary and their ambiguity can be exploited according to context. One such notion is that of 'sacrifice', and I begin with this example because I do not want to suggest that the exploitation of ambiguity is specially characteristic of the contemporary Church in its present mood. The Christian meaning of the word 'sacrifice' lies pre-eminently in the redemption wrought by the death and passion of Christ. It is extended, however, to cover the sufferings of soldiers and civilians in wartime, and the soldiers' rôle becomes analogous to the redemptive act of God in Christ. The religious vocabulary shifts ambiguously to legitimate and even to sanctify warfare. Society and God's Israel become metaphorically interchangeable.

A very similar ambiguity is today exploited in relation to 'Christian liberty'. The 'glorious liberty' of the sons of God as expounded in the New Testament has not much to do with political democracy, let alone with 'liberation'. Nevertheless, phrases like 'set us free' can be slid across from the religious context into a vaguely liberationist context. A concept in Christian theology is half-appropriated to validate a particular political position. In a very parallel manner, whole ranges of vocabulary can be reused and reset in an existential, indeed atheist, perspective. Don Cupitt, for example, uses the old words but totally unhinges their direction and reference by using the controlling term 'God' to mean that ethical path which is the object of one's most serious choice.

But there is a further shift which needs examining. It is held that the exemplary acts of God in Christ can be efficacious in *social* situations. This is in spite of the fact that the death of Christ upon the cross for the redemption of mankind had no political efficacity whatever. The Romans were not reconciled with the Zealots. Jerusalem did not know the things which belonged to her peace and was captured in AD70 and destroyed in AD135.

Nevertheless, the rôle of love at the level of persons, that is between man and God, man and man is transferred to the level of political process. A reconciling agency is posited in social disputes and confrontations which repeats or works analogously to the redemption wrought by Christ. There is thus an optimism of love and reconciliation applied at the level of political process. Now, as I shall indicate below, I do not want to suggest that political processes work according to a completely determinate set of 'system dynamics', or that reconciling gestures are not possible on the part of representative persons or ordinary individuals. But the optimism built into this particular vocabulary does seem to me quite misplaced. Whether reconciliation, even costly reconciliation, 'works' depends largely on specific features of the social context. Many contexts are entirely recalcitrant.

Such optimism is, I believe, part of a general liberal presupposition about harmony reworked by reference to traditional theology. It is also closely linked to a vocabulary about the unity of the Church.

The disunity of the Church is conceived as due to culpable sin. Christian disunity and conflict is not seen as socially and existentially inherent, but as due to bad moral management ('our sinful divisions') which is now about to be cleared up by the Holy Spirit. In a paradoxical way the Church has adopted a superficial liberal and enlightened view, about the roots of religious and political conflict and the possibilities of harmony. I say 'paradoxical' because historically this same view identified religion *itself* as the main source of conflicts, whereas it is now clear that these occur at the system level of political process without any disbenefit of religion whatever.

These presuppositions about conflict, generated in the interstices of liberalism and semi-liberalized Christianity, are matched and supplemented by a conventional 'Book of Wisdom' which contains the commonsense view of travellers on the Clapham omnibus. Where the Church might speak of reconciliation, the people on the bus are inclined to say that really grown men ought to be able to get together and come to some agreement. According to proverbial wisdom, social confrontation derives in great measure from the intransigent wills of leaders. If goodwill is injected into the situation a proper compromise will result. Indeed, 'goodwill' is a concept spanning both the theological realm and this proverbial wisdom. This is the one reason why Christmas can be so inclusive a celebration, mixing faith with humanistic invocations of 'goodwill'. But beyond 'goodwill' there is further assumption also rooted in proverbial wisdom: that when the long-term history is taken into account, the moral balance between antagonists is roughly equal. It follows that there is also a policy to be followed where compromise is the proper reflection of that moral balance. However, the existence of such a policy is actually just an act of faith.

Parallel to the individualist presumption concerning 'goodwill' is an emphasis on 'people'. Now, it seems to me that while the Christian reference to 'people' is entirely proper, indeed to be applauded and supported, it is easily distorted into an attitude which would make policy dependent on particular images of people suffering, especially where these can be dramatized (as they now are) on television. Policy whose ultimate concern is 'people' cannot work by extrapolations from dramatized pictures of this or that cost at the personal level. This is a very difficult area for ecclesiastical spokesmen, since it is not easy to maintain a vision where 'people' are of ultimate moment and yet avoid being diverted by dramatized images. The images are 'true', but they are not enough of the truth to provide a basis for policy. Much suffering cannot be shown in personal pictures.

Parallel with the aspirations to harmony is an emphasis on 'community'. Those who are engaged in the promotion of lasting social bonds can hardly avoid being influenced by communitarian nostal-

gia. Yet in any situation costs will be considerable in terms of mori-
bund communities. This is not to say that change may be embraced
at any price: that would be to justify any pyramid of sacrifice in the
name of those who might ultimately benefit. All the same, I think
it reasonable to suggest that religious comment is often weakened
by communitarian nostalgia just as much as by an individualist
presumption. The point must be put very cautiously because the
emphasis on 'people' and 'community' includes and emphasizes
precisely the social costs of policy which I believe a radically econ-
omistic approach ignores at its peril. In other words, I believe that
in spite of sentimentality about 'community' there is a hard-headed
critique of economism which ought to be pursued. The Church is
still embedded in relationships and networks of family and local
tradition and understands that people hold to their roots and solidarities and are not movable at will or the call of economic
rationality.*

The last point I would make about religious comment concerns
its level of specificity. Clearly, clergy and Christians generally have
to avoid staying safely at the level of the great and good works.
Equally they have to speak out in certain situations at the limit
where moral ambiguity is much less present than normal. Cardinal
Sin, Bishop Tutu and Cardinal Glemp are in such a situation. But
most situations, *taken overall* are deeply ambiguous. I do not see that
the *general* situation in France, for example, justifies spokesmen
speaking 'in the name of Christ' as to which party should be supported, though the Church retains the right to defend its own specific interests within the polity. Conversely, localized situations and
particular issues may be much less ambiguous, and quite rightly
attract some ecclesiastical or Christian comment, though I think it
may be wise to adopt broad ethical grounds rather than invoking
Christianity. This is a matter of judgement. There are parts of France,
La Vendée, for example, where movements related to Action Catho-
lique have adopted a vigorous rôle in economic and moral transformations in rural life. But, in any case, many particular issues do not
yield a clear ethical judgement: Scottish devolution, for instance, or
television in Welsh.

The nuclear debate is held to be a prime instance of an issue
yielding a moral conclusion and therefore rightly attracting specifically Christian comment. But, although, for example, I do not myself
favour Trident, it seems to me that the issue is poised in terms of
'nicely calculated less or more'. With *all* the options so dangerous
to humanity it is odd that anybody can anathematize other believers
in the name of Christ. The whole debate over 'the Bomb' is one

* The history of Oldham since the sixties is a terrible illustration of the way architects
and rational planners of urban 'renewal' ignore the roots, needs and solidarities of
people.

where false dramatizations of good and evil, on all sides, actually damage our capacity to take very cool and carefully calculated ethical decisions.

Once we are in a situation of ambiguity then technical questions, notably long-term prediction of outcomes in terms of specialist knowledge, become very important. Notoriously, the predictions may be inadequate, but one must at least seek for knowledge which offers predictions above random. On the whole, Christian comment turns to the immediate human image rather than the long-term consequence. Quite often what is called 'prophecy' consists of demonstrations, tableaux, the invocation of pictures, the use of the name of Christ as a rhetorical reinforcement, the deployment of the big words behind a limited, contingent position. (Of course the attempt to characterize issues as *solely* technical is just a ruse to prevent Christian incursions into awkward areas.)

When the Church engages in comment it brings specialist knowledge and specific analyses to bear in particular areas, notably peace and colour, but it avoids specificity in relation to central issues where the argument becomes economic and turns on the crucial opportunity costs of e.g. inflation as distinct from unemployment. How much unemployment, for example, *is* acceptable as a consequence of the monopolistic position of trade unions, over-high real wages and monetarist policy? Is the economic criterion ever to be applied in pit closures, and if not, then are the long-term consequences for other workers acceptable?* Now, any responsible comment cannot stay in the relative safety of large words or calls for unity, but must stake out a technical argument for a given policy, in which all the costs for given groups and values are shouldered and accepted not for the duration of the comment but the relatively long-term duration inherent in acts of political responsibility. To do this, of course, would bring the Church down to the level of ordinary political action, and might involve it in the constrictions and stereotypical characterizations attendant on all political debate. So, it does not do this, except only in relation to those issues of peace and race I have just mentioned. What the Church does do is to act implicitly as if there are diverse rôles available in political debate.

One is the commenting rôle, which stands back somewhat from specificity, technicality and party identification. Another is the politically active rôle for which specificity, technicality and party identification is the politically active rôle for which specificity, technicality and party identification are necessary. Yet another is the rôle of the

---

* It is interesting that when the leaders of the NUM made clear to Church leaders that they would not abide by TUC guidelines the Archbishop of York said it was 'not for them to judge', though disapproval could be taken as implied, and had probably been voiced privately. But, of course, a public judgement would have involved the Church at the *nub* of a life and death economic and political struggle.

leader of a relatively deprived minority not ever likely to have direct political responsibility at least in that rôle. The Rev Jesse Jackson plays precisely this part which offers him a free rhetoric only trimmed at the edges to the real constraints of political exigency. It is the first and third of these rôles which in different circumstances the Church feels able to take up. It can comment, and it can engage in free rhetoric for particular and relatively (or absolutely) deprived minorities. It eschews the rôle of the direct political activist, except in very special circumstances e.g. Nicaragua.

Christian commentators do not only rely on a theory of complementary rôles in the making of political comment. They are also aware of the different opportunities for comment dependent on context. One cannot say anything at all times. It is obviously the case that a Christian qua citizen may speak his mind in the public forum on whatever subject he chooses. It is also clear that a bishop may, *speaking as a citizen*, vent a particular opinion, though there are dangers in constant comment or in becoming a focus of controversy in the Church. The real problems arise when a bishop speaks 'in the name of Christ', which easily implies that he speaks for the Church as a body; these problems are accentuated when he speaks in a liturgical context. The liturgical context is seen as one in which the great and good words are embedded in paradigmatic action, and is not to be lightly made use of to pronounce on ambiguous political issues.

I have to make one further comment on the general nature of religious rhetoric before turning to what I believe to be the general objective constraints within which it operates. Religious rhetoric is an expression of a basic grammar written into a society by virtue of having accepted and slowly absorbed a given religion. I say 'slowly absorbed' because I think the process whereby a culture is stamped with the basic grammar of a religion can take a very long time: centuries. The endless recitations and repetitions of liturgy and homiletics are part of the slow process of writing in the grammar. Certain exemplary pictures and perspectives have to be so reinforced that they form a whole world taken-for-granted.

This basic grammar or structure of perspectives and pictures is quite tightly organized. This is not to say that it yields a single logical line, but it does give rise to a group of logical lines, expanding organically from the basic root. One line or another will come into view in the course of history as possessing special relevance, according to the thrust of varying circumstances. The circumstances 'select' the relevant branch of religious logic, which then seems to occupy the whole foreground, while the rest of Christianity is mostly recited somnambulistically. The long sleep of liturgy is one in which all the great archetypes are maintained while just one picture escapes from sleep and looms large in consciousness.

I stress this strict but branching grammar because what I am about to say may suggest that religious rhetoric exhibits a shoddy shapelessness. On the contrary, it is an architecture of precise balances in which one fault can widen and undermine a whole structure. A misconstruction at point A will ramify through the most distant parts of the theological edifice.

But that said, there is also fantastic scope for variant readings. You have only to think of the myriad implications of a parable. The injunction to make friends with the Mammon of Unrighteousness is a classic focus of varying interpretation; but there is hardly a single story which cannot be pushed in the required direction. The Parable of the Talents can be given a very Protestant reading with the emphasis on using money and resources with all due diligence. Going out into the highways and byways to compel the wanderers and uninvited to the marriage feast can be deployed so as to justify ecclesiastical coercion. There are always coronation psalms to crown Kings and Magnificats to console the lowly.

Notoriously proverbs come in twos to allow you either to look before you leap or else to act immediately because he who hesitates is lost. The religious sign is both A and not A, so that the cross stands simultaneously for the non-violent martyr and the Christian crusader. Indeed, the religious sign, like the political sign, is often most powerful when alive with dynamic contradiction. Few people notice the contradictions within the sign. They receive only the sense of the 'field' within which the sign operates. The cross is 'in the field', and that is enough. Prophets and priests, like politicians, have licence to contradict themselves, because so much of their diction consists of signs and pictures. Like Walt Whitman they can say:

> Do I contradict myself?
> Very well then, I contradict myself,
> (I am large, I contain multitudes).

Indeed, you will never pull in the multitudes unless you *do* contradict yourself.

I mentioned the importance of establishing the correct 'field'. Religious and political vocabularies have to be so deployed as to convince listeners that a speech is authentically 'in line'. This reference back sets the speaker in the correct genealogy and is much more important than logic and consistency. The messenger always cites his credentials and does so by the invocation of correct words and the pronouncement of statutory curses. A great deal of what a religious or political commentator does consists in proper verbal stationing. Every picture has to be 'framed' in all senses of the word 'framed'.

Now, how does this flexible medium of comment and vision engage with the permanent conditions and contingent limits of social reality? Well, in one way it refuses to engage. We, as we absorb the sermon and the political speech, segregate it from what we know about the world, that knowledge which we have either by tangible experience or professional expertise. The statements are bracketed, partly for safety, and often because their purchase in the world we deal with 'out there' is so small. This indeed is *itself* one of the prime conditions of social life. At one moment in one context we accept a world of rhetorical devising. At another time we operate according to the understood limitations and requirements of mundane exist-ence. We understand perfectly well that the sermon or political prophecy must be disengaged from the world in order for it and the world to survive. The rhetorical vessels and their fluid contents have to be put in a specially segregated area, roped off from ordinary secular space. That is the first and great condition of the real world: the understood segregation of comment from facts.

What then of these facts, belonging to the semi-determinate world of system dynamics? Put in that way it may seem we are speaking of reality which can be expounded only in sociological theory. But we are also speaking of a world which we know by commonsense. We have a preliminary and pretheoretical sense of what the con-stants and the constraints are. Name any sphere of human action, like the operation of the stock market, and we have a commonsens-ical apprehension as to how it has to be worked. I want to use that apprehension to build up a few statements about conditions, constraints, predictabilities and limits. Each situation, whether it be the market or a union negotiation, or a diplomatic exchange, gener-ates its typical script which we know almost by heart. That well-known script requires only a touch of theory to give us our general conditions.

The *most* general condition is that indicated and manifested by the existence of the script itself. In everyday terms we know that scripts are, as we say, 'all too predictable'. A script emerges from aggregate behaviour. Each contributor to a situation is unique but the overall consequence will be the set script for that situation. A contributor may even withdraw and refuse to say his set piece, but the play of social dynamics will then proceed without him. Political choice is not individual choice writ large, but something operative within very strict margins. This is not to say that certain conditions may not be specified where the individual contribution is much greater than normal. A Lenin or a Woodrow Wilson makes a differ-ence. Without Margaret Thatcher the train of semi-determined scripts accompanying the course of the Falklands' War might not have been set off.

The next most general condition is the narrowing of options, boxing actors in a corner. That is not quite the way to put it, since if strictly true, options would in time disappear altogether. But there is, in a given situation, a steady narrowing down of choice and closing off of options. The commentator or sermonizer will speak in terms of what would have been possible *if* such and such had not already taken place, but each sequence of choices solidifies into a trajectory. You can see this most clearly in the sequence which precedes a war. A relatively open system has a specific, pre-existing tendency to closure, which sucks decisions forward faster and faster towards the vortex of the whirlpool. Many industrial situations have narrowed and narrowed over time till the script becomes totally formulaic. People are inducted into rôles with formulae attached and can no longer even imagine a slightly different performance. The logic of society consists in considerable measure of these 'locks' which are specially resistant to speeches and sermons. In ordinary talk we recognize these locks when we refer to 'knee-jerk reactions' and 'vicious spirals'.

Take the existence of a party and the constraints inherent in party organization as a prime case of system dynamics and 'locks'. A party is itself a kind of lock: the lock of antagonistic horns which cannot disengage. There is a paradox in this, which is that *nothing* can happen without these constricting rival solidarities. The general social condition illustrated here is that the limited solidarities and their stock rivalries are necessary. The constrictions they generate form the preconditions of any creative political action. So that the individual who constantly consults conscience in his adhesion to party and in his political decisions is abnormal. He even sometimes makes relatively moral outcomes more difficult to achieve. The point has to be very carefully stated. The process itself tends to grind conscience out of existence and to promote the amoral playing of set games. A characteristic instance was provided by those American foreign policy experts who infiltrated Albanians into Hoxha's Albania, knowing they would be killed, but accepting *no* moral responsibility. That is a profound *déformation professionells*. But the individual conscience as it is conceived and expressed by moral commentary and by sermonizing is unreal. The moral vantage point seized by the sermon is a false one.

The real constraint of political adherence and the morality inherent in it can be formulated more humanly perhaps by setting out the situation of the individual participant in a system of aggregate political behaviour. The politician has made an initial judgement that the goals and policies of a party are closer, though perhaps only marginally closer, to his conception of the social good than other parties. Once he joins that party he must obey a set of group imperatives at least partly rooted in the brute need to survive. Thus, he must accept the leadership in crucial matters, and refrain from dissociating himself from policy except in extreme circumstances and in matters understood to be decisions of conscience alone. All this amounts to a severe circumscription on his acts and expressions of opinion. He cannot speak the truth freely. Beyond that he has to contend in public that crucial differences turn on the election of his party and he has to present other parties in stereotypes and caricatures. The failures of those other parties must be attributed to their policies not to events and circumstances beyond their control. Above all within his own party he will experience a strong impulsion to exert pressure against all those who, in any way, ignore these constraints. He knows that survival depends on solidarity, and solidarity on threat and obloquy. Fear is the bond of fraternity as much as faith or love.

These constraining conditions of political association operate both above and below the level of the party, say at the level of nations and trade unions. The differences of level may be blurred since a party may define itself as coextensive with a future revolutionary nation, combining the loyalties of a whole society with those of a millennial political sect. Or a party may see itself as the idealized historic core of the nation. A trade union may, of course, be assimilated to such parties and display the same holistic loyalties. It may also by virtue of the ecology of certain industries become almost coextensive with the solidarity of a complete community and this in turn may overlap a regional loyalty: miners in South Wales cherish communal and regional solidarities as well as union loyalties. But analytically, one can suggest there are variations in the constraints operative as between unions and nations, below and above the level of party.

A union or trade association exists mainly for the advancement of the interests of its members, though it may also control standards of performance and entry, and define a professional ethic. The rôle of such an association is governed by the logic of leverage. If it can police entry and demand a closed shop that increases leverage: power breeds power. If it can cause rapid distress or disrupt an essential function, that likewise is a source of power, sometimes so clear and obvious that it need hardly be exercised. Of course, those who lead such associations and unions will appeal to more general notions than their own limited interests, and may well invoke the interests of a whole class even as they pursue policies which will impoverish or put out of employment other members of that class. Historically, the solidarity of classes has rarely been more than the contingent, and fleeting overlap of sectional interests. The concept of fairness deployed in negotiations will depend on the strength of the association or union. If it is very strong there is less need to deploy general concepts of fairness. And so on. The logic of leverage includes a use of fear and force parallel to that which sustains the fraternity of parties, above all else the weapon of excommunication. It includes the appeal to ancient solidarities built up in previous situations which may be deployed whatever the character of contemporary disputes. And there is, of course, a necessary appeal to potent myths and martyrologies.

At the level of nations, all the constraints which operate in trade associations and the party are reinforced. The solidarity and the fraternity of nations is not incidentally holistic but inherently holistic. Membership of the nation involves and expresses the very fact of social existence itself, not just the aspect of political action or economic interest. Nationality subsumes these and transcends them with an all-embracing claim. It is possible to be apolitical; you can sometimes avoid joining a union; to be stateless is to be bereft of social existence as such. Meanings are mediated through the nation's language, and the past through its charter myths, stories and selective history. National service is rarely regarded as optional and obedience in that service is defined as a duty correlative to citizen rights.

The deployment of themes and motives with an all-inclusive and religious weight and resonance is matched by a quite stark acknowledgement of the notion of national interest, above all in international disputes. Sometimes this will be loaded with an additional freight of political messanism, whereby the national interest is made co-extensive with a doctrine of universal human liberation, as in Russia and America. Indeed, a nation can sometimes summon up the fearful and ultimate fraternities of the millennial sect: such a nation has a mythology which organizes all life with the depth and range of membership in the Jehovah's Witnesses. (Parenthetically, when this happens a war is launched between the millennial national society and the millennial sect very much more ferocious than the intermittent war between secular élites and ecclesiastical élites.)

To the constraints of national fraternity and national interest, even at their most minimal, must be added the conditions of international political bargaining and exchange. These are most clear in wartime but never cease to operate. Such relationships are congeries of force, though cross-national fraternities can build up if the logic of alliances stays constant sufficiently long for co-operation to yield ties of friendship, particularly among peoples with similar material, political, religious and historic culture. This will push interested rivalries below the level of naked conflict to the level, for example, of Britain's war against France in World War I and America's war against Britain in World War II.

Those who play the key rôles in articulating these fields of international force act within a small range of options. They attend to a logic which will bend the internationalism of universal religions or universal schemes of political liberation. National interest will triumph over Islamic unity. Wars between communist states will be even more ferocious than ordinary wars because national interest will represent itself as the true guardian of the universal hope. A

Richelieu will pursue the national interest of France not the international interest of Catholicism. The Vatican is a special case, but the logic of geopolitics is followed without remission as Irish and Ukrainian Catholics at different times have discovered. And this logic means attention to the average tendencies of international actors i.e. the almost determinate script, generated by the net effect of average tendencies rooted in the checks, balances and imbalances of power.

How then does the grammar and rhetoric of religion relate to these constraints? Clearly, I cannot discuss here the application of the fundamental grammar of religion since it provides a taken-for-granted medium of everything said even when it has undergone major secular metamorphoses. My book on *The Breaking of the Image* (1980) was concerned with that problem. But something can be said about the fluid rhetoric of religion by way of a sketch of typical situations. Most of what I have said hitherto has had something of an Anglo-American provenance even though I have referred in passing to very different situations where the Church is related to Third World minorities or élites or exploited groups or to whole repressed nations, like Poland, Lithuania and Croatia. Let me then conclude by a typology of situations and the way Christian rhetoric may relate to them.

There is, first of all, the situation in the North European Protestant world, where the Church has been very extensively marginalized. It is clear that the Church feels that its services as a source of social legitimation are more dispensable than they were, and it will only give full transcendental insurance and assurance to the nation when the issue is survival, as in all-out war. Otherwise it will characteristically express reservations about the justice of particular wars and the means by which they are prosecuted. As for internal conflicts it will distance itself both from radical right and left and take up positions in the politics of welfare. It will align itself with the characteristic emphases of the service professions, of which it is now one among many. Ecclesiastical comment will emphasize broad issues of urban decay, race and peace, eschew detailed economic arguments, and avoid most direct economic conflicts. This comment will be heard respectfully, and occasionally (as in relation to the Nationality Bill) be heeded. Mostly it will be just noted but otherwise ignored or dismissed as naive. I should add that in my opinion Protestant influence on society works more at the level of cultural motifs and moral cultures rather than through ecclesiastical comment.

In North America, the situation is different. Whereas in Scandinavia and Britain churches have been gently floated down a central tide of semi-secularity at the level of communications (e.g. the BBC) and state institutions, in America there is a genuine pluralism which enables massive areas of conservative religiosity, Protestant and Roman Catholic, to retain vitality. Thus apart from the liberalized mainstream Protestant denominations, like Methodism, which pursue the same left-centre comment found in Northern Europe, there are massive religious pressure groups capable of maintaining themselves indefinitely, by an all-embracing institutional life and especially by the use of private ownership of modern communications. The 'Moral Majority', so-called, has to be listened to, at least at election times. Moreover, the Roman Catholic Church can elaborate what Cardinal Bernardin called a consistent and comprehensive moral position, on such matters as abortion, nuclear war, and (in the near future) economic policy. No doubt the American electorate concerns itself mainly with domestic issues of employment and the rate of inflation but the liberal Protestant, conservative Protestant and Roman Catholic sectors can operate as fairly effective pressure groups, and genuinely influence opinion. Of course, this will run into certain barriers, notably the separation of church and state, but it is interesting that Cuomo and Geraldine Ferraro felt obliged to defend their distinction between what they accept personally as Roman Catholics and what they propose as public policy. They had to stake out their political rôle *vis-à-vis* their obedience to ecclesiastical pronouncement such as those of Archbishop O'Connor.

In Catholic Europe, there is a combination of the marginalization which has occurred in Protestant Europe with more integral relationships. Roman Catholic Europe has been racked by a more prolonged and bitter war between ecclesiastical and secular élites than elsewhere. To the extent that the ecclesiastical élites have been partially marginalized, they have to maintain their base in the process of socialization, and this has given rise to renewed tension over schools, in France, Spain, Italy and, above all, Malta. The Church remains integral enough in many sectors, either to express their traditionalism or to take a part in their development which may well lead away from traditionalism. Thus it has been an integral and indeed rather radical element in the shifting economic and moral transformations of the French countryside. But there has been a war within Catholicism itself, for control of the extensive social and inclusive networks with which the Church in Europe tries to maintain itself. Thus in Dutch Catholicism, which established a very extensive network of cultural defence, there has been a social schism between critical elements, associated with the 'knowledge class' and the traditional social sectors. The network lost cohesion and gained criticality. Political comment grew and church practice declined.

The overall result of this situation has been a partial withdrawal in most countries from identification with the older *'integriste'* position or the more recent Christian Democratic position, and the emergence of varying degrees of radicalization. Given that the Church does retain some of its old command of an inclusive social network its voice has some impact. Obviously this impact is enormously increased where the identification of the Church with repressed nationship means that it can be 'integral' in the old sense and *also* engage in radical criticism. In Poland Christian symbols stand for national survival and are now closely linked to the struggle for representative institutions. Indeed, the Church almost profits by the demolition of these institutions since it then becomes the residual legatee of popular aspiration. Were representative institutions to emerge they would gradually channel more secular impulses, and might even rival the Church, though the fund of goodwill towards the Church and respect for its pronouncements could not easily be dissipated.

There is no way easily to summarize the Central and South American situations, though these provide the main theatres for an influential liberation theology. In several countries, like Brazil and Chile, the Catholic Church has both remained integral and been partially separated from secular élites and can thus channel popular discontents and radical criticisms. However, it is not the only religious force: both countries have experienced massive Protestant inundations, and Brazil in particular is affected by widespread cults like Umbanda and Spiritism. In other countries like Venezuela it was never really integral and was effectively subjugated in struggles with radical liberals. Thus it is weak, as well as divided between a majority who broadly support and are happy to 'ornament' the state, and a growing minority who are engaged in popular movements. The political impact of the Church is almost nil. In yet other countries, like Argentina, there remain substantial elements of the *'integriste'* Catholicism. In parts of Central America, as is well-known, the Church is estranged from the ruling group, and sides with a rebel movement. In Nicaragua it had a delicate task, in that the Sandinista Government was engaged in very extensive re-socializations, especially of the young, and the specific rôle of the Church in the future is not clear. In places like El Salvador and the Phillipines, the Church can be a massive constraint on dictatorial power.

The remaining situations must be summarized even more briefly. In part of Africa the Church gradually became identified either with exploited and repressed groups as in Namibia or with the new élites, who had been mostly equipped by Christian education. This position allows the Church to channel anti-colonial protest and also to retain enough moral capital to challenge the aggrandizements of the new élites, as in Zimbabwe and in Uganda. In other areas of Africa, the Church may represent a territorially based section of the population, over against an Islamic government as in Southern Sudan, or have connections with particular sectors within a wider federation, as Catholicism had with the autonomist aspirations of Biafra. In parts of Asia, like Japan and India, the Church is likely to be inserted in relatively educated and 'progressive' sections of the population and make a political contribution consonant with that social position. And in the kind of conditions existing in South Korea it may be a major focus of social criticism.

Clearly, there is a vast range of situations in which ecclesiastical or religious comment may be heard, and these are funnelled, focused and affected in a very complex way by the Vatican and bodies like the World Council of Churches. Most of my comments on the political language of the churches were concerned with the relatively marginal situation of churches in N W Europe. A much more extensive analysis would be needed to embrace all the relevant situations, from Poland to El Salvador, from Namibia to South Korea.

Chapter 5
The Church's Debate on Social Affairs
Digby Anderson

1. Background

In 1984 I was involved in editing a collection of essays by sociologists and economists analysing church, mostly but not entirely Church of England, publications on social and economic matters[1] and in 1985–6 in editing a series of reports from Jewish,[2] Protestant,[3] Catholic,[4] and rationalist[5] scholars on religious and ethical thinking about poverty. During this time there was an increasing number of church statements on social-political questions, particularly during the miners' strike and connected with the *Faith in the City*[6] report and the Chief Rabbi's report *From Doom to Hope*[7] in England, and the American Catholic bishops' pastoral letter *Catholic Social Teaching in the US Economy*.[8] This essay is simply a number of reflections on that debate.

'Simply' is perhaps not quite the right word. There are many fascinating aspects to the debate which I ignore here: ecclesiological questions about what sort of authority the various documents have and the extent to which publications and their ideologies reflect organizational changes in, especially, the Church of England, particularly those of synodical government. Again, one can analyse, as David Martin has, the sociological explanations for the changing ideological disposition of the clergy, for instance, in their reduced status.

I have chosen to ask some other questions. Moreover, I have also chosen an approach, or rather have had an approach imposed on me. The recent pronouncements from persons purporting in some, usually ambivalent way, to speak for the Church of England or even the Gospel have contained more than their fair share of rhetoric, a rhetoric arrogating to their recommendations some privileged entitlement to compassion in which much manipulative allocation of complex policies into heroes and villains has been made and seductive terms of slippery connotation such as 'care' and 'need' have been artfully deployed. Bluntly, against sentimental calls to side with the poor, careful realism cuts no ice. Rhetoric demands rhetoric, a rhetoric which shows dramatically how empty and, in the end, so unhelpful to the genuinely poor, so much care-talk is.

2.   The mischaracterization of the debate: it is not about whether there should be a social gospel

Let us start by correcting a misunderstanding. The debate, at least that in which I am interested is not about whether the Church has a right to speak on socio-economic issues. Of course it has. It may on occasions have an obligation to do so. The view that the Church should ignore them and concentrate on unworldly or next-worldly matters is not one anyone in the orthodox Christian (or I imagine Jewish) tradition can hold. The error in it is not as much its devaluation of this world as its opposition of the two worlds since it is precisely through restored manhood, through God-given and God-redeemed creatureliness, through love of neighbour, through proper use of creation, through the Incarnation, through the Church and her sacraments, i.e. it is through this world that one comes to things eternal. Christian living is in but not of the world, in the world but under the shadow of eternity, the things of this world made all the more important by being seen in the light of the divine scheme of redemption.

So I am at one with those who preach a social gospel. Indeed, precisely because the social gospel is central, it should be taken seriously. It should not be used as an excuse to spray the real problems of the needy with talcum powder talk about care, share and community, that now totally meaningless rhetoric of the sixties, or licence an impatience which makes us grab at certain seductive secular Utopias which promise much but whose actual incarnations have so far to deliver anything except collectivized suffering.

3.   Church publications not social enough

My original complaint was that the gospel had not been social enough, or some others might add, evangelical enough, in the sense that it had not been based on a thorough enough sociological, economic, biblical and theological analysis. Bluntly, if the poor are worth helping, they are worth tough, realistic thinking. All too often Church reports on socio-economic issues were ideologically partisan, economically ill-informed, sociologically naive, sentimental rather than loving, and theologically dessicated. Those are the complaints documented and illustrated in *The Kindness that Kills*[9] in its analysis of 24 publications on topics ranging from racism through unemployment, welfare, and the closed shop to the rôle of multi-nationals.

Subsequently I had cause to analyse a longer list: let me illustrate some typical products. There are Church reports which assert that 'Poverty is always evil because it is the outcome of the wickedness of the rich'.[10] This idea seems extraordinarily popular among Church writers. It begs economic questions of whether poverty levels in different societies are indeed caused by the riches of the rich rather than a host of other natural, economic or cultural factors.[11] It begs sociological questions about whether societies can plausibly be divided among a simplistic Marxist schema of two and only two classes in dichotomic opposition, or whether there are not important variations within such classes, of whether class or some other stratification is more important, and it begs philosophical or analytical questions about the relationship between inequality and poverty.[12] The quotation is not, unfortunately an isolated example. David Sheppard is addicted to similar Cowboys and Indians sociology[13] and this dichotomic class schema, if it deserves so grand a name as schema, is incorporated into *Faith in the City*[14] along with similarly questionable and Marxist, yes, Marxist notions of such as alienation. What is objectionable is not so much the concepts themselves but the fact that they are not argued, they are asserted or even taken up casually as a matter of preference: 'let's look at the world this way'. The authors are free to make the invitation, but the reader is equally free and in my view should be encouraged to reply, 'If you cannot show me why you have chosen that perspective rather than another, I prefer to refuse your invitation'. I would go further and suggest that other dichotomies such as 'inner city' and yet more, for example, the now fashionable 'north-south divide' are similarly infantile, and a sign that their users are interested in rhetoric rather than serious analysis on behalf of those in need.

My apologies. We were getting a flavour of the Church publications. There are Church publications explicitly critical of capitalism asserting 'the basic ethos of capitalism is definitely anti-Christian',[15] asserting that God is biased toward materially poor people and against materially rich people,[16] announcing that Marxism like Christianity is about 'enhancing human dignity, freedom, creativity and wholeness',[17] attacking multi-national companies,[18] denigrating the motives of businessmen,[19] praising Fidel Castro,[20] arguing the unions' case for enforced unionization,[21] denouncing government attempts to borrow and spend less public money,[22] spurning wealth creation[23] or imprisoning it in a permanent subordinate clause – 'while we accept the real importance of wealth creation . . . ' followed by the main business of the day which is spending other people's money. Reports blame free enterprise for unemployment and see intervention and collectivization as its cure,[24] demand the political redistribution of wealth from successful to unsuccessful economies,[25] assert that educational performance depends simplistically on educational expenditure,[26] assume that Britain is characterized by 'institutional racism'[27] and that its police discriminate against ethnic minorities,[28] advocate, minor reforms aside, more of the same nationalized welfare system and manage to do so as if Britain were a ruthless individualist economy rather than a society in which 50 percent of the population receive substantial income in wages or handouts from the state. These are all views which are legitimate but they are views which are in dispute, which need argument and to every one there are other opposing but equally respectable views. So the first batch of complaints is that the publications are partisan and less than adequately argued.

4.   Church views show no respect for sociology

A second is that many of them share a very odd sociology. Sociology is about how large, often unpleasant animals called humans manage to live together in huge numbers in a co-ordinated and orderly way, even their conflicts manifesting order. It is about why societies do not fall apart. And much of it is about how this order is spontaneously generated and maintained, that is, it is not the result of rulers imposing it according to a blueprint. The fundamental sociological attitude, whether the sociologist be in favour or not of political tinkering with society, is profound respect for society, the respect of friend for friend or foe for powerful enemy, a respect for that multitude of inter-locking institutions, exchanges and values which are society. He knows that it will defeat simple-minded attempts to engineer ideologically prescribed outcomes and that paradox and waywardness as much as intended outcome are the characteristics of social intervention, especially at national governmental level. With respect go modest, realistic goals and a certain scepticism. Enthusiasm is as much a sociological heresy as Knox showed it to be the theological heresy.

Next to none of the Church reports have learned this respect, which is strange, for it is really a respect for the sociability of humans themselves, a sociability which can even organize and contain their own capacities for evil and is essential for an order of fallen creatures. The failure to respect society has three consequences. First, it means the aims of the publications and indeed, one must presume, of the interventions they advocate are ridiculously unrealistic. Second, it means that they do not appreciate how many of their goals can be achieved by naturally occurring elements in society rather than interference by the polity. Third, it leads to social policy without sociology, or rather social policy without an explicit, thought-out sociology. Buried in those reports are colossal and highly questionable assumptions about, for example, progress, about rationality, about the rôle and availability of knowledge in and of society, the rôle of tradition, prejudice, stigma, prediction. To generalize, the sociology so often assumed seems one which accepts uncritically linear progress, has a nineteenth century view of rationality and science, is nervous about absolute values, conventions and tradition, despises social cements such as prejudice and stigma, and is optimistic about prediction and planning. Deep in the heart of these publications is what Hayek called constructivism.

5. The failure to appreciate naturally occurring welfare agencies

If society is bigger than the polity, its elements do not necessarily work against those of the polity. As Herbert Spencer pointed out, there are three sources of welfare in society, the state, voluntary organizations and informal welfare, the welfare provided by family, neighbours and friends. He might have added the welfare provided by organizations whose payment and advantage lies in satisfying the people's expressed desires, i.e. market-based enterprise, for indeed profits are won by providing what people want and need. The informal sector is and will always be bigger than the other two. There is no foreseeable possibility of the state bringing up all children and looking after all the elderly, let alone, God forbid, of it providing company, conversation and love. Thus those who would reduce suffering and maximize welfare are bound to value the informal sector. The Chief Rabbi, for instance, in a report,[29] suggested to currently poor minorities that his people had been helped out of the ghetto, not by the manipulations of politicians, but by their strong family structure and traditional values emphasizing hard work and impeccable behaviour which gave no cause for reproach to the majority culture.

Look, I beg you, through the many long pages of *Faith in the City* and you will find next to no mention of the family as a solution to urban social problems – quite incredible in a text of Christian provenance. Precious little on hard work or immaculate public behaviour either. Worse, this omission, as unsociological as it is un-Christian, was not enough for church spokesmen. They actually attacked the Chief Rabbi for saying what they were too in awe of current secular fashions to think, or, let us be charitable, had forgotten. For nearly 20 years, since *Putting Asunder*, the Church of England, individual bishops and priests apart, has been mealy-mouthed about its endorsement of the traditional family and those two decades have seen the family's decline so that expenditure on unmarried families has risen, in the same period, from £15m to £2,000m and to a point where one in three of the 'inner-city' children is being brought up without a father with all the attendant problems of delinquency and poor educational performance. I will not dwell on the thousands of unborn children who died to satisfy modern relativist ethics and an easy relationship with secular progressivism or the appalling AIDS carnage for which failure to speak out about homosexual buggery was partially responsible.

But the reason for the mealy-mouthed relativism is even more instructive. Firm lines could not be preached on morals for the majority because they would stigmatize the minority who could not attain them. We should be caring for the unfortunate not preaching standards. Quite apart from noting that such reticence never stopped the authors from firm and even mandatory lines on capitalism or racism – never any worry about stigmatizing a capitalist or racist – the excuse is patently absurd. Only the Church in the twentieth century could fail to see the difference between public pronouncements in which firm lines are essential and remedial personal pastoral care into which other considerations enter. Once again it is a sociological confusion about institutions and how they maintain rules yet keep rule-breakers within themselves.

6.   And modesty about intervention

Respect for society teaches modesty in intervention. After most of the reports discussed above and the reaction to them, the Board for Social Responsibility engaged on a rather different project. *Goals for a Future Society* does not prescribe partisan solutions and, perhaps learning from past criticisms, is a well-intentioned attempt to seek a range of views on future social policy. That said, and although its authors' good faith is obvious, they still do not understand the divergence between themselves and certain critics which is not over different solutions but whether ambitious, centralized and widely-discussed plans *of any kind* cure undoubted social ills.

Goals is a 'consultative document inviting responses' from many institutions – a series of questions. About what? About the future. No caution, modesty or precision here: the sky, or at least the stars are the limit. It is implicit Utopianism in full flood.

> How can women . . . structure their lives . . . in ways that are rewarding and satisfying. . . . How can increased family stability best be achieved . . . how urgent a problem does racialism pose for the welfare of the nation? . . . What policy should we adopt as a society to the older and commercialized areas. . . . Does a bright future owe a debt to the past? What should be the goals [of non-workers] for living? What goals for life can . . . be set before people of average or below-average ability? What new attitudes do we need to have to our work . . . to maintain status or esteem at acceptable levels? What about the duration of education? . . . Should the . . . black economy be encouraged? Ought overtime to be banned . . . Will pressures to federalize the United Kingdom grow? . . . Will power gravitate inevitably to officials? Are our prisons congested because of a breakdown in public morality or because of society's failure. . . . ? Is it possible that we might increase our share

of world economic activity? . . . What are legitimate areas of public spending? . . . Is unhappiness in Western society due to some extent (I like that 'to some extent') to a materialist attitude to life? Should our goals . . . be constrained by environmental considerations . . . What are the chief creative possibilities you see in the situation of Britain today?

We would like you to share with us your views on these matters. In the light of your contributions, and our reflection on them, we would hope to produce for the widest possible discussion a statement from the Church of England on the kind of goals we should be taking seriously for the coming years.

The BSR, in response to criticisms of ideological narrowness, has mistakenly devised a project of *topical* vastness. The imprecision and enormous number of questions (I've mentioned perhaps a twentieth of the pamphlet) are calculated to maximize the return from ideologues and windbags. And what will the BSR do with them? They are not designed to be representative or amenable to any methodology known to social science. In so far as they will give a range of views, that exists. If the Church is taking up stargazing, there is no need to set up a project and invite the witches of Endor to send in predictions by November. They, contrary to the then Bishop of Birmingham, BSC Chairman's preface, have published their forecasts already. There's a lot of futurology about, most of it inevitably nonsense. Why did the BSR not do a simple literature search and have their panel of contemporary Nebudcadnezzars award already-published forecasts marks for economic and sociological astrology?

It would all be an unfunny joke but for two matters. One reason for wanting to guess the future and set goals for it is the assumption that society is centrally knowable, plannable and malleable, what Hayek calls aptly 'the fatal conceit'. The Bishop clearly thought that collective planned goal-setting is how better societies are achieved. There is not much evidence for it. Social improvements have largely resulted from individuals following not precise goals but guidelines (including those of the Church), chosen freely or through tradition and without much theoretical or explicit consideration let alone formal discussion. Progress derives from the interaction of individuals' dispersed initiatives at muddling through life. We should be wary of the BSR's wish for 'us', some collective whatnot, to change attitudes, fix goals and manipulate status and esteem, wary of its desirability and practicality.

The likely BSR response to this would be that its aim is not to fix policies but to encourage discussion, general vision, testing of attitudes, that sort of thing. However, discussion is not best started by banks of imprecise questions about the future. The Bishop asserted that 'there is much fear and uncertainty today because . . . we have no clear goals'. The opposite is more likely. There is nothing so calculated to engender fear and uncertainty as endlessly discussing all the imaginable happenings of the future and scorning habit, tradition and unarticulated values. They, not bureaucratically-organized windbaggery, are the foundations of society and foundations that have proved able to adjust to change without so much as a page of a 'consultative document'.

7.   And are the publications good theology?

We have not talked much theology. I have already said that my complaint is largely sociological. But I must draw your attention to certain texts which suggest that there might be as much bias in theological interpretation as there clearly is in sociological interpretation. The texts speak for themselves. I have selected only two.

First, since those who condemn liberal capitalism make much use of the Hebrew canon, Our Lord not giving them much ammunition Himself and often manifestly avoiding invitations to authorize the first century equivalent of the Board of Social Responsibility, it may be useful to see what other interpretive traditions have made of the Hebrew canon. Here for example is Rabbi Jonathan Sacks, the Chief Rabbi designate and also Director of Jews' College London which trains the orthodox rabbinate in Britain.[30] Dr Sacks has harsh things to say about those who would make the prophets, so popular among Christian socialists, central at the expense of the Mosaic law.

> The one thing Judaism rules out *ab initio*, by specific biblical command, is a bias to the poor . . . compassion . . . must not distort judgement.

The rabbinic tradition is not concerned with side-taking but with

> the preservation of impartiality, the balance of claims, the reciprocity of rights and obligations, the interdependence of apparently opposed interests. . . .

Also, in contrast, Rabbi Sacks offers little comfort to those who would draw any simplistic political message from their reading of the Old Testament, whether about strikes, social security payments or exploitation. According to rabbinic tradition the gifts of this world are to be enjoyed: 'In the world to come a man will have to face judgement for every legitimate pleasure which he denied himself', precisely because poverty is evil, precisely because no-one should impoverish himself to relieve the poverty of others and excessive charity is therefore 'not piety but folly'; charity is good but the best charity is that which helps the poor rise to independence and work:

> The highest [charity] is that of the person who assists the poor . . . with a gift or a loan or by accepting him into a business partnership or by helping him find employment.

Poverty relief is good, but income redistribution should not be pursued simplistically, i.e., without considering other virtues such as output, economy and efficiency with which it may conflict; the poor should be helped but the poor are those who lack sufficient income, not those who simply have less income than others:

> you are commanded to maintain [the poor man], but you are not commanded to make him rich.

Or if your idea of authority is not so much Scripture as the Church tradition, look at a recent study of the late-scholastics working in the Thomist tradition in Salamanca and elsewhere in Spain from the fifteenth to seventeenth century.[31]

The author, Alejandro Chafuen, traces their influence through Samuel Pudendorf and the course of study Francis Hutcheson arranged for Adam Smith on to the author of the free enterprise bible himself.

On common ownership

> After man's loss of innocence, it becomes necessary for each individual to share in the things of this world, in real estate or moveable riches. . . . If universal love won't induce people to take care of things, private interest will. Hence, privately owned goods will multiply. Had they remained in common possession, the opposite would be true.
>
> Thomas de Mercade, 1571

> A donkey owned by many wolves is soon eaten.
>
> Proverb often cited by late scholastics

> We know that the fields are not going to be efficiently tilled in common ownership, and that there will not be peace in the republic, so we see that it is efficient to undertake the division of goods.
>
> Domingo de Banez, 1594

> . . . private property is necessary for human life for three reasons. First, because each person takes more trouble to care for something that is his sole responsibility than what is held in common or by many – for in such a case each individual shirks the work and leaves the responsibility to somebody else, which is what happens when too many officials are involved. Second, because human affairs are more efficiently organized if each person has his own responsibility to discharge; there would be chaos if everybody cared for everything. Third, because men live together in greater peace where everyone is content with his own. We do, in fact, notice that quarrels often break out amongst men who hold things in common without distinction.
>
> St Thomas Aquinas, *Summa Theologica*

In summary, Late Scholastic thought provides several arguments in favour of private property:

1. Private property helps to ensure justice. Evil exists because men are sinners. If goods were communally owned, it would be the

evil men 'and even the thieves and misers' who would profit most, since they would take more from the barn and put less into it. Good men, on the other hand, would contribute more and profit less. The fact that the most immoral people dominate society represents a harmful element and a distortion of natural order.

2. Private property is useful for the preservation of peace and harmony among men. Whenever goods are held in common, disputes are inevitable.

3. Privately owned productive goods are more fruitful because it is natural for men to take better care of what is theirs than of what belongs to everybody; hence the medieval proverb quoted above.

4. Private property is convenient for maintaining order in society, and it promotes free social co-operation. If everything were held in common, people would refuse to perform the less pleasant jobs.

5. No man (not even a priest) can detach himself from temporal goods. Original sin brings with it the problem of scarcity, which is the source of economic problems (i.e., the difference between unlimited needs and limited resources).

On public finance

According to the Late Scholastics, people are much more careless when they spend public money than when they spend their own. This causes expenditures to increase more than they should. In 1619, Pedro Fernandez Navarrete, 'Canonist, Chaplain and Secretary to His High Majesty', published a book of advice for the preservation of the Spanish monarchy. According to him Spain's major problem was emigration prompted by the high taxes people had to pay to finance public spending. His conclusion was that the best thing a king could do to enlarge his kingdom was to be moderate in spending.

> The origin of poverty is high taxes. In continual fear of tax collectors, [farmers] prefer to abandon their land, so they can avoid their vexations. As King Teodorico said, the only agreeable country is one where no man is afraid of tax collectors.
>
> Pedro Fernandez Navarrete, 1619

> He who imposes high taxes receives from very few.
>
> Ibid.

> The king is not going to be poor if the vassals are rich, because riches are better kept in the hands of the subjects than in the thrice-locked coffins of the State Treasurers, who go bankrupt daily.
>
> Ibid.

On profit

Among the motives which justify profits, St Thomas mentioned the following: (1) to provide for the businessman's household; (2) to help the poor; (3) to ensure that the country does not run short of essential supplies; (4) to compensate the businessman's work; (5) to improve the merchandise. . . . He also ascribed legitimacy to profits obtained from price variations in response to local changes as well as those earned through the lapse of time. Furthermore, he allowed for profits which would compensate the risks of transport and delivery.

Summary of *Summa Theologica* II–II

Once again, the point is not partisan. It is simply that, if the inter-relationship of economy and theology is important, then its study should take account of such interpretations as well as Tawney's and others' view that Christianity and a free economy are enemies.

8.   And debate itself

Let me end on a controversial note, questioning something progress-ive church people hold dear, even dearer than high public spending. One reaction to these criticisms is a tactical retreat. Dear critic, they say, what you argue is most interesting, but it is based on a misunderstanding. These reports are not meant to be a rigorous analysis, they are just starters for debate. Hmmn. Well suppose that is so. Suppose that the new idol is not political social activism itself but debate, is it a better idol? The contemporary Church of England is indeed a talking shop. Synodical government is a windbag's char-ter. But what is it for? Calculate, if you will, the man and woman hours which will be spent debating *Faith in the City*, then cost them, not forgetting that the Church of England is a middle-class insti-tution. Remember every hour debating is an hour not visiting the sick, the bereaved, the lonely. And contemplate the spectacle of a church so keen to talk about the importance of persuading politicians to solve the needy's problems that it has no time actually to do that itself.

Chapter 6
Utopias in the Modern World
Robert Van de Weyer

When Thomas More wrote *Utopia* (1516) he knew it was a dangerous book. Its glowing description of a communist, peace-loving society was a stinging condemnation of Tudor England, in which bishops and noblemen enjoyed huge wealth while a starving peasant could be hanged for stealing food. But More himself was ambitious for high political office, and wished to express his radical political ideas without jeopardizing his career. So he put the account of Utopia into the mouth of a rugged seafarer, Raphael Hythlody – whose name is a Greek word-play meaning 'expert in nonsense' – while he put into his own mouth remarks of gentle scepticism, doubting whether Utopian ideas would work in civilized Europe!

Utopian ideas have always been more subversive than straightforward political argument. Those who pride themselves on their worldly wisdom dismiss each new Utopian scheme as impractical and unrealistic. Yet the insights embedded within the scheme will lodge in people's imaginations, and nag at orthodox political attitudes. More's book, fantastic though it is, remains the only English work of political theory written in the sixteenth century still read today. But if Utopian ideas can enjoy such power, Utopian communities, where the ideas are put into practice, can pose an even greater threat to the political and cultural order. When in the fourth and fifth centuries young men in their thousands wandered off into deserts and forests to set up monasteries, the ecclesiastical authorities were quick to condemn them as heretical madmen. The Protestant Reformation was nurtured in communist – and pacifist – Christian communities in central Europe which were viciously persecuted; and although Luther and Calvin compromised these early ideals, groups like the Quakers and the Menonnites soon sprang up to renew the Utopian life style of the original reformers.

In the wake of the Industrial Revolution there was a flowering of Utopian ideas and communities, as people sought an alternative to free-market capitalism: in Britain Robert Owen, with his co-operative ventures and New Harmony Colony, was the leading figure, while in France men like Saint-Simon emerged with ideas remarkably similar to those of Thomas More. Engels contemptuously labelled these pioneers 'Utopian Socialists' – the first time, to my knowledge, that the word 'Utopia' was used as an insult – but Karl Marx's vision of a communist society, in which the state has withered away and people live in co-operative harmony with one another, makes Thomas More's ideas seem positively hard-headed.

Today, I believe, we are witnessing a new wave of Utopian thinking, in response to the huge and rapid changes taking place in the world economy. It is too early to do more than speculate as to the nature of the current economic revolution and its social implications. But it is already clear that the orthodox ideologies which emerged in the nineteenth century – free-market capitalism and state socialism – are pathetically inadequate to cope with these changes. Thus the search is now on for new political theories that can speak to the needs of our time. And it is hardly surprising that a new generation of Utopian idealists is emerging.

I am proud to confess that I am part of that generation. I have been knocking around the Utopian movement for the best part of two decades. And for the past ten years I have been involved in establishing a Christian community which – though we hesitate to use the term – is Utopian in its ideals. In preparing to start the community I was grimly aware that most such projects fail, breaking up after a year or two in bitter acrimony, leaving a debris of broken marriages and lost fortunes. So I spent some years studying communities, asking why some work and others flop. Strangely the most productive part of this research was a year spent in Ethiopia, looking at the life of the ancient monasteries there. They have survived almost unchanged for fifteen centuries, following precisely the pattern of the first monasteries of the Egyptian desert. The loose-knit structure of the Ethiopian monastery seemed ideally suited to a community of families; and so in most important respects we have adopted this model.

What I should like to do, then, is to look at our Utopian experience, and see to what extent our community should be regarded as subversive – or, to put it more gently, how our way of life could contribute to the search for a new ideology.

Commitment and change

Alvin Toffler wrote almost two decades ago of 'future shock'; that our highly mobile society was having disastrous psychological and social consequences. Benedict, writing his monastic rule in the sixth century, emphasized the importance of 'stability': the monk must become firmly rooted in a particular community, since love and trust between the brethren can only grow if they are permanently committed to one another.

In our community we do not take life vows, and formally only commit ourselves for one year at a time. But from the outset we realized that people should intend to spend several years in the community; and I suspect that most of us now see ourselves as remaining members for the rest of our lives. In Benedict's rule 'stability' means literally staying in one place; in Ethiopia the monk is committed only to a rule of life, and may occasionally move to another monastery if it seems desirable. We have adopted the Ethiopian pattern: and indeed some years ago I moved from our original group at Little Gidding to found a new branch at Leighton Bromswold, five miles away. But for all of us it is vital that we feel wholly committed to the community – none of us is free just to leave because things get a bit tough.

As a consequence bonds between members have become very strong over the years. There is that same relaxed intimacy that one finds in a good family: people feel no need to impress one another, or to earn each other's good will, but can be open and easy in each other's company. The children within the community are remarkably protective towards one another – and, of course, bicker in the way that members of the same family always do. Paradoxically, this intimacy between members strengthens rather than weakens traditional family ties, and demands a more rigorous standard of sexual morality than has become common in Western society. In a highly mobile context marriages can break up, and new partnerships be formed in a new place, with little social disruption. In a stable community family relationships must also be stable, and there must be far greater social pressure on marriages to remain intact through difficult periods. Indeed, communities which sit lightly on traditional morality, allowing a high degree of sexual freedom, invariably collapse.

Flexibility and mobility – these are the watch-words of modern free-market capitalism, as espoused by the New Right. I hesitate to say that our Utopia is rather rigid, but it certainly intends to be immobile. To believe in life-long monogamy, and to put down firm roots in a particular place with a particular bunch of people – these are an affront to the prevailing values of our society. The villages around us are rapidly becoming 'yuppified', as we are in easy reach of Cambridge and the other nerve centres of the East Anglian post-industrial boom. Having lived in the area almost eleven years I am now one of the longest standing inhabitants – apart from a few retired farm labourers. And, as the local vicar, I am aware that my wife and I, along with the other couples in the community, are peculiar in our sexual habits. The famous statistic of one in three marriages ending in divorce vastly underestimates, in my view, the degree of sexual mobility in our society – especially amongst the affluent members of my generation.

Stewardship and property

One of the problems of pure communism is where one draws the boundaries of common ownership: is it the nuclear family which shares its wealth; or is it the village, the nation, or the whole world? In most Utopian writings, including Thomas More's book, the nation is the unit which owns wealth. In monasteries, of course, it is either the individual monastery or the Order to which it belongs. This question of boundaries is not merely academic, but is crucial to the way in which decisions are made and resources allocated. Whatever unit owns the wealth must also determine how income is distributed, and, indeed, what work individuals do.

Many Utopian communities which have incorporated families have come unstuck because they have tried to share all income and possessions. Quickly the community finds itself in a dilemma: either it must establish a quite sophisticated bureaucracy whose decisions are binding on all members; or it is liable to collapse into indolent poverty. The brute fact is that self-interest is a necessary motivation for all of us, especially where the work we have to do is dull or unpleasant. And the larger the group which shares income the weaker that motive becomes: to put it crudely, if I, as a member of a communist community of fifty people, were to give up work, I personally would only be two percent poorer. Thus such communism requires an authoritarian bureaucracy to determine what and how much work I must do. There is a further, no less fatal, objection to pure communism: the authority of the community will inevitably cut across the traditional authority that parents have over their children, and that families have over their own affairs. Thus communism inevitably weakens family bonds – a point which Thomas More never considered.

Needless to say, we do not practise communism in our community. Nonetheless we are wholly committed to the principle which underlies communism: that our economic lives must be conducted within a firm moral framework. We are not simply free to pursue the highest income for ourselves. In our rule of life there is quite strict discipline of stewardship, in which members of the community must each year review their use of time and money, considering carefully how to allocate their resources between their immediate family, the community and other commitments. But, more importantly, the personal relationships within the community exert a strong influence on people's economic decisions. Although there are considerable differences in personal income and wealth, there is almost no difference in standards of living. Richer members make in all sorts of seen and unseen ways a larger material contribution to the community; people are spontaneously very generous with their time, which could otherwise be used to earn more money; and the levels of consumption above the norm within the community would be regarded as offensive, earning disapproval rather than envy. Thus the strength of personal relationships within the community has a profound economic effect.

This makes us seem even more peculiar in the eyes of our yuppy neighbours. While new cars, kitchen fittings and house extensions spring up like wild flowers in the nearby villages, we struggle to get our P and R registration cars through another MOT. And while we are happy to give money directly to local worthy causes, our neighbours insist on lavish fund-raising events in which they get full value for what they give. At one time people thought we must have some hidden source of wealth; now they just think we are odd.

Freedom and power

The political conflict between Right and Left which has raged for two centuries in capitalist society is a reflection of the conflict that lies at the heart of capitalism itself. As Thomas Hobbes saw clearly – a century before the Industrial Revolution – a society which puts economic power solely in the hands of individuals will always tend to degenerate into a 'war of all against all'; thus the power of the State must check the freedom of the individual. Right and Left – America and Russia, come to that – differ only in where the balance is struck.

Utopian ideas transcend that division. The power of the community over the lives of individuals derives from the personal commitment of those individuals, and is sustained by their mutual trust. Correspondingly that same trust allows the community to vest authority for particular aspects of its life in individuals, without need of bureaucratic control. The challenge for any community is to find actual structures in which that trust is give practical expression. Ultimate authority must lie in the community as a whole, so the Quaker method of striving for unanimity has much to commend it: it prevents the group dividing into parties and factions, which any crude voting system tends to encourage. But Quaker style consensus is time-consuming to achieve: and, more importantly, can stifle the creative spirit of the individual. We have adopted the structure of the Ethiopian monastery in which 'pastors' are chosen by unanimous consent. They advise and encourage, but have no executive power; and they in turn appoint, after consulting members, particular people to manage the various spheres of the community's life. Like any structure this has its dangers, but its advantage is that it gives individual managers a high degree of freedom in making decisions, while retaining ultimate power in the hands of the whole community.

It is tempting to imagine that this structure – or something similar – offers a direct alternative to right wing and left wing models of social organization. But in fact the political implications are more subtle than that. Both free-market capitalism and state socialism are methods of organizing large, impersonal groups – the national or even the world economy. By their nature they destroy the cohesion and authority of small groups, be it the extended family, the village or whatever. The Utopian approach reasserts the authority of the small group, based on personal bonds of trust, and regards such groups as the necessary building blocks of any large-scale organization. In this century it was Mahatma Gandhi who understood this most clearly. For him the true alternative to British rule was not an authoritarian Indian government in Delhi, or, worse still, rampant capitalism: rather, it was what he called 'Panchayat Raj' – the independence of the local village. This was both an economic and a political creed: the extended family and the village should seek a high degree of economic self-sufficiency, and this in turn would lead to a natural harmony in which state coercion and weapons of war would no longer be necessary.

Idealism and reality

Utopian communities always evoke strong reactions. Most people quite naturally feel threatened by their very existence, and nervously try to brush them aside as weird and half-baked. They will anxiously look for some scandal which will prove they are corrupt and immoral; and failing that they will accuse them of being self-righteous and priggish. I know that from personal experience. When we started not only our neighbours but also visitors would constantly be on the look-out for sexual misdemeanours and financial corruption; and no doubt comparatively minor offences, which would pass unremarked in ordinary society, would have made juicy reading in a Sunday paper. But when we turned out to be boringly moral and honest, those determined to oppose us decided we were too holy and stuck-up.

But there are equally strong feelings in the other direction. There are many people in our neighbourhood who have come to respect and like the community – especially the farmers and the labourers who still survive in the council houses and unmodernized cottages. To put it at its lowest, we are regarded as a lot more pleasant than most of the affluent commuters that have moved in. And we attract genuine seekers from far and wide, who come to share our life for a few hours, days or weeks, trying to sort out their own values and ideals.

There is no direct link between Utopian communities and political theories. Although we are often asked to give our support to particular political causes, as a community we have steadfastly refused to do so. Most of our members are fairly apolitical, and have no inclination to try and connect the life of the community with the political issues of our time. At general elections our votes probably cancel each other out. Yet undoubtedly Utopian communities are political entities. The opposition they evoke proves that. They are a living affront to the dominant moral and political attitudes of our society. And they are a practical test-bed of alternative values.

I believe that Utopian communities are politically and morally highly influential, not through direct pressure but through their example. In the early and mid-nineteenth century, for example, the Utopian socialists were enormously influential; and their ideas have an awkward habit of reasserting themselves in left-wing discussions. But, more importantly, I believe that Utopian ideas are essential if the society which emerges from the present revolution is to be just, humane and peaceable. My own modest contribution to Utopian literature, a book called *Wickwyn*, is an attempt to show how the current crisis could lead quite naturally to a society with many Utopian characteristics. Yet the response which that book has evoked has taught me a harsh lesson. It was a soft book, designed to lead people gently towards Utopian ideas; but that has allowed people too easily to dismiss it as – to quote a letter to me – 'insanely optimistic'. The lesson is that those of us of Utopian inclination, if we venture into the merciless world of political debate, must be prepared to argue with all the hard logic which our opponents muster. If I write another political book, as I intend to, my natural Christian meekness will be much less conspicuous!

Chapter 7

Religion and Utopia
Krishan Kumar

I

Three minutes, I thought, would be enough to suggest the obvious and intimate connection between religion and Utopia; and so, not wishing to waste everybody's time, I initially declined the Director's kind invitation to give the address on which this essay is based. It seemed hardly worth spelling out what was so familiar and evident. I thought of general religious concepts such as *salvation, redemption, hope, fulfilment, perfection* and *perfectibility*. I thought of specific ideas within the Judaeo-Christian tradition: 'the Garden of Eden', 'Paradise', 'the end of days', 'the New Jerusalem', 'the millennium'. Was not Utopia replete with these sentiments and associations? Could we even think of Utopia without them? And was not this why a good number of theologians, such as Paul Tillich and Martin Buber, had felt drawn to Utopias, recognizing a natural affinity between religion and Utopia? Here, for instance, is Martin Buber justifying his faith in messianic or prophetic socialism: 'Religion without socialism is disembodied spirit, and hence not authentic spirit; socialism without religion is body, emptied of spirit, hence also not genuine body.'[1]

Further reflection only seemed to confirm this initial sense of the near-identity of religion and Utopia. After all, was not the very first Utopia, the eponymous Utopia, written by a Catholic martyr who became a saint (Thomas More, *Utopia*, 1516)? And similarly with the classic Utopias of the sixteenth and seventeenth century – the group that includes Campanella's *City of the Sun*, Andreae's *Christianopolis*, Bacon's *New Atlantis*: these were written by men who were either priests or monks or who held deeply religious convictions which come out clearly in their Utopias. In one important sense all their Utopias were varieties of 'Christianopolis', the Christian Utopia, the ideal Christian Commonwealth. This was so whether their Utopias were mainly moral and social, as with More, or whether they were concerned with the potentialities of the new science, as with Campanella, Bacon, and Leibniz. In the latter case we get what Comenius called 'pansophias', ideal societies based on scientific knowledge and techniques. But it is made absolutely clear that science is seen as the means both to a better knowledge of God and to the creation of a truly Christian society. For both Campanella and Bacon that is, in the end, the only justification for giving science and scientists so elevated a place in their Utopias.[2]

Then there is the clear and powerful influence of monasticism on the modern Utopia. More, we know, spent four years with the monks at the Charterhouse, and wrestled with the question of whether to become a monk himself. The monastic life seems to have been the one he preferred above all others. Certainly his Utopia has strongly monastic features: communal living, involving the community of property and dwelling, as well as communal meals; plain, uniform dress; a serious though by no means a solemn ethos, with a devotion to work, study, and contemplation. We find these monastic features recurring repeatedly in subsequent Utopias – from the House of Salomon in *New Atlantis* to the monastic yearnings of the very secular Saint-Simonians of nineteenth-century France.

Here, we may say, religion seems to have contributed to Utopia not just spiritual content but institutional form as well.

I don't think, though, that there can be any doubt that of all the links between religion and Utopia the most important is the idea of the millennium. This is Judaism's main contribution to Christian Utopianism. Millenarianism is clearly a development of Jewish messianism. And the critical thing here is that the Jewish idea of the Messiah is – as so well brought out by Gershom Scholem[3] – of a decidedly *human* person. A political or military Deliverer, of the House of David, will arise and will gather together all the Jews from all the corners of the earth, and he will restore them to their original home where they will live in peace and prosperity under the law, the *Torah*. There will be an 'end of days' and the inauguration of the 'Days of the Messiah'. The Age or Reign of the Messiah is hence on this earth: it is a public and political State of goodness and freedom, not a matter of personal or individual salvation, or of life in the hereafter.

This idea is kept very much alive in Christian millenarianism. The Council of Ephesus pronounced millenarianism a heresy in 431, and the orthodox view throughout the Middle Ages was Augustinian: which meant a denial of a new earthly millennium following the second coming of Christ (for Augustine, the one and only earthly millennium had already begun with the advent of Christ). But we know how impossible the Church found it to prevent alternative interpretations arising, mainly in the form of commentaries on the *Book of Daniel* and the *Revelation* of St John the Divine. *Revelation* in particular gave rise to the standard pattern of millenarian belief. Christ's second coming would be accompanied by the emergence of the Antichrist and victory over him. There would be a first Resurrection and a first Judgement. Then would ensue Christ's thousand-year reign of peace, joy and freedom on earth. That would be followed by a second Resurrection and a second and last Judgement, and the final end of earthly existence. But up to that final point, Christian millenarianism shared with Jewish messianism the belief that the new providential dispensation would take place on earth.

The millenarian belief became even more explosive when mixed with the 'Three Ages' philosophy of Joachim of Fiore.[4] Joachim's 'Third Age of the Holy Spirit' had much in common with the character of the millennium as generally understood. This Third Age of freedom had already begun, Joachim proclaimed, and with it the authority of Pope, priests and the whole ecclesiastical hierarchy had fallen away. It was in fact largely in a Joachimite form that millenarian ideas inspired so many of the radical movements of Christian Utopianism: the Anabaptists of Münster, the Diggers, Ranters, and Fifth Monarchists of the English Civil war, the Shakers and the Oneida community of nineteenth-century America.

Even when millenarianism and Joachimism had ceased to be overtly important in Utopian strivings, they continued to exercise considerable subterranean power. As a structure of thought, as an evolutionary philosophy of history, they were fairly evidently the inspiration of many of the nineteenth-century social philosophies, such as those of Fichte, Hegel, Marx, Comte, and others.[5] In so far as Marxism and Positivism can be said to have a Utopian character – and I think they have – then religious thinking clearly underpins much modern Utopianism. The Third Age could erupt as the Third International or the Third Reich with the same apocalyptic fury.

Coming more directly to the Utopia itself, as a literary form or genre, there is the view that Christianity established the dominant myth or archetype behind Utopian (and anti-Utopian) thought: the myth of Paradise and the Fall. Here there is seen a close correspondence between the structure of Utopian thought and the Judaeo-Christian linear view of history as having a beginning, a middle, and an end (rather than, as in the pagan classical view, as cyclical). 'The Bible', says David Lodge, 'can be read as Utopian fiction; and the Apocalyptic tradition, which Frank Kermode takes as a model for all fictions, is clearly a major theme in Utopian literature, particularly of the "Science fiction" variety, so often concerned with the end or near-end of the world.'[6] The theme of the Fall, a concern with origins and beginnings rather than endings, is most often to be found in the anti-Utopian form, as in William Golding's *Lord of the Flies* and *The Inheritors*; the apocalyptic ending, the glorious dawn that awaits humanity, is to be seen at its clearest in the Utopian fiction of H G Wells, as in *The World Set Free* and *The Shape of Things to Come*.

David Lodge points out that even where, as in the case of Wells, explicitly Christian notions like original sin are repudiated, 'the archetypes are apt to enter by the back door'. He draws some interesting parallels between Wells's moral fable *The War of the Worlds* and Milton's *Paradise Lost*: in both accounts a foolish and arrogant humanity is routed by a ruthless extra-terrestrial intelligence but is saved at the last by providence from complete destruction. *Paradise Lost*, says Lodge, 'as well as being the major transmitter of the Genesis myth in English, is also the first great work of science fiction, complete with War in the Air and interplanetary travel.' Moreover, both Milton's poem and the myth of the Fall can be interpreted either optimistically or pessimistically. We can either deny the irreversibility of the Fall and look forward to redemption or the millennium. Or we can accept the fact of inevitable suffering and man's sinful state during his worldly existence. The first view leads us to Utopia, the second to anti-Utopia; the first, to take twentieth-century examples, gives us Wells's *A Modern Utopia*, the second Huxley's *Brave New World*. (I shall not deal here with anti-Utopia – merely to say that everyting that is said about Utopia can also be said about anti-Utopia – only, as it were, in reverse.)

II

I have, I am afraid, taken far more than three minutes to state the obvious. I have been expanding on my initial impression that, even if religion and Utopia are not the same thing, they seem so closely related that Utopia might better be studied by theologians and philosophers of religion than by historians or social theorists, let alone literary critics.

I now want to take a further generous measure of three minutes to qualify this view very severely. In doing so I shall state something equally obvious. At least, it was pretty obvious to an earlier generation of thinkers, but as with so many matters that seemed clear in the past we have managed to cloud it with our cleverness. I want to argue that, despite a powerful religious (Christian) influence on the Utopian enterprise and on the supplying of many Utopian themes, religion and Utopia are quite different things and ultimately point in very different directions. In other words, when Thomas More coined a new word, in a typically witty conflation of two Greek words (*outopia* = no place, *eutopia* = the good place), he also invented a new thing, a new literary form with a new social content capable of expressing different possibilities from traditional religious ideology.

This, as I say, used to be obvious, and is obvious now to most people not caught up in the thickets of Utopian studies. But such is the vogue for myths and archetypes, such an urge to uncover the anthropological roots of some well-nigh universal 'Utopian propensity', that some simple historical and typological distinctions are in danger of being overlooked. It was because I myself came increasingly to be impressed by this, and to feel that there was some danger of others being carried away by current fashions, that I changed my mind and accepted the Director's invitation to speak. The only justification for my appearing before you, then, must be to re-assert some rather obvious yet neglected truths.

The first thing to note is that the literary form of Utopia, a tradition of Utopian thinking and writing, is not to be found anywhere outside Western cultures. Utopia, like science and capitalism, is a European invention – and for much the same reasons, and in the same kind of historical conditions.[7]

Now of course this suggests that – as with science and capitalism – there is some intrinsic connection between – not Utopia and religion in general but – Utopia and *Christianity*. But this should not lead us to reduce Utopia to some variant of Christianity. We recognize, for instance, that in the case of science (or secularization) there is some kind of 'elective affinity' between the world-view of science and that of Christianity. But on the whole we consider it unhelpful to reduce science to religion, for we acknowledge a fundamental difference of method and orientation (or intent). So with Utopia and Christianity. Christian civilization gives rise, uniquely, to Utopia, as it does, uniquely, to capitalism, science, and secularization. (For Utopia, I think the essential or at least most important link is in fact the millennial idea, which despite traces elsewhere seems distinctively Judaeo-Christian in its prominence.) But Utopia is not Christianity.

We can put it even more strongly: the 'Christian Utopia' is a contradiction in terms. This too is obvious as soon as we think about it. There is, there must be, a fundamental antagonism between the forms and concerns of religion and the forms and concerns of Utopia. That is, of course, why Utopia is not to be found in non-Western cultures, dominated as they have traditionally been by typical 'other-worldly' religions (and why Utopia has arisen only in a culture whose religion produced a powerful 'this-worldly' variety). Religion can never be more than secondarily concerned about life on this earth. Even where a religion has a Paradise concept, and many do, the attempt to anticipate or to realize the Paradise on earth is ultimately blasphemous and impious. It is an arrogant usurpation of the omnipotence of God, who alone can bring in the new dispensation. And for all the strength of the millennial (and perfectibilist or Pelagian) strand in Christianity, this in the end is true for Christianity as well. 'My Kingdom is not of this world'. Augustine, with his anti-millenarian, anti-Pelagian emphasis, is in the end the dominant influence in churchly Christianity (just as, perhaps, the anti-apocalyptic Maimonides is within Judaism). As Bishop Goodman put it, reproving the millenarians of seventeenth-century England, 'if Paradise were to be replanted on earth, God had never expelled man from Paradise.' It was the religion in their radicalism that prevented the Civil War sects from arriving at a truly Utopian conception of society. The problem was, as Christopher Hill says, that 'however radical their conclusions, however heretical their theology, their escape route from theology was theological.'[8]

Ultimately, then, to the Christian, Utopia must always be 'the perennial heresy.'[9] Theologically that seems absolutely the right position.

I have, some of you will have noticed, refrained from defining either religion or Utopia. I shall persist in this refusal. Definitions are far less helpful than might first appear, certainly in the human sciences. The commonly understood meanings of both religion and Utopia will suffice for my purposes. From the context and use of both terms so far you will already have gathered my understanding of them. But in the case of Utopia at least perhaps I should make explicit the implications of what I have just said. Utopia, then, is a secular, rational form of inquiry concerned with the transformation or reconstruction of human life on earth. It is, for all the overtones of fantasy and 'no-whereness', essentially a form of sociology (as H G Wells recognized, although he got the historical priority right when he said that sociology was a form of Utopian inquiry)[10].

Now this of course leaves me immediately open to the charge of tautology. Since I have defined Utopia in such a way as to exclude religion, then obviously religion and Utopia must be incompatible. The point I want to make, however, is that in writing his *Utopia* Thomas More inaugurated a tradition of Utopian social inquiry which carried certain characteristic hallmarks and attributes, certain postulates about man, society, and nature as well as certain formal literary conventions. The Utopian tradition has been more or less continuous since More. Writers working in the tradition are aware of their predecessors and of the conventions of the genre, which they themselves elaborate and develop. From this tradition – of some four hundred years – it is not difficult to pick out a series of elements which most students of Utopias would be prepared to agree constituted the principal features of the Utopian enterprise. This is not the place to offer such a list, but it is certain that it would include that secular and rational character which I have highlighted. Utopia, like secularism in general, comes out of religion, and as with secularism carries the impress of its parentage as well as of its revolt against it. In that sense it is true, and helpful – tautology is a venial sin – to define Utopia at least in part as the absence or exclusion of religious preoccupations. But religion, having seeded Utopia, gave birth to a child which like all healthy children developed its own autonomous and independent character.

III

If we accept that More, in inventing Utopia, broke with the religious world-view of medieval Europe, then this helps us to explain certain features about More's own Utopia and most later ones as well.

It explains why More made his Utopians pagans, not Christians. More's Utopia was described by his biographer R W Chambers as 'a pagan state founded on Reason and Philosophy', and that is a good description of its general character – rational, utilitarian, moderately hedonistic. So too Campanella's Solarians in the *City of the Sun* are pagans. And while the inhabitants of Bensalem in Bacon's *New Atlantis* have been converted to Christianity (by a special appearance of Christ among them), most scholars agree that the Christianity is a very thin veneer over the exuberantly scientific, Promethean, enterprise represented by the House of Salomon. We may in fact see this as a general feature of the 'Christian Utopia', the 'Christianopolis', of the sixteenth and seventeenth centuries: the religious shell often contains a hard rational, scientific, and ultimately secular kernel.

This way of seeing Utopia also connects it, in a more or less self-evident way, with the historical circumstances in which it arose: the period of the Renaissance and the Reformation. We need to remember that More's *Utopia* (1516) appeared in the same decade as Machiavelli's *The Prince* (1513), and shows the same influence of classical republicanism and Hellenic rationalism which we find among so many Renaissance humanists. (Also, perhaps we should add, the same satirical playfulness that the humanists enjoyed in Lucian, Horace, and Persius.) But this is also the decade, of course – the devil's decade? – of Luther's Ninety-Five Theses, which he nailed to the church door at Wittenberg in 1517. So Utopia partakes of the same current of thought and society that was destroying the unity of Western Christendom and leading eventually to the secularization of society (for where there are so many discordant voices they must eventually silence each other). This took time, of course. The immediate effect of the Protestant Reformation was to produce a wave of 'religious Utopianism', in the teachings of Thomas Müntzer, Andreae, Comenius, Winstanley and others. But Luther and Calvin, re-asserting Augustinianism, had made a stand on the centrality of original sin and had made clear their strong hostility to Pelagian ideas of perfectibility. Radical thought, and *a fortiori* Utopian thought inevitably had to go secular, as is obvious from the eighteenth century onwards.

Original sin deserves a further note. Its rejection, explicitly or implicitly, is the starting-point for most Utopian speculation. H G Wells made of this almost a defining condition of Utopia: 'The leading principle of the Utopian religion is the repudiation of the doctrine of original sin.'[11] Most students of Utopia have accepted that this must be so. If Utopia is the perfect society, then men must be perfectible (although not of course 'naturally good', or else the whole Utopian project becomes redundant). No concept of 'fallen' or 'sinful' man must be allowed to stand in the way of this perfectibility. Moreover, unaided reason must suffice to achieve the state of human perfection.

It is this feature of Utopianism that has produced some of the strongest reactions to it from more orthodox Christians such as G K Chesterton and C S Lewis. In both their cases Wells, as the greatest representative of twentieth-century Utopianism, was the victim of their sustained invective. It was *a propos* Wells that Chesterton produced his memorable quip:

> The weakness of all Utopias is this, that they take the greatest difficulty of man (i.e. original sin) and assume it to be overcome, and then give an elaborate account of the overcoming of the smaller ones. They first assume that no man will want more than his share, and then are very ingenious in explaining whether his share will be delivered by motor car or balloon.[12]

It was not just original sin, as a principal item in the baggage of Christianity, that the Utopians threw overboard. The European voyages of discovery supplied the sense of Christianity as something ethno-centric and particular. To Enlightment thinkers such as Voltaire and Diderot Christianity represented the narrowness and parochialism of traditional thought at its worst. The eighteenth-century discovered Man as an anthropological unity stretched across many cultures and religions. No one religion could possibly provide the philosophical and moral synthesis required to establish the framework for future human evolution. Utopia therefore did not simply borrow from the travel literature of strange lands and exotic cultures that the European voyages produced (although that borrowing was an important stage in the development of Utopia – Raphael Hythloday we should remember, discovered Utopia as a result of accompanying Amerigo Vespucci on his voyages). Inspired by the vision of a unified humanity it steadily discarded its bounded and local character – an undiscovered island, a lost civilization, a hidden valley. It reached out for a Utopia that encompassed the whole globe and even the whole universe.[13] Wells again made the canonical claim: 'No less than a planet will serve the purpose of a modern Utopia.' This could of course allow religion in by the back door (increasingly its only port of entry into the modern mind); but if so only on severely qualified terms. If religion was to have any place in Utopian thinking about mankind's future, it was as a distinctly secularized religion – the religion of humanism, Comtism, Marxism, or science.

One final feature of Utopia needs to be mentioned, in stressing its separation from religion. I have not so far mentioned the name that is for many people, even more than More's, synonymous with Utopia. I mean of course Plato, and his *Republic*. I do not in fact think that the *Republic* is a true Utopia, although classical Utopianism is another story for which there fortunately is not time. But there is no doubt that for most writers of Utopias it has been a towering presence – in the case of Wells as much as that of More. I am not referring so much here to the endless reappearance of philosopher-kings in Utopia – Wells's Samurai, Huxley's Controllers, Orwell's Inner Party members. What is more important is the Platonic cast or character of the typical Utopia: its rational, Hellenic, conception. This sets it apart from any construction which has a marked providentialist or salvationist character. Plato's *Republic* draws on – or creates – the Hellenic tradition of the 'ideal city': a man-made, rationally-constructed order of human perfection. This may well be seen as a microcosmic reflection of a divine order, or a heavenly city: but the crucial thing is that the earthly city can in principle be as perfect as the heavenly city because men may become god-like. This Hellenic conception seems clearly to underlie the neo-Platonist architectural Utopias of the Renaissance – the ideal cities of Alberti, Filarete, Patrizi, and Leonardo. It is if anything even more hubristic in later architectural Utopias – L'Enfant's plan for Washington DC, Le Corbusier's design for *la ville radieuse*. And from a different direction, something of the same idea reappears in Bacon's claim that science can reverse the consequences of the Fall. The 'pure knowledge of nature and universality' will lead to the 'restitution and reinvesting of man to the sovereignty and power which he had in his first state of creation.' So, just as the architectural Utopia, the scientific Utopia continued the Hellenic tradition with its motif of 'men like gods'.

IV

Let me finish with this reflection on Religion and Utopia. I have been stressing the differences between Christianity and Utopia. Despite this, a case can, I think, be made out for saying that Christian conceptions and impulses sustain and encourage Utopianism right down into the nineteenth century and perhaps even later. Using a Freudian metaphor we might say that Christianity is the 'Unconscious' of Utopia. In other words, while Utopia expresses a distinct ambition and enterprise which is different from Christianity, some kind of transcendentalism, such as the idea of a Paradise lost and a Paradise to be regained, may well have provided much of the emotional and expressive force behind the Utopian endeavour. It is a view of this sort which underlies the recent claim of the Manuels, in their impressive *Utopian Thought in the West*, that by the late nineteenth century Utopia was on the wane, because religion was on the wane and secularization was the dominant tendency. So, Utopia is not religion; but no religion, no Utopia.

This position can be debated endlessly, in all its aspects. For one thing, it is by no means clear that Utopia has declined in the twentieth century; certainly it experienced a vigorous revival in the post-1945 period. But accepting for the moment that there is such a connection between religion (Christianity) and Utopia, could it not be argued that *Marxism or socialism* has come to play the role that Christianity played for the earlier Utopias? Does not Marxism in particular offer a 'secularized transcendentalism' as the basis for nineteenth- and twentieth-century Utopias? Marxism provides a complete theodicy (a justification of the ways of History to man); it links past, present, and future in a meaningful sequence; and on the basis of a particular theory of man and history it holds out the promise of a heaven on earth (the classless communist society). As with Christianity, Marxism leads constantly to attempts to picture this future heaven, to prefigure it, to anticipate it, to force it into being ('prematurely', etc.), to dream about it. All this nourishes a modern Utopianism that starts in the late nineteenth century and runs throughout the twentieth century (Bellamy's *Looking Backward*, Morris's *News From Nowhere*, Wells's *A Modern Utopia*, Marcuse's *Essay on Liberation*, the idea of the Soviet Utopia, the Israeli Kibbutz as Utopia, to take some well-known examples).

And, as some confirmation of this view, it is the lapsed 'true believer', the heretics and renegades from socialism, who producce the bitterest images of *anti-Utopia* – Zamyatin's *We*, Koestler's *Darkness at Noon*, Orwell's *Nineteen Eighty-Four*, the whole group of Western intellectuals who suffer the disillusion of the 'god that failed' – James Burnham, Whittaker Chambers, John Strachey, Richard Crossman, and others.

What is perhaps even more interesting, and provides an ironic twist to our story, is that in many of these cases the ground of the anti-Utopian critique is provided by religion. The Utopia of socialism is attacked as hubris, as an absurd and eventually catastrophic attempt to set up the perfect rational society with the material of 'fallen man'. Much of the form and substance of the anti-Utopian critique comes in fact from Dostoevsky's examination of the consequences of the decline of religion in *The Brothers Karamazov*. The 'legend of the Grand Inquisitor' from that novel is rehearsed in the dialogue between the Controller and the Savage in *Brave New World*, and between O'Brien and Winston Smith in *Nineteen Eighty-Four*. The general theme of anti-Utopia follows the Legend: Utopia can provide happiness and security but at the price of freedom. Following Berdyaev, the anti-Utopians argue that freedom is not to be found in realizing the 'perfection' of Utopias, but in the imperfection of a necessarily untidy and 'irrational' human society – a society that can never be more than a faint simulacrum of the City of God. Men are not and never can become gods. To act as such leads to disaster.

With this, the relation of religion to Utopia begins to become more complicated. In the twentieth century religion can be found on the side of Utopia (Martin Buber) as well as of anti-Utopia (Berdyaev). The simple dichotomies I have set up begin to look too simple, to waver and crumble. This is a good time therefore to stop. But the current situation of Utopia does at least throw into relief one of the main themes of this talk: the close affinity of Christianity to Utopia, and at the same time the enormous distance between them.

Chapter 8
Was Marx a Religious Thinker?

David McLellan

It is common to equate the ideas of Marx (and those of his followers) with some sort of *ersatz* religion. But I wish to suggest that the question in my title should be answered in the negative. Of course, I am well aware that the question itself is obscure or, at the very least, conceptually complex. What sort of religion is being referred to here and what do we mean by 'religion' anyway? Equally, what sort of Marx is being referred to here and is there some describable essence at the core of Marx's thought and that of his followers? In a very vague sense, there is obviously some connection if not continuity between Marx and the Judaeo-Christian tradition. Marx was, after all, a Jew, and his Jewishness, it might be thought, must have had some sort of effect on his thought – I shall be going into exactly how much in a minute. Equally, Marx was deeply involved with the cultural heritage of Western Europe – a heritage which had itself been informed by Christianity for many centuries. To take only the most obvious example, Hegel's whole system of thought can be seen as an attempt to adapt Protestant Christianity to the *Zeitgeist*. And in as far as Marx is viewed as a disciple of Hegel (another question with which I shall be dealing at greater length shortly), the filiation of ideas is clear.

Nevertheless, what I do wish to contest is the overly facile and conceptually unrigorous assimilation of Marx and religion. Karl Popper, for example, affirms the religious character of Marx's thought on the basis of its being what he calls an 'oracular philosophy'.[1] Berdiaeff tells us that 'if communism is opposed to all religion, it is less in the name of the social system that it embodies than because it is itself a religion. For it wishes to be a religion fit to replace Christianity, it claims to answer the religious aspirations of the human soul and give a meaning to life. Communism sees itself as universal, it wishes to control all existence and not simply some of its aspects.'[2] Again, Pareto, with a psychological reductionism typical of so many of these approaches calls socialism a 'lay religion',[3] a non-rational faith of the lower classes. And, finally, Schumpeter declares categorically:

> Marxism *is* a religion. To the believer it presents, first, a system of
> ultimate ends that embody the meaning of life and are absolute standards

by which to judge events and actions; and secondly a guide to those ends which implies a plan of salvation and the indication of the evil from which mankind, or a chosen section of mankind, is to be saved.[4]

However much truth the above statements may contain as a matter of participant observation, they do not give us a clear answer to our question. For they amount to characterizing any form of totalitarianism – or even any 'ism' at all – as religious. But a clear answer is only forthcoming, if at all, through the use of rather rigorous definitions which are necessarily prescriptive and therefore essentially contestable. It is from this point of view that I want to deny that Marx was a religious thinker. For such a characterization of Marx does an injustice, through conceptual woolliness, both to Marx and to religion. To Marx, because it does not take seriously either his own self-description or the clear implications of his science of society. To religion, because it tends to rob it of its essential transcendence by subjecting it to currently fashionable secularizing trends.

Enough by way of introduction. The first substantial question I wish to pose within the above framework is: what continuity, if any, is there between Marx and the Jewish religious tradition? The allotting of a substantial place to his Jewishness in the interpretation of Marx's thought is one that tends to come more from the Right than from the Left – Adolf Hitler is only the most obnoxious example. Yet writers of the most diverse political and religious views would share Edmund Wilson's characterization of Marx as 'the great secular rabbi of his century'.[5] But there is surprisingly little evidence for what is so widespread a view.

Marx was indeed a Jew in the clear sense that he was born of Jewish parents. But he was not a Jew in a religious, cultural or national sense. His father was a man of the Enlightenment, a Deist, a Voltairean and there is no evidence that Marx knew very much about Judaism. Isaac Deutscher, in his book *The Non-Jewish Jew* claimed that Marx 'transcended' his Judaism:[6] but unlike, say, his contemporary Heine, Marx had no Judaism to transcend. Of course, Marx was descended on both his mother's and his father's side from a long line of rabbis: but to suppose that this had a very substantial effect on his thought is to indulge in speculation about inherited racial characteristics which has surely been shown to be as untenable in theory as it is baleful in practice. Even sociologically, the link between Marx's Jewishness and his socialism is tenuous. It has plausibly been argued that anti-semitism of one sort or another is the reason at least for there being so many Jews among the early socialists: those who are marginalized in society see and experience its deficiencies and are therefore more ready to advocate its change.

But Marx became an outsider in Germany because he was a political radical, not because he was a Jew. The frustration of his proposed career as a university lecturer was due in the first instance to the Government's dismissal from his university post of Marx's chief mentor Bruno Bauer – and the suppression of Marx's newspaper the *Rheinische Zeitung* which precipitated his self-imposed exile was due solely to its radical tone. Baptized Jews could and did rise to high academic positions in mid-nineteenth century Germany.

But in spite of all this, parallels have been drawn between Marx's thought and Judaic conceptions in two main areas. Firstly, Marx, it is said, was a secularized version of an Old Testament prophet; and, secondly, Marx's idea of the mission of the proletariat parallels that of the 'chosen people'. As for Marx as a prophet, those who indulge in such descriptions very rarely give any close attention to the concept of 'prophecy'. If by prophecy is meant the foretelling of the future then this is not relevant to the Hebrew prophets, and, in any case, Marx was very sparing of such predictions. If – more in keeping with the present discussion – the concept *does* refer to the views and attitudes of the Old Testament prophets, again it is misleading so to characterize Marx. It is true that Marx read the prophets and made many references to them. And, like the prophets, he denounced the ruling strata of society and announced their imminent doom and destruction. But the prophets did not recomend revolution and had no social or political programme, advocating, as they did, a return to a simple and more traditional way of life based on the precepts of Jehovah. What Marx shared with the prophets had little that was distinctively Jewish about it – and it is shared by many non-Jewish socialists from Weitling to Lenin.

As for the substitution of the proletariat as 'chosen class' for chosen people, this was even less substance. The idea was put at its most succinct by Toynbee:

> Marx has taken the goddess 'Historical necessity' in place of YHWH for his deity, and the internal proletariat of the Western world in place of Jewry for his chosen people, and his messianic kingdom is conceived of as a dictatorship of the proletariat; but the salient features of the Jewish apocalypse protrude through this threadbare disguise.[7]

And it is worked out at length in the massive psycho-biography of Arnold Kunzli. However, Marx himself never drew any parallel between the rôle of the Jewish people and that of the proletariat. Moreover, the two cases are very different: the Jews have been chosen by the direct will of God and are constantly threatened by disloyalty to their vocation. The destiny of the proletariat, on the other hand, is determined by the socio-economic laws of history which are beyond their control. In conclusion, the most that could be said is that the typical concerns of the Judaic religion for equality, justice, reason and a this-worldly ethic (as against certain versions of Christianity) do certainly find an echo in Marx's work. But this is not enough to distinguish him from other thinkers of non-Jewish origin.

So let us now turn to what Marx himself says of religion. As is well known, there is little. And what little there is sounds very negative. It is true that the origins of Marxism are to be found, at least in part, in French Socialism which had, in the 1830s and 1840s a profound neo-religious tinge to it. Engels recalls the disciples of Louis Blanc when faced with Germany atheism asking in a puzzled tone: 'L'atheisme c'est donc votre religion?' But it is quite clear that Marx and Engels did their best to distance themselves from the vague forms of communism which just regarded it as Christianity in practice. The most striking document in this respect is the circular against Kisege of 1847 which prescribes in the most trenchant manner any admixture of socialism and religion.

But it would be wrong to deduce from this that Marx saw no *historical* connection between Christianity and socialism or indeed that he thought religious doctrines to be quite straighforwardly false. Marx was no simple eighteenth-century rationalist/materialist. For the famous phrase about religion being the opium of the people reveals a much more positive attitude than that of his predecessors. The common view that this represents a condemnation of religion is false. In the nineteenth century opium was widely used as a pain-killing medicine and the phrase of Marx simply points up the consolations offered by religion in the face of the sufferings involved in human existence. The origin of the phrase, moreover, lies in Kant's discussion of 'Religion with the bounds of a pure Reason' – and Kant was no atheist.

At the very least religion was for Marx a necessary stage in historical development. He says most strikingly in an addendum to *Capital* only recently published:

> The domination of the capitalist over the worker is thus the domination of the thing over man, of dead labour over living labour, of the product over the producer; for the commodities which become the means of domination (in fact only over the worker) are themselves merely the results of the productive process, *its* products.
>
> At the level of material production, the true process of social life – which is nothing but the productive process – we find the same relationship as obtains at the level of ideology, in religion: the subject is transformed into object and vice versa.
>
> From the historical point of view, this inversion represents a transitional phase which is necessary in order to force the majority of humanity to produce wealth for itself by inexorably developing the productive forces of social labour which alone can constitute the material basis for a free human society. It is necessary to go through this antagon-

istic form, just as it is necessary at first to give man's spiritual forces a religious form by erecting them into autonomous power over against him.[8]

And it could be posited from this that Marx saw the same kind of historical continuity between Christianity and Marxism as he did between capitalism and communism.

Marx's description of religion as 'the recognition of mankind by means of a detour, by a mediator'[9] implies a kind of *Aufhebung* of religion in socialism, a continual suppression and supercession of religious conceptions. Of course, this is itself a strong and continuous current in Christian theology. In the Kingdom of God there will be no room for the kind of signs, symbols and language that currently make up the phenomenon of religion. When we know even as we are known, the sort of representations that we now find necessary will be dispensable. This *via negativa* culminates in the view that even to predicate existence of God loses its meaning and importance. This idea of the immanence of God found its social expression in the millenarian movements connected with the immense industrial and agrarian revolutions that heralded the modern age and themselves gave birth to socialism. The conceptions of Thomas Münzer, given prominence by Engels, are only the most striking example. The conclusion here is not at all that Marxism is a secularized religion – only that there is no direct and categorical opposition between the Marxism of Marx and religion.

But this conclusion crucially depends on an interpretation of Marx. Let us glance therefore at the various interpretations that Marx's thought has been subject to. For Marx is no more accessible to us directly than is any other thinker: we all perceive him through some sort of hermeneutic tradition.

The Marxist tradition, like the Jewish and the Christian, has its own orthodoxy. This orthodoxy proclaims that Marxism is a science. And such a science had been held to be incompatible with religious belief on two grounds. The first, and more straightforward one, is that Marxism contains a materialist metaphysic. If, as alleged, 'the unity of the world consists in its materiality'[10] then all statements, including religious ones, are ultimately reducible to statements about the movement of matter. Secondly, religion can be dismissed not in metaphysical, but in functional terms: religion is an instrument of class rule, an ideological bulwark of the dominant class. This view, too, contains a covert ontology, both in its simplistic equation of the origin of a belief with its truth value and its assumption that religious assertions must always be a cloak for something else – obviously so in the case of conservative religion but equally so in the case of radical religious movements – Anabaptists, Cargo Cults – which must be cloaks for political demands. The traditional Marxist metaphor from heavy engineering – that of base and superstructure – tends to put religion on the tip-top of the superstructure and thus at the furthest remove from 'reality'. Incidentally, it is this approach which explains why so much Marxist writing on religion is so bad. Marx has often been taken, along with Weber and Durkheim, to be one of the three founding fathers of sociology. As far as religion is concerned, the contributions of Marxists to our understanding of religion seems, often in contrast to those writing in a Weberian or Durkheimian tradition, to be usually very poor. This is not always for lack of interest – it is just that many Marxists could not take religion seriously. Marx himself devoted little time to a study of religion – indeed his famous pregnant aphorisms on religion are nothing but, as he himself says, a repetition of Feuerbach.

Although the orthodox Communist view has been that Marxism as a science implies that religion is some sort of an illusion, there is another view of Marxism as a science that does allow room for legitimate religious belief. Marxism, it is said, is the science of society, a description of how society works: for normative judgements about society we shall have to go elsewhere. This has a respectable Marxist pedigree and indeed became the dominant interpretation of Marxism during the two decades preceding the First World War. With the growing prestige of natural science, Marxism came to be seen as a similar 'science' of society and Marx's method was seen as akin to that of Darwin. It was Engels himself who declared at Marx's graveside: 'Just as Darwin discovered the law of development of organic nature, so Marx discovered the law of development of human nature.'[11] The growth of mass Marxist movements, too, particularly in Germany, called forth an exposition of Marxism that was clear, simple and comprehensive. And the neo-Darwinian interpretation of Marx (that came to be known as dialectical materialism) seemed to fit the bill admirably – all the more so as it seemed to bring the added psychological advantage of an assured eventual victory. A typical example of this approach is the following passage from Kautsky, referred to as the 'Pope' of Marxism at the time, from the end of his book on ethics:

> Neither can social democracy as the organization of the proletariat in its class struggle do without the moral ideal, without moral revulsion against exploitation and class domination. But this ideal can gain no assistance from scientific socialism . . . Of course, in socialism the researcher is also a fighter . . . Thus, for example, in Marx the working of a moral ideal breaks through in his scientific research but he is always at pains, and rightly so, to banish it from his work, in as far as it is possible . . . Science has only to do with the knowledge of necessity.[12]

Nevertheless, as with nature, you can pitchfork values out but they will come rushing back. And indeed they did with a revival of

Kantianism inside Marxism. Faced with the apparent autonomy of the material world, Kant had embraced the divorce of facts from values and attempted to construct a moral system that was justified in its own terms, and without reference to the world. As such, it was obviously compatible with a neo-Darwinian Marxism reduced to an allegedly scientific account of the laws of motion and society. Kantian morality could be laid on top of Marxist science and socialism could have both its Marxist facts and its Kantian values.

As for Christianity, this jejune interpretation of Marxism allows an even bolder conclusion than that of Kautsky and Hilferding. For if, as came very slowly to concluded, Darwinism in one shape or form is not necessarily incompatible with the Christian religion – then why should neo-Darwinian Marxism be incompatible? What harm could Christianity see in a mere science of society? I call to mind here the storm caused in Rome when the eminent Jesuit professor Gustav Wetter suggested that if the Church wanted to teach a realist epistemology in its seminaries, it would do better to adopt the more up-to-date one evolved by Leninist dialectical materialism than the rather *passé* versions elaborated by Aquinas from Aristotle. This may have been a joke – indeed, knowing Fr Wetter, I suspect it was. But the serious point remains.

Nevertheless, I am unhappy with this neat – over-neat – solution to our problem. This is no dialogue, let alone any dialectic. It is simply a division of labour. One of the most depressing aspects of some contemporary intellectual life is the compartmentalization of knowledge. The cobbler should stick to his last, it is said. We all have our 'fields'. No politics is sport. Leave nuclear power to the experts etc. But it seems to me that much of the most interesting work is done, certainly in the social sciences, on the borderlines or 'interface', as the contemporary expression has it, between two disciplines; where, instead of sleeping peacefully side by side, disciplines engaged in fruitful intercourse. Of course, it may well be safer to stick to one's last and one can obviously see why, under certain circumstances, party and church have adopted the 'safe' option of carving out a piece of ideological territory which is exclusively theirs to till as they wish without any alien interference. But the very roots of the Marxist and Judaeo-Christian traditions preclude this option – to be true to themselves they have to live dangerously.

For Christianity this may seem obvious: only the most perverse fixation on such statements as 'render unto Caesar' or 'my kingdom is not of this world' could lead to the view that Christianity is only concerned with disembodied values and is essentially an 'other-worldly' religion. But what of Marxism?

Marxism, too, is far richer and more comprehensive than the account of Kautsky and Hilferding would suggest. As soon as Marxists have forgotten Engels's statement that the 'German working class movement is the inheritor of classical German philosophy',[13] they have become the worse for it – not only in changing the world, but even in interpreting it. Classical German philosophy here means primarily Hegel. It is almost no exaggeration to say, in the title of a recent book by the late Alvin Gouldner, that there are two Marxisms. The criterion for their separation is the extent to which they display an interest for, and understanding of, Hegel's philosophy.

The type of Marxism which (I am claiming) is correlated with an understanding of Hegel is that which puts emphasis on the importance of working class consciousness, of class struggle, on the self-activity of the working class movement, and on the subjective side in general as opposed to those who either put their trust in some sort of almost natural inevitability about the collapse of capitalism or those who, while wishing to intervene actively in history, operate through some agency not evidently expressive of the consciousness and desires of the working class. The distinction, more briefly, is between those Marxists who wish to change the world through the activity of the working class and those who wish either just to interpret the world or who use their interpretation in such a way that they bypass working class activities. And it is claimed that the first set are influenced by Hegel and that the second are not.

Marx called himself Hegel's 'disciple' and set great store by the 'rational kernel' in Hegel's dialectic. The only materialism known to him was historical materialism, the doctrine that man's response to his natural needs – his economic activity – was the key to understanding history. In his third thesis on Feuerbach, for example, he rejected eighteenth-century French materialism and held the subjective element to be ineradicable – a view which (I believe) remained central to his thought. 'Philosophic' questions about what the world consisted of were alien to his approach. And equally it could be said that Marx believed in the self-emancipation of the proletariat, though owing to the lack of mass proletarian political parties during Marx's lifetime he was not in a position to comment on some of the problems that would arise later. In spite of certain affinities with some of Marx's later work, with Engels the situation is somewhat different. Although Engels acknowledged a debt to Hegel (and devoted a considerable time to expounding it), his views diverged from those of Marx. In Engels's interpretation, Hegel's achievement was to have discovered the general laws of motion of the world conceived of as a process of interconnected change and development; and almost always Engels connects these dialectical laws with developments in the natural sciences.

I do not merely wish to claim that some element of Hegel is essential to any, in some sense, 'right' Marxism. I do indeed think that it can be shown that one version is more in keeping with the spirit of Marx and with those who wish to change the world rather than to interpret it. I wish to suggest, more specifically, that in the relationship of Marxism to religion a dialectical, Hegelian Marxism is capable of a more fruitful approach. The only approaches open to 'scientific' Marxism are either negation or exclusion, saying of religion either 'it is false' or 'it has nothing to do with me'. And we can see that this is borne out by a glance at the classical Marxist thinkers. Although Marx said little about religion, most of what he *did* say – connected with the subject of alienation, for example, and evidently under Hegelian influence – has provided much food for Christian thought without, of course, making Marx himself into any sort of a Christian. Engels, on the other hand, as indicated earlier, is rather more sparse when it comes to material for dialogue – except in his early period, which is of course precisely the time when he was busy secularizing his Young Hegelian views. Kautsky and the Second International Marxists have no time for Hegel and – correspondingly so I am arguing – no interest in the content of religion. (I should add here, as I have been somewhat denigrating Kautsky, that from a sociological, historical point of view his large book on *The Origins of Christianity* is a most impressive piece of work. But this does not affect my argument). Lenin's views of religion as 'mediaeval mildew' or 'one of the most odious things on earth' and of the idea of God as a concept of 'inexpressible foulness'[14] go hand in hand with the simplistic materialism of *Materialism and Empiriocriticism*: Lenin's views are much more muted after his serious study of Hegel in the war years. Stalin reinforced, in philosophy at least, the worst aspects of Leninism and had as little time for religion as he did for Hegel – except as an added support for Russian patriotism during Hitler's war. Certain sections of the Frankfurt School, Gramsci, the later Sartre have all conserved something of the legacy of Hegel and they talk, in some respects, the same language as Christianity. It is significant that one of the factors leading to a loss of interest in Marxist-Christian dialogue in France was the growing popularity of the anti-humanist, anti-Hegelian, anti-religious Marxism of structuralist inspiration a la Althusser. After so much muddying of the waters by such as Roger Garaudy when it was difficult to spot the difference between progressive Communists and left-wing Catholics, many a Party member must have breathed a very heavy sigh of relief when at last there arose an intellectual leader whose version of Marxist doctrine was of a rigour and ridigity that precluded any sort of conversation with wayward Christians, existentialists and the like.

What I have been outlining above is not just an academic exercise in the history of ideas. I believe that it matters which kind of Marxism or socialism is adopted by those who are inclined to espouse such ideas. It would be a mistake for those on the Left to fail to leave some space for religion in their approach to society and politics. Religion in some shape or form has been a deep and enduring aspect of human activity – and there is every reason to think that this will continue to be so for at least the near future. Benign neglect or outright rejection by the Left will mean that the immense power of religion can be captured by the ideologies of the Right. Consider here the rôle of the so-called 'moral majority' in America and the way by which, almost by default, a whole string of repressive social measures appear to many there to have behind them the weight of the whole Judeao-Christian tradition.

For the religious side, though, too, the consideration is appropriate that the Marxist attitude to religion is a function of the kind of religion they see. Marx's idea of God as a projection of alienated man whereby God becomes rich in proportion as man becomes poor does indeed apply to a lot of the extreme Lutheranism of the time with its belief in the utter corruption of human nature, unbridgable gulf between God and man, salvation therefore *fide sola* etc. And Engels's views are undoubtedly coloured by the appalling Pietism of his Wuppertal background. Lenin's extreme views on religion quoted above are rendered entirely intelligible by the even more appalling mixture of other worldly spirituality and this worldly subordination to Tsarist autocracy that characterized the Russian Orthodox Church of his time. The question therefore confronting religious people with progressive social and political views is whether, without prejudicing their faith, they can present a face in which Marxists can see reflected much of their own aspirations for humanity. It is a question which, for the present at least, I must leave open. But it is only obscured by those who wish to portray Marx himself as a religious thinker. As I said earlier, such a position does scant justice either to the richness of Marx's own thought or to the tenets of religion.

Chapter 9

Christianity under Communist Rule*

John Lawrence

The subject of this essay is Christianity in countries under Communist rule. My experience is of Eastern Europe in general and the Soviet Union in particular, but I shall have something to say about China, Ethiopia and Latin America. I do not like to isolate Christianity from other faiths, and I shall say something about Islam, but there is not enough evidence at any rate not enough available to me – for me to say anything useful about how Buddhists have fared under Communist rule, and surprisingly little about Judaism.

I begin by asking whether there is common ground between Christianity and Communism. Can one be both a Marxist and a Christian? In some sense this must be possible because there are people who say they are both; but what do they mean by that? There are different kinds of Christians and Marx himself is reported to have said 'décidément je ne suis pas Marxiste'. So some latitude must be allowed to exist among the followers of Marx also. But classical Marxism regards religion as a distorted and false reflection of exterior reality, which is due to social causes and can be eliminated by the elimination of those causes. Reorganize society on Marxist principles and religion will disappear of its own accord, if not at once, then by degrees. For the purpose of this discussion I take a Christian to be anyone who says with the earliest church 'Jesus is Lord' and worships the one true God, Father Son and Holy Spirit. Such persons can obviously not accept that religion is a false reflection of reality, but they may think none the less that Marx's analysis of class conflict and the role of economic factors in history has hit the nail on the head and therefore that the adoption of a programme based on his thought will lead to a beneficient transformation of human society.

Marx had grasped something important but, it seems to me, that there is something missing in his ideas. Otherwise their application would hardly have encountered so many difficulties. His thought was based on an analysis of Victorian industrialism, a system that has now passed away: and his analysis bears only a fitful relation to the world of the late twentieth century. But it is perfectly legitimate for a Christian, or anyone else, to hold that, in spite of all the changes that have taken place, Marx's analysis still holds good in

* This was prepared before the overthrow of the Communist régimes in Eastern Europe

all its essentials and that it provides a liberating principle. Christians who hold this view may well maintain that Marx's view of religion was based on run of the mill Victorian religion and does not apply to a purified Christianity, such as they now hope to see. Or, they may think that Marx, for all his acumen, failed to understand what Christians believe. I like the story of the Cuban Catholic, who said 'We are as atheist as they are. We don't believe in the God they don't believe in.'

Can one be both a Communist and a Christian? This is altogether a different question, and the answer must be 'not without self-deception'. A Communist is a specifically *Leninist* Marxist and Lenin gave a special twist to Marxism. He was not a bad man in the way that Hitler or Stalin were bad, but there was a 'lie in his soul' with the result that he built lies and cruelty into the foundation of his system. In Leninism moreover, there is no picking and choosing. And Communism is by definition Leninist. The system is all embracing. Party discipline is strict and it was Lenin who built cruelty into the system and thought control, with its corollary of official lies which must never be contradicted. Lenin also greatly strengthened the atheist element in Marxism, holding firmly that 'every religious idea, every idea of God, even flirting with the idea of God, is unutterable vileness'. It was axiomatic among the Bolshevik leaders who seized power in 1917 that religion would have to be exterminated. This did not exclude temporary tactical concessions to the churches or even tactical alliances. And there are countries where Party members have not always been required to renounce the church at once as a condition of Party membership. But such concessions are tactical and do not connote any weakening of the belief that in the end religion must be utterly eradicated. There have indeed been devout Christians in the West, such as the late 'Red Dean' of Canterbury and others, some of whom I have known, who have supported the Communist Party and may indeed sometimes have been card carrying Party Members. I do not question their sincerity but I believe them to have been victims of self-deception.

Yet there is a certain structural resemblance between Marxism and Christianity. Marxism has a Messianic element, which no doubt has some connection with Karl Marx's Jewish background. This has been taken up by some of the Latin American Liberation Theologians and is helping to restore dynamism to their Christian theology, a dynamism which is scriptural but had been weakened over the centuries by the influence of Greece's more static philosophy. Moreover the Communist form of Marxism has a more particular resemblance to the Russian form of Christianity, a thesis that is developed by Berdyaev in his great book *The Origins of Russian Communism*. Communism as we have it, arose out of the nineteenth-century Russian revolutionary intelligentsia, who had rejected the Russian

Orthodox Church but had been brought up under its influence and carried some of its ways of thought into the revolutionary movement. That is the theme that I have developed at greater length in *The Hammer and the Cross*, the book which I wrote for BBC Publications, and which was published in 1986.

It might have been hoped that this partial structural resemblance would provide some common ground, but in practice this has not been so. The explanation lies in the character and experience of Lenin himself and in the way in which he moulded Bolshevism. Lenin's teaching is inseparable from Communism in ways that even Communists are often not fully aware of. Here again, Berdyaev, himself a Marxist before he became a Christian, is enlightening. Lenin, he wrote, was not so much a theoretician of Marxism as a 'theoretician of revolution; everything he wrote was but a treatment of the theory and practice of revolution . . . Hence his narrowness of outlook, his concentration upon one thing, the poverty and asceticism of his thought, the elementary nature of the slogans addressed to the will. Lenin . . . read a great deal and studied much, but for a definite purpose, for conflict and action and for controversial purposes in order to settle accounts with heresies and deviations . . . He fought for wholeness and consistence in the conflict, which was impossible without an integrated dogmatic outlook, without a dogmatic confession of faith, without orthodoxy. He permitted any method in the fight to achieve revolution. Lenin's revolutionary principles had a moral source; he could not endure injustice, oppression and exploitation, but he became so obsessed with the maximalist revolutionary idea, that in the end he lost the immediate sense of the difference between good and evil; he lost the direct relation to living people; he permitted fraud, deceit, violence, cruelty. He was not a vicious man, he was not even particularly ambitious or a great lover of power, but the sole obsession of a single idea led to a narrowing of thought, and to a moral transformation, which permitted entirely immoral methods in carrying on the conflict.'*

It should be added that Lenin was not a truthful person. Indeed he positively revelled in a lie, if it served the purposes of the Revolution. His followers have too often claimed that what suits the Communist Party is the truth. In practice this easily comes to mean that the truth is what suits the ruling group in the Party for the time being. And widening the argument from Lenin to the movement which he founded, 'Bolshevism made use of the Russian traditions of government by imposition. It made use of the characteristics of the Russian mind in all its incompatability with the secularized bourgeois society. It made use of its religious instinct, its dogmatism

* *(The Origin of Russian Communism*, pp. 138–40, slightly condensed.)

and maximalism, its search after social justice and the Kingdom of God upon earth, its capacity for sacrifice and the patient bearing of suffering, and also of its manifestations of coarseness and cruelty. It made use of Russian Messianism and faith in Russia's own path of development. It made use of the historic cleavage between the masses and the cultured classes, of the popular mistrust of the latter . . . It absorbed also the sectarian spirit of the Russian intelligentsia.'*

But have there not been changes since Lenin died? The short answer is 'When Communists are in opposition, yes. Where they are in power, "no".' In the Soviet Union there is not a flicker of interest in Western neo-Marxism. Stalin applied Lenin's teaching with great thoroughness but he added nothing to its substance. Leninism remains frozen.

This however, does not exclude much tactical variation in the Kremlin's attitude to religion. For instance the persecution of Islam did not start till about 1928 because the Soviet Government was not yet strong enough in central Asia and other Moslem regions to risk antagonizing the great majority of the inhabitants. In the case of the Russian Orthodox Church persecution began sooner. There were originally two reasons for this persecution, one ideological and the other pragmatic. All religion was considered dangerous because it was thought to be opposed to science and to give pie in the sky, thereby deflecting effort from the harvesting of the 'solid joys and lasting treasure' of the earthly paradise promised by the revolution. And equally important at this stage, the Church was thought to be counter revolutionary. However, a quarter of a century later the great patriotism shown by the Russian Orthodox Church in the Second World War proved vital to the national resistance. So there was a marked easing of the persecution; and the accusation that the Church was disloyal was heard no more. But the ideological hostility remained and has led to a second wave of persecution which started twenty-five years ago and is still going on.

The Russian Orthodox Church has always had a strong hold on the emotions of the Russians as an incarnation of the nation but from about 1840 positive belief in Christianity tended to be out of fashion in enlightened society. There have been striking exceptions but in general the tide was flowing against religious belief until the eve of the Revolution. And for more than forty years after 1917 the tone was set by the continuing atheist intelligentsia. There was, however, from about 1850 a thin stream of profound theological and philosophic thought, which came to a head in the last years of Tsarism. This *aggiornamento* was rudely cut short in 1917 but in the last twenty years the works of Berdyaev, Bulgakov and other

* (Op. cit., pp. 168–9 slightly condensed.)

religious writers of the beginning of this century have again become very influential in Russia. To return to the time before the Revolution, while sophisticated Russians were luxuriating in doubts, simple people continued to believe, and the quality of their belief has been too often underrated. In most respects the great Russian writers give us the best history that there will ever be of Russia in the nineteenth century, but in this respect they are misleading. The religion of the peasants was rejected by sceptics, while sophisticated believers either sentimentalized it or looked down on it as something that their enlightened souls had outgrown. Even Dostoyevsky misses something important. To my mind the truth of the matter is better shown in a funny little book, *The Religion of the Russian People* by Pierre Pascal, the doyen of French Slavonic scholars. (In parenthesis I am proud to say that I was instrumental in getting this book translated into English.) The fact is that Russian religion is far more thoughtful than has been generally allowed. The peasants were generally illiterate, though latterly not so illiterate as has often been assumed, but they were no more stupid than other people and they were intensely interested in religion. Religious differences formed a lively subject of debate among them since at least the middle of the seventeenth century. After all one does not need a formal education to see that the Christian religion raises certain *prima facie* difficulties and that the differences between denominations are important, even if not quite so important as church people have often made out. The Russian peasants did not think they were interested in theology and probably did not know what the word meant. Indeed there were endless complaints about their ignorance. But they were not so simple as is often assumed.

Of course they were not all religious or all intelligent but many of them were both. Their discussions however, were not verbalized in the Western European style. They thought in images, which were not easily understood by the Frenchified educated classes who grew up after Peter the Great, nor by many of the clergy who, so far as they were educated at all, had generally received an education that was superficially Western. With exceptions I do not think the peasants learnt much from the parish priests. Their teachers were rather worship, icons, and *startsy*. The liturgical year of the Orthodox Church is exceedingly complex and not all of the services are immediately 'understanded of the people' but Orthodox worship returns to the same themes over and over again. It may not render up its secrets until the fortieth hearing, but persistence is rewarded. Moreover the great variety of Orthodox iconography in churches and very often in private houses provides a commentary on the whole of the Church's year, a sort of pictorial *targum*. The importance of the secular clergy was that through the continuity of worship they provided for the right glorification of God. The word Orthodoxy (or in Slavoinc *Pravoslaviye*) means not only right opinion but right glory and in those churches of the East, which call themselves Orthodox the second meaning can be more important than the first. The clergy had been taught above all to celebrate the Liturgy. Until recently they were not generally expected to preach.

If the teaching office of the clergy was less important, its place was taken by the monasteries and more particularly by *startsy* or elders. The office of a *starets* is not defined in canons and it is not often that an abbot or a bishop is a *starets*. The office is charismatic; and is universally recognized by the mass of the faithful. The greatest of all *startsy* was St Seraphim of Sarov who died in 1833. The most famous *starets* in imaginative literature is Father Zosima in *The Brothers Karamazov*. The peasants would travel many thousands of miles on foot to visit a famous *starets* and it was from their pilgrimage to holy places and holy men that they learnt to explore the depths of faith. I have dwelt at some length on the positive side of the peasant religion, because it is hardly possible to understand either the survival of Christian faith under persecution or its naturalization in the harsh new world of Soviet rule without knowing something of the silent contribution made by a simple but thoughtful faith.

After the Revolution, when the persecution began, those who walk with religion 'when she goes in her silver slippers', soon went their way. The intelligentsia by and large remained sceptical or at best indifferent. The visible structure of the churches was almost completely destroyed. Countless bishops, monks and nuns, priests and simple believers disappeared into the Gulag; by the end of the thirties no more than three hundred Orthodox churches at the most remained open for worship in the whole vast Soviet Empire. It was thought that public religion could be destroyed by closing churches and liquidating the clergy. And any private religion that remained could be dealt with by the systematic destruction of icons and religious books, by atheist propaganda and by relentless pressure on believers. All this had a considerable result but not so much as was expected. Tens of millions grew up without, as far as appearances go, any knowledge of religion. Yet the pressure and the persecution did not achieve their purpose. In 1937 there was a census, and its results were never published. It is generally believed that the reason for this is that they showed a persistence of religious beliefs which the Kremlin found unacceptable.

Four years later, when Hitler attacked, it became clear that the support of the Russian Orthodox Church was necessary for national unity. Without it the Soviet state would hardly have survived Hitler's attack. So the Moscow Patriarchate was restored, the Kremlin allowed a number of churches to reopen for worship, a few monasteries and convents began to function again, and after the war theological education on a modest scale was once more allowed.

Behind the German lines, while Hitler did not exactly encourage religion, the people were allowed to open the churches and there was a revival of open religious life throughout that great part of European Russia, which had been overrun by the invaders. Conditions varied from place to place, but in the north west the Pskov Spiritual Mission undertook a remarkable work of re-evangelization, some of the results of which remain to this day. All this was not so much a rebirth of faith as an uncovering of what had always been there, mainly among simple people. This was the time when I myself began to know Russia well, and I detected very few signs of religious interest among educated people.

When peace came, much of the wartime gains were retained. By now there were about twenty thousand Orthodox churches open for worship, not a great number for one sixth of the land surface of the earth, but a great improvement on a few years earlier. The Kremlin's calculation seems to have been that, when the last *babushka* died, religion would cease to exist. In the meantime it was the lesser evil to tolerate the Church, while keeping the hierarchy under strict control. But this control had to be carefully moderated. If the Party interfered too much religion would go underground, where it would be much harder to control. The Party's yoke was none the less heavy but this mattered less than might be expected because the *startsy* continued to operate, though in extreme secrecy. The faithful gave canonical obedience to the hierarchy, but moral and spiritual authority was reserved to the *startsy*. This very Orthodox solution to a difficult problem is puzzling to Western Christians, but it works surprisingly well. I have never heard anything but the vaguest indications of where the *startsy* are to be found, while they are alive, but after his death in 1978 the work of Father Tavrion of Riga was given some discreet publicity. If it is asked how persons, whose existence is kept so private, are able to exercise their influence, the answer is that trusted messengers keep communications with them open. It is a mistake to suppose that there is now an extensive underground branch of the Russian Orthodox Church but there are many aspects of church life which are kept from inquisitive gaze. Stalin's own daughter was secretly baptized not by a priest operating in secret but by the incumbent of a Moscow church who lawfully and openly conducted services every day in his church.

It will be asked what was the quality of the faith now disclosed? It seems to me that the faith of the simple believers and of the intelligentsia had met in the concentration camps and had fused together. Such faith was equally at home in tradition and in the modern world, though it is not always fully articulate in verbal terms.

The middle generation might at this time seem to be lost to the Church but the older generation, who had grown up before the persecution, were still alive. The grandmothers very often quietly handed on to their grandchildren the essentials of Christian belief. Soon after the war it started to become clear that something had gone wrong with the Party's tactics. Those churches which were open were crowded with worshippers, who were not all old women. A significant section of a younger generation, who had been born after the Revolution, were coming into the Church. I give by way of illustration one instance which happens to have come to my notice. Just before Christmas one year in a mining town in the Ukraine a young lad was feeling very bored. There was absolutely nothing to do in the evening, except perhaps to get drunk. So his mother said 'Come along, dear, and see for a change what I like. Come to church'. So he went that evening and went back the next day and every day for a week. At the beginning he knew next to nothing about Christianity. At the end of the week he was on his way to the priesthood. Now he is a bishop. At first only a few of those younger people who came into the Church were well educated, but in 1958 I noticed in church for the first time a few faces of the intelligentsia. I made a note of this at the time but did not feel sure enough of my facts to say anything about it in public. In the next few years, however, the trickle became a flood and by 1963, the last complete year of Khrushchev's rule, the mood of the educated classes was changing visibly. What had happened?

Belief in Marxism had collapsed even among Party members killed by the cruelty, lies and corruption of the system. But until the death of Stalin people were too frightened to talk. So much so that most of them did not know what they thought. When Stalin died in 1953, there was no sudden change, but every year people began to talk a little more freely until, rather suddenly as it seemed to me, the cup overflowed and everyone seemed to be saying 'I do not believe a word of the Marxist ideology. No more does anyone else, least of all the Party members.'

If the Russians had been British or French, they might have settled down to an aimless unbelief, but the Russian nature abhors a spiritual vacuum. In spite of all the cynicism and corruption of Soviet life Russians still believe in right and wrong more than we do nowadays. The universe is not a sphinx without a secret. If the meaning of life is not found in Marxism it must be sought elsewhere. The Russians are intensely patriotic, so they turned to the Russian past and wherever they looked they found the Russian Orthodox Church.

The atmosphere of the intelligentsia is now wholly changed. Above all it is the younger educated people who have been coming into church. A few years ago, a dissident intellectual, Levitin-Krasnov, then newly come to the West, calculated that 'only about 15 percent' of the students at Moscow University were believers. This may seem a high proportion, when one considers the quality of their faith and the price at which it has been purchased. I should add that, if young people are in the forefront, the older generations including members of the Party have also been deeply affected. Buried emotions have re-emerged. Many on entering a church did not know why they had come. One gifted, charming and intelligent girl stayed for two hours apparently transfixed. When she left a priest asked her 'Do you understand Slavonic?' 'No'. 'Did you understand what was happening?' 'Very little.' 'Then why did you stay?' 'I do not know but you will tell me, and then I will be baptized.' And she was.

Such stories are many and their varying forms are revealing. Many will say 'When I began to go to church, I knew for the first time who I was.' 'All this unreality suddenly fell away and I began to live for the first time.' Those who know the falsity of so much in Soviet life will understand such feelings, but of course all this did not happen at once. Alexander Ogorodnikov has described the predicament of himself and his friends, which is typical of an important section of Soviet youth. 'My friends and I grew up in atheist families. Each of us has undergone a complex, sometimes agonizing, path of spiritual questioning. From Marxist convictions via nihilism and the complete negation of any ideology, via attraction to the 'hippy' life style, we have come to the Church.'

The upshot of this complicated evolution is that it is now being said once more 'See how these Christians love one another'. And the contrast is perhaps more striking than it was in pagan Rome. Soviet rule encourages informers and informers make people exceedingly circumspect. Circumspection of this intensity merges inevitably into hypocrisy. Shortages are normal and the best way to get on is to work the system ruthlessly. In these circumstances treachery and stabbing in the back are almost taken for granted. To be relieved from such a life is indeed relief. Not that church life is perfect. There are informers in church, too. Trust the KGB for that. Moreover, 'the flesh is bruckle and the fiend is slee'. But when every discount has been made, the change from a society, where it is almost the rule to trample one's neighbour under foot, to a community where everyone helps, may well seem a change from night to day. At any rate it brings out the decency and kindliness which are so often just below the surface in Russian life.

These facts may easily tempt one to exaggerate. Doubtless there are more seekers than finders and there may be more worshippers of Bacchus or Mammon than of the one true God. To sum up, the traditional peasant religion may have lost ground in the last twenty years, while Christian faith has undoubtedly gained ground among the educated classes. On balance it is clear that religion is becoming stronger.

The evidence for a religious revival is, indeed, copious, but it is impossible to quantify. Very many believers find it necessary to conceal their faith and may only go to church when they are away from home. It is easier to escape notice in a big city but even so anyone holding a responsible position and particularly any member of the Party would almost certainly find it advisable to keep his faith dark.

The unexpected strength of religion prompted a new wave of persecution which was prepared in the late fifties and got fully under way in the early sixties. This was not so savage as Stalin's persecution but it has been more insidious. Instead of trying to crush religion from without, it tries to undermine it from within by placing compliant persons or even agents of the KGB in key positions. It may be doubted whether atheist agents are often planted in the Church from without but strenuous efforts are made to 'turn' members of the clergy and then to get them placed in high positions. This policy which is pursued unrelentingly has had some success, but many good priests, bishops and monks succeed in resisting the pressure and are not by any means always prevented from carrying on an effective ministry.

To complete the story it should be added that by the last year or two of Brezhnev's reign the Kremlin found it necessary to increase further the pressure on religious believers of all kinds. *Christian Prisoners in the USSR*, a Keston College staff study, gives an illuminating quotation from Yuri Belov. 'Recently a KGB official said openly to an arrested believer during interrogation: "religion is a crime which we are tolerating just for the time being".' I doubt whether this KGB interrogator meant to imply that merely going to church is in all circumstances a crime even by Soviet law but rather that any evangelistic or charitable activity outside the four walls of a church building was a crime in the Party's eyes, even if it is not yet inscribed in the statute book.

So far I have concentrated on the Russian Orthodox Church, though much of what I have said would apply to other beliefs. It is time now to consider them. Before dealing with Jews and Moslems I shall deal briefly with other forms of Christianity. There were in Tsarist Russia very many and very various sects. This has not changed, but there is no need to catalogue all Russian sects here, though many of them are very interesting and some of them are large. The most important of the Protestant churches is the Baptist Church. An atheist Russian friend with good Party credentials once asked me why it is that the best elements in the working class are becoming Baptists? The question gives the picture. The Russian Baptists are the same sort of people as those who founded the Trade Unions, the Co-operative movement and the Workers' Educational Association in this country. I would add that the Russian Baptists are a necessary element in the country's spiritual health. I once heard a Russian Orthodox bishop say that the Baptists had been raised up by God in this century so that the Gospel might be heard in places where no Orthodox priest could go. The Russian Baptists have all the Protestant virtues; yet their spirituality is not so far removed from the Orthodox as is commonly supposed. There is an element in the Russian character which is naturally Protestant and I believe that this element has deep roots in Russian religious life, going back to at least the seventeenth century, and that when properly understood, it will enrich Orthodoxy. Lord Radstock, whose preaching had much to do with the spread of evangelicalism in Russia in the last century, always intended that his converts should remain in the Orthodox Church, but they were driven out by Pobedonostsev, the reactionary Procurator of the Holy Synod.

Roman Catholicism hardly exists among the Russians but it is the national religion of any Poles still remaining in the Soviet Union, and of the Lithuanians who are as ardent in their faith as are the Poles, with whom they share so much history. To be a Lithuanian is to be a Catholic. The Lithuanians did not come permanently under Soviet rule until the end of the war. So they escaped the earlier and fiercest persecution. They have suffered much in the last forty years but their Church has never been reduced to the abject condition of the Russian Orthodox Church before 1941. Their inspiring resistance to Party pressure has been well chronicled in the *Samizdat Chronicle of the Lithuanian Catholic Church*, and in Michael Bordeaux's book *Land of Crosses*.

The Ukraine is in the main Orthodox but the western Ukraine was under Polish rule so long that Catholicism in its Uniate form has become the religion of the people. This branch of Catholicism is totally illegal in the Soviet Union for political reasons, but the people retain their Uniate faith and practise it stubbornly in secret. I have no time now to go into this intricate history in any detail but it helps to remember that the religious history of much of Eastern Europe is more than a little like that of Ireland. Religion decides allegiance, memory lasts for centuries. So the instinctive reaction of any Russian to Catholicism is like that of an Irish Catholic towards Protestantism. In the western Ukraine the fact that so much of the population is stubbornly loyal to its Uniate Catholic faith is often taken by Russians to denote that they will never be fully loyal to a state whose dominant element is Russian. Such non-theological factors greatly complicate the spiritual relations of different churches.

The Soviet Union is a multi-national state, as was the Russian Empire before it. This essay is not a political treatise, but it is important to remember the impact of political factors. The Russian Orthodox Church is always felt, even by unbelievers, to be a force of Russian patriotism, while the Catholics, the Lutherans of Latvia and Estonia, the Autocephalous Orthodox Church of Georgia, the Gregorian Church of Armenia and above all the 45 million Moslems are felt to be forces of separation.

The religious condition of the Jews is perplexing. Until twenty-five years ago the Jewish intelligentsia was as atheist as the Russian intelligentsia, but recently there has undoubtedly been some spiritual renewal among them, which seems to owe little to the few synagogues that are open and much to ancestral tradition. There are some remarkable Jewish converts to Christianity and it seems that when a Russian Jew turns to religion nowadays, he is as likely as not to turn to Christianity. But there are cases of Jews who got their first lessons of Hebrew in a Christian setting, perhaps from some elderly priest and then gravitated back to their own ancestral religion. As always, it is difficult to distinguish the ethnic from the religious elements both in the Jewish consciousness and in the reasons for their ill treatment. In some ways the relations between Jews and Gentiles are immensely better than before the Revolution but it should not be concealed that anti-semitism is sometimes found in the Church in places where one would least expect it, as well as in a highly developed form in the Communist Party. I am sure that there is more to say about Soviet Jewry but we must wait for research which only Jews can carry out.

Islam in the Soviet Union has maintained its position distinctly better than either Christianity or Judaism. No more than between 400 and 450 mosques are open for worship in the whole area of Soviet Islam and the clergy are in general politically more subservient than the clergy of any of the Christian churches. But the Muslim clergy, few though they are, are well educated and their published sermons can be outspoken in claiming the superiority of Islam over Marxism. Their few publications sometimes reach a high intellectual level. Muslim religious life, however, is not expressed so much in the mosques as in the cult of Holy Places, in the almost universal retention of Muslim customs such as circumcision, religious burial, etc., and above all the all-pervading, though illegal, Sufi religious brotherhoods. These are described by Alexander Bennigsen and Marie Broxup as 'well structured hierarchical organizations, bound by absolute dedication'. According to recent Soviet sources they are 'mass organizations numbering hundreds of thousands of adepts'. Indeed, Soviet sociologists state that more than half the total Muslim population of certain tribal areas in the North Caucasus belong to such a brotherhood. When some of these Muslim tribes were exiled from their homelands during and after the war, the result was that they spread the Sufi brotherhoods to areas where they had not previously existed. In parts of the Caucasus the policy of persecuting Islam has not only strengthened faith, but has produced an anti-Russian xenophobia, which has made life for Russians and Armenians so unpleasant that their proportion of the population is declining, sometimes rapidly. These facts would scarcely be credible if they did not come from Soviet official sources, which would have no motive for magnifying the influence of Islam, indeed very much to the contrary. So strong is the influence of Islamic society that someone who does not believe in God is well advised to keep it quiet. Party officials must presumably make some pretence of atheism on public occasions when the Russians are watching. Once when the headmistress of a school in Turkestan was showing it off to some foreigners, she rashly said that since she had studied astronomy she no longer believed in God. Without thinking I burst out 'Astronomy has nothing to do with it'. She had no answer and I shall never forget the look of triumph on her colleagues faces. There must be many other such embarrassing scenes on official occasions but it seems clear that most Muslim Party officials are accepted by fellow Muslims as 'ours'. Presumably a little incense burnt on the altar of Caesar can be overlooked; but it must be galling, for the Muslims despise the Russians as their former subjects in the days of Tartar rule. And the Russians despise Tartars in return. In Russian it is even ruder to call someone 'Aziat' (Asiatic) than in English to call him a Nigger. In many parts of the Soviet Union Christians and Muslims have long lived side by side but in those parts which I know there is very little social contact between them. Russians do not learn Turki or Persian and Muslims can be slow and unwilling learners of Russian.

It should be added that, so far as my own observations of Central Asia have gone, while there is only a little contact between believers of the two faiths, the old Islamic hostility to Christianity has gone. There are a few Christians living in Central Asia who are ready for a deeper exploration of belief together with their Muslim brothers but in Soviet conditions this would be difficult and I see little sign that many Muslims are yet ready for it. But I shall never forget the beaming smile and warm handshake that I got when I chanced on a private meeting of a group of Muslim women at prayers in one of the tombs at Samarkand, and was able to show my sympathies.

What developments have taken place among Soviet Muslims in the last sixty years? The old hostility between Shia and Sunni seems to be a thing of the past. The position of women has changed. There is still talk of bride price but the women go unveiled in the streets, stride out with confidence and look men straight in the face. Before the Revolution the Muslims of the Russian Empire, or at any rate the Tartars of the middle Volga, were a well educated, forward looking, relatively prosperous group who were striving to bring Islam into the twentieth century. Their grandchildren, as might indeed be expected, have made great advances educationally and technologically and at any rate in Central Asia they are far more prosperous. Morever, their numbers are rapidly increasing, while the Russians and other Slav peoples are barely holding their own demographically. The Muslims look forward to an increasing weight in the Soviet Union and in that sense Soviet Islam is aggressive. Latterly there has been some influence from the Ayatollahs across the Persian border but Soviet Islam is not in general fundamentalist. It is, however, conservative, as Christians also under Communist rule are generally conservative. And it has resisted Communist penetration to a remarkable extent. Marxism is a doctrine that grew up within Christendom and no Christian society appears to have the antibodies required to reject it as a transplant. But the closed nature of the tribal and clan Islamic society of the Caucasus and Central Asia has proved well adapted to reject any attempt to graft Leninist Marxism on to it. So Leninism never gets inside Soviet Muslim society. Soviet Muslims share most of the discontents of the other peoples of the Soviet Union, but, in general they have distanced themselves from the movements of dissent among the Christian peoples of the Soviet Empire.

Turning from the Soviet Union first to the satellites and then to China, Ethiopia and Cuba, one finds much to confirm the picture of relations between Christianity and Communism in countries under Communist rule. The differences are very interesting but what concerns us here are the similarities. In all the Soviet satellites of Eastern Europe all religion is persecuted. Everywhere the churches have shown unexpected strength and in most cases they have emerged stronger than before and sometimes amazingly stronger. In China Catholicism has on the whole held its ground but Protestantism has undergone a spectacular increase. Before 1949 there were less than a million Protestant Christians. For the first ten years of Communist rule persecution reduced the visible presence of the Church very low. For the next ten years during the Cultural Revolution, persecution was redoubled, but when the smoke began to clear away, it transpired that there were more Christians than before. Many, many more. The official estimate is between three and five million Protestants but it is generally agreed that this is a gross underestimate. Informed guesses vary between 20 million and 50 million. No one knows the true figure, but it is clear that the spread of the Gospel has broken through all the controls imposed. A new church is now opened every day on the average in China, and there are countless house churches which escape all enumeration.

In Ethiopia the Derg, which is under Leninist control, thought at first that they could abolish Christianity and Islam by cutting off their sources of supply, but leaked documents show clearly that this has not worked. I conclude this mini survey with some extracts from a document used for training Party workers in Addis Ababa, which illustrates the devious methods used also in other Communist countries.

> Try to have loyal Party members infiltrate all Christian groups and gatherings . . . Forbid attendance at religious services, especially by young people. Confiscate the papers of those who attend and make them wait interminably to have their papers returned, for days on end . . . If the ban on church attendance proves to be ineffectual, have the church leaders thrown into prison, do not bring any precise charge against him (sic) . . . Close the churches, allow the local authorities to treat the Christians in their respective areas as they see fit. Let it always be local officials of lower rank who close the churches or who arrest believers. In this way the government cannot be accused of being hostile to believers . . . Deny the existence of religious persecution . . . If it is absolutely necessary to get rid of an important Christian leader, have him disappear. Do not announce his death . . . Allow the churches the right to exist, as long as they give the government the right to control the choice of their leaders and to define their orientation.

Throughout this inquiry it is remarkable how much agreement there now is between experts on the situation of religion in the Soviet Empire, in China and even in Ethiopia. Regarding Cuba and Nicaragua there is wide disagreement and I will not attempt to say who is right. Perhaps the Marxism of Latin America is never properly Leninist. Or perhaps it has not had time to show its true colours. So for this purpose it must be left aside as providing no certain evidence. But the Soviet Union, the rest of Eastern Europe, China and Ethiopia provide abundant and surprisingly homogeneous evidence.

What can we conclude? It is evident that religion in general and the Christian religion in particular have a persistent strength and resilience which cannot easily be accounted for by a seculiar view of life. That does not prove the truth of any particular religion or even of some vaguely religious view of life but it must give pause to any who think that religion is on the way out, whether they are scientists, philosophers, journalists, politicians, academics, poets or anyone else. A hundred years ago on a day of full tide on Dover Beach, Matthew Arnold wrote:

> The Sea of Faith
> was once, too, at the full . . .
> But now I only hear
> Its melancholy, long, withdrawing roar

In Western Europe this withdrawal still continues, but not in most of the world and certainly not in the Soviet Union and its satellites or in China or Ethiopia. Both Christians and other theists will conclude that God, who works in a mysterious way, has once more made the wrath of man to praise Him.

The experience of Communist rule also shows the immense strength of tradition in religion, particularly where faith is under pressure. Russia is Orthodox in spite of all and, though a Russian atheist will think that all religion is bad, he is likely to think also that the Orthodox Church is better than other churches. A Soviet VIP was visiting a British university and was shocked when he was shown the chapel. But he was doubly shocked when he found that it was a 'Protestant chapel'. Many Russians detect resemblances between the Anglican and Orthodox churches and this is counted in favour of Anglicans too, even by atheists.

This deep attachment to national religious tradition is not confined to Russians or to Christians. An Uzbek will be a Muslim, and in the rare event of his conversion to Christianity, he will cease to be an Uzbek. Even the Eskimos and other peoples of the Siberian north when presented with a cult of Lenin as a first stage to Communism, seem first to have absorbed Lenin into their bear cult, which can be traced back to Paleolithic times, and then to have pushed Lenin into the background. (R.C.L. 1985.) Coming nearer home, a Pole or a Lithuanian is a Roman Catholic, an Armenian is a member of his own national church, and so on, not merely in the sense that religion is inherited with nationality, but in the deeper sense that something in him reverberates to his national faith. When I have looked at icons with non-believing Intourist guides, they have sometimes asked me shyly what something means. 'What is that cow or that donkey? Why are they there?' Or the Presentation of Christ in the temple. So I repeat the *Nunc Dimittis*. The girl responds with 'Oh, how beautiful. I remember my mother telling me something like that. How very beautiful.'

So religion appears to be indestructible and religious tradition to be very durable. And negatively it seems clear that Communist rule has not transformed the character of man in the way that all orthodox Leninists expected.

Chapter 10

Nicaragua: the Theology and Political Economy of Liberation

David Ormrod

The Nicaraguan revolution is unique in several respects. At an early stage, the principles of political pluralism, a non-aligned foreign policy, and a mixed economy were put into effect. Roughly sixty percent of the national income is generated in the private sector. It remains to be seen how these principles will develop in the period of post-war reconstruction. But one thing is certain: the active and continuing mass participation of Christians has distinguished this from all previous socialist revolutions. The Nicaraguan Minister of Culture, Miguel Ernesto Vijil-Icaza, puts it like this:

> This is the first Revolution in history that has proclaimed that there is no contradiction between Christian faith and the struggle for social change; the first that has not seen borders between the believer and the consistent revolutionary.[1]

This new situation has enormous significance for the future of political and social change in Latin America, where the bulk of the population is Christian and where, by the end of this century, more than half the membership of the Roman Catholic Church will be found. It follows that revolutionary movements in the sub-continent will not succeed without the active presence and support of Christians; and that the opposition of the Roman Catholic hierarchy, if it fails to moderate the revolutionary process (as seems likely), may permanently divide the Church. So the Nicaraguan revolution, which represents a large-scale realization of the praxis of liberation theology, has potentially momentous consequences for the whole of Latin America and for the future of the Church.

Several large questions follow from this unique Christian participation in insurrectionary movements and revolutionary change. How do pro-Sandinista Christians view the use of violence and the limits of non-violence? How and why did the Catholic hierarchy move from a position of mild support for the revolution to one of criticism and outright opposition, and in some cases, encouragement of the counter-revolution? What is the special character of the encounter between Christians and Marxism in Nicaragua? The first question – that of non-violence – does not have the same significance in Western Europe, where the issue is often discussed in absolute terms, as it does in the dictatorships of Latin America, and so I am tempted to side-step it. However I think that many Nicaraguan Christians would say that Christian commitment in their situation demands struggle, and that the use of violence is one of many forms of struggle. Furthermore, whilst the insurrection was necessarily violent, the revolution itself has been remarkable for its non-violence. The second question – that of the Church's rôle in the counter-revolution – has been and continues to be exhaustively discussed in a number of reliable and accessible publications.[2] The third question, about the interrelationship between Christianity and Marxism, has been given little attention, but deserves much more. According to Philip Berryman, author of one of the best accounts of the rôle of Christians in the Central American revolutions, none of the major exponents of liberation theology have devoted systematic attention to Marxism as such. 'That the theologians have not devoted themselves to a more direct confrontation with Marxism – or, more appositely, Marxisms, does not mean that the time for such confrontations may not eventually come. Indeed, there is reason to believe that developments in Central America may demand precisely such work'.[3]

It seems to me that 'direct confrontation' is unlikely, given the extent to which certain strands of Marxist thinking have been absorbed and integrated into liberation theology. And perhaps Berryman underestimates the self-conscious way in which this integration has been effected, certainly in the seminal text of Gustavo Gutierrez. The conditions for a Christian-Marxist dialogue, as it was understood and practised in Europe during the 1960s, simply do not exist in Nicaragua. The basis for those dialogues depended upon at least a majority of the participants maintaining distinct religious and political commitments. And in any case, some liberation theologians, took their own dissatisfaction with these European dialogues, which they had carefully followed, as a starting point. Gutierrez wrote of the need to get away from 'the well-trodden paths of dialogue' and explore the possibilities of creative innovation by confronting high-level theory with practice: 'Grassroots experience in social praxis is fundamental'.[4]

It is of course well known that liberation theology emphasizes the centrality of praxis: that theological reflection should be rooted in the activity of Christians in today's world. Christian commitment results in activity, and that activity gives rise to reflection. So it follows that we cannot understand liberation theology simply as a chapter in the history of ideas. It would be a mistake to attempt to trace a pattern of development from one text to another, or from one church statement to another, even if those statements have the significance and authority of the Medellin documents of 1968. Indeed, the Conference of Latin American Bishops at Medellin was

so significant precisely because, in applying the ideas of Vatican II
on Church renewal to the local situation, basic communities were
established and pastoral agents were trained who were enabled to
work out their own response to events. The fact that progress made
at Medellin was, according to some commentators, halted or neutra-
lized at Puebla in 1979 merely underlines the practical limitations of
official statements.[5] The most radical break with previous thinking
that Medellin and Puebla established was not so much the often
quoted 'option for the poor' – which has frequently emerged in
progressive Christian movements without placing socialism, let
alone revolution, on the agenda – as the insistence that the structures
of Latin American society were fundamentally flawed. It was at
Medellin that the notion of 'structural sin' was first accepted.

With the unfolding of events in Nicaragua, it has become impossible to define the present scope of liberation theology in terms of its
origins as a clerical movement. As David McLellan usefully reminds
us, liberation theology began as 'a clerical movement of younger
theologians whose studies in Europe had led them to abandon traditional Thomism in favour of biblical and patristic sources and the
salvation history contained therein'.[6] But, as the prominent Jesuit
theologian Cesar Jerez has explained, it came as a serious shock to
the higher authorities in the Church that there existed a concrete
historical project behind liberation theology. This theology, he says,
'takes the Kingdom of God seriously, considering that this Kingdom
begins here and now'. And because it is a reflection on events
that have a time and a place, the social sciences have become
an important part of this theology. But what kind of social
science? Is it possible, Jerez asks, to utilize non-dogmatic Marxist
perspectives selectively, complementing them by Latin American
viewpoints?[7]

In broad outline then, these questions and observations indicate
how we might approach the relationship between Christians and
Marxism in Nicaragua, mediated in part, through liberation theology. First of all, we need to understand the rôles which Christians
have played in the revolutionary process. (And the word 'process'
is a key word in Nicaragua, signifying constant change, the absence
of dogma, either theological, or political, and a flux of events
in which all can participate.) Secondly we need to understand
what kind of Marxism has been utilized, perhaps selectively, as a
tool of analysis for transforming this particular society. Finally,
because Sandinista Marxism differs substantially from orthodox
Marxism-Leninism, I will comment on the impact which the
Nicaraguan situation is having in mainstream Christian circles in
Eastern Europe.

Christians and the revolution

Although the Roman Catholic hierarchy within Nicaragua quickly withdrew its initial support for the revolution, relations between Church and State improved towards the end of 1986, with the establishment of a joint commission to settle various outstanding problems. The expelled bishops, Vega and Carballo, were allowed to return, and Radio Catolica was reopened. The increasing sacrifices demanded by the war, both material and human, forced the bishops towards a strategy of gradual reconciliation with the people, well before the signing of the peace accords. And the provocative actions of the Archbishop of Managua, Cardinal Obando y Bravo, who for some years provided the religious focus for the conservative opposition, proved to be an increasing embarrassment to the Vatican. During the 1987 investigation of Colonel Oliver North's clandestine operations, the truth of earlier newspaper allegations was established when it was shown that Obando received at least $125,000 for his personal anti-Sandinista campaign, probably through CIA channels. In spite of this, the Cardinal now heads the country's National Commission for Reconciliation, and his earlier hostility to the Government is played down by the Sandinistas.[8]

It is of course true that the Church hierarchy, particularly through Cardinal Obando, played a major part in undermining the Somoza dictatorsip. Most Christians, in the 1970s, hoped to see the demise of the Somoza régime and the majority probably envisaged a social democratic alternative. Divisions amongst Christians existed, but these were substantially obscured in the series of 'opposition fronts' which were formed in the late 1970s, in which the Sandinistas participated. The insurrection was a popular movement led by the FSLN, but the first provisional cabinet was formed from social democratic and conservative elements as well as the Sandinistas. So the first stirrings of Church opposition in 1980–1 can to some extent be seen as the inevitable by-product of a process in which the socialist charcter of the revolution was consolidated.[9]

In general, it would be true to say that opposition from the higher levels of the Church, because of its increasingly provocative character in a war situation, has only served to build up grassroots Christian support. This was most clearly seen in the 'Evangelical Insurrection' of the summer of 1985 led by Miguel d'Escoto, Minister of Foreign Affairs. Conor Cruise O'Brien described it as a way of waging spiritual war against Obando through the form of a sacred drama. At what was probably the lowest point of Church–State relations, d'Escoto began a fast for peace, followed by a great journey across Nicaragua, an extended Via crucis, or Way of the Cross, in which he was joined by several thousand people at different stages.

At Esteli, Bishop Ardón opened his cathedral to the pilgrims, and before a crowd of 20,000 embraced d'Escoto and declared that the motives of the pilgrimage were 'of authentic Christian Faith in the pursuit of peace and life'. For the first time, the façade of unity maintained by the Nicaraguan hierarchy had broken. Visitors and letters of support arrived from all over the world, including personal visits from the deputy foreign ministers of the Contadora group and the Brazilian Bishop Pedro Casaldaliga. Supported by 23 other Brazilian bishops and the Archbishop of Sâo Paulo, Casaldaliga engaged in what he described as a mission of 'ecclesiastical co-responsibility' for Nicaraguan Christians abandoned by their nominal leaders.[10]

In contrast to the Church hierarchy, the bulk of the Christian population has maintained its support for the revolution. The clergy, in daily contact with the poor, have tended to provide active support and a small minority participated in the armed insurrection. It was in the base communities that the earliest Christian contacts with the FSLN were made in the late 1960s. The Christian Sandinista Luis Serra has described the five most important characteristics of the Nicaraguan communities: (1) Bible study was linked with critical reflection on existing social reality; (2) evangelical activity was based on the Church's 'option for the poor'; (3) the liturgy was simplified and popular language and music were introduced; (4) impetus was given to organizing the lay community so that they could deal in a collective manner with the problems that surrounded them; and (5) responsibility for evangelical work was assumed by laymen as well as clergy.[11] By 1979, there were about 300 such communities in Managua alone.

As social conditions deteriorated, and particularly after the Managua earthquake of 1972 which created unlimited opportunities for corruption and misappropriation of foreign aid by the Somozas, increasing numbers of Christians were drawn to the communities and into relief projects. The work of Christian organization amongst the poor was viewed by the dictatorship as subversive in itself, and from the beginning, the communities and the clergy associated with them were persecuted by the National Guard. 'Disappearances' became common and human rights violations reached such a pitch that the Catholic hierarchy and religious orders issued several international protests. Faced with this spiral of legalized violence, the radicalization of Christian activists followed.[12] Dom Helder Camara called for the application of 'liberating moral pressure', but in the face of brutal repression, many came to realize by the mid-70s that association with the FSLN was essential. It was through groups such as Fr Uriel Molina's Christian Revolutionary Movement, founded in 1971 in the Barrio Rigueiro of Managua, that many young people entered the FSLN. In 1975, the national leadership of the majority fraction within the FSLN accepted non-Marxist Christians into membership. Joining the insurrection, for many, seemed to be the next logical step. The exceptionally brutal character of the National Guard's activities and the fairly rapid course of the insurrectionary movement probably account for the fact that few Christian Sandinistas have thought it necessary to justify their 'option for counterviolence'. This contrasts with the situation in the Philippines, for example, where Hechanova and others have considered a 'moral theology of violence'.[13]

Luis Serra has argued convincingly that those who try to explain Christian participation in the revolution in terms of organizational and theological changes fostered by the Catholic and Protestant churches are mistaken. Rather than Vatican II, Medellin and the progressive encyclicals of Paul VI, Serra suggests that the confluence of structural crisis in the Nicaraguan economy, the increasingly repressive character of the Somoza régime and the activity of the FSLN gave the impetus to popular insurrection and the incorportion of Christians into the struggle.[14] Cesar Jerez would not go as far as this, and regards the encyclicals and bishops' conferences as 'significant stages' to be assimilated alongside other important elements – particularly the new contribution of lay people, the growth of strong nationalist feelings, and the development of a 'non-dogmatic Latin American socialist tradition.[15] Both points of view are useful in helping Europeans to understand the course of events in Nicaragua, but it would be unfortunate if Serra's remarks are taken as indicating that Christians were merely co-opted by the FSLN and allocated subordinate rôles. Given the fact that Christians occupy leading positions in government, the administration and popular organizations, it is evident that they have exercised a formative and creative influence in consolidating the revolution and building the new society.

As well as the three priests in government whose careers have been followed by European journalists, the brothers Ernesto and Fernando Cardenal, and Miguel d'Escoto, there is a larger number of less well-known Catholic laypeople with ministerial positions, such as Vijil-Icaza. As many as half the members of the cabinet are practising Christians. A number of Christian institutions have played key rôles in the process of reconstruction. In anticipation of the possibility that the counter-revolution would attempt to manipulate Christian opinion, two Jesuit-sponsored institutions from the anti-Somoza period were strengthened: CEPA, the Centre for Training Peasant Leadership, and the IHCA, the Central American Historical Institute which has produced discussion guides on the aims of the Sandinista revolution and Christianity, and publishes *Envio*, a monthly magazine of analysis of Nicaraguan affairs. The latter is directed by a distinguished Jesuit, Alvaro Arguello, and has close links with the Jesuit University in Managua, the University of Central America (UCA). This institution, in turn, is directed by Cesar Jerez, perhaps the best-known liberation theologian in Nicaragua. In August 1979, the Antonio Valdivieso Centre was founded as an ecumenical centre for theological reflection and publishing, and for solidarity and project work. Its director, Uriel Molina, explained its rôle as 'the Christian mission in the new Nicaragua . . . we belong to the liberation theology movement, but are inspired by the major waves of Roman Catholic and Protestant theology'.[16]

These examples show that Christians in Nicaragua have responded to new opportunities in an extremely positive way, unique in the history of socialist revolutions. As Serra suggests, in Gramscian language, they have enabled themselves to become the organic intellectuals of the people, genuinely articulating popular aspirations. The earlier idea of a strategic alliance between religious and atheistic socialists, has, according to Serra, given way to 'an intimate, practical, and theoretical amalgam found in the same persons and organizational structures.'[17] Some of these individuals, with FSLN membership, have come together in a loose organization known as Christians in the Revolution, which Vijil-Icaza describes as an umbrella group or a network. Significantly, it is affiliated to the Socialist International through its membership of the SI's religious wing, the International League of Religious Socialists. Jerez, in his five-fold typology of Sandinista practice in relation to religion describes Christian Sandinistas as a minority of people who have abandoned the dogmatic Marxist-Leninist view of religion, who are neither disillusioned with nor confused by the institutional church, and whose Christian and revolutionary beliefs are expressed in the conviction 'that there is no contradiction between being Christians, active members of the people of God, and being Sandinista revolutionaries.' He goes on to say, ' . . . they feel consoled by firmly adhering to what they believe to be Jesus Christ's mandate: "You are the light of the world, you are the salt of the earth".'[18]

Of course, official Sandinista policy on religion maintains that matters of religious judgement should be regarded as the responsibility of the churches and private individuals, and that when Christian Sandinistas intervene in religious discussions, they do so as individual Christians. But it also recognizes the motivation provided by religious faith in the revolutionary process. In so far as some writers have argued that 'religion is a tool for the alienation of people and serves to justify the exploitation of one class by another', the statement suggests that this is true only in relation to specific historical periods, and implies that it has no universal validity.

Christians and Marxism

The relationship between Christianity and Marxism has obviously been mediated in part through liberation theology. But in terms of the Nicaraguan situation, we must recognize that the encounter has taken place pragmatically, within the broad ideological framework of Sandinismo. And Sandinismo is compounded of three elements, namely, nationalism, non-dogmatic Marxism, and popular Christianity. Leading Sandinistas who are not Christian frequently use religious language and Christian imagery. It is reported that Comandante Thomás Borge, Minister of the Interior and one of the founders of the FSLN, 'speaks with passion of the Earthly Paradise and of Hell and the Antichrist.' President Ortega has addressed crowds with the slogan 'People of Sandino! People of Christ!'[19] And in the cult of the revolutionary dead, the 'Heroes and Martyrs' of the revolution are frequently acknowledged as being 'presente' – still with us. At a more reflective level, the large component of social Catholicism in Sandinismo is clearly shaped by the Medellin emphasis on unjust social and economic structures, and of course on liberation theology which itself has incorporated elements of Marxist analysis. So within Sandinismo, there arises an all-important point of contact between non-atheistic pragmatic Marxism and the Marxism of liberation theology. And to break it down even further, this 'non-dogmatic Marxism' which Jerez refers to is a loose form of economic Marxism, as distinct from political or philosophical Marxism. It is, in fact, dependency theory.

It is surprising that this common preoccupation with dependency theory amongst Nicaraguan Christians and socialists has not been analysed in a detailed way in the literature about religion and the revolution. Dependency theory originated in Latin America during the 1960s when economic stagnation was setting in and development programmes were seen to be failing, and when popular movements were gathering strength. Kennedy's 'Alliance of Progress' of 1961 was soon recognized as a transparent means of staving off radical political and economic restructuring, and theoretical as well as practical explanations were required to explain the inadequacies of developmentalism. Nowadays, there are several different schools of dependency thinking in Latin America, North America and Europe.[20]

Dependency theory maintains that capitalist development in one part of the world necessarily creates underdevelopment in another – indeed, it sees the development of underdevelopment as a condition for capitalist growth. The capitalist countries at the core of the world-system extract the surplus from peripheral countries such as Nicaragua. Orthodox Marxist-Leninism, on the other hand, maintains that capitalist accumulation proceeds via the labour process: capital extracts a surplus from labour, and a progressive process of capitalist expansion will undermine and transform pre-capitalist modes of production. Lenin's original theory of imperialism explained how the export of capital would further extend capitalism on a global scale. In broad terms, the class-based analysis of orthodox Marxism-Leninism is overtaken by a geopolitical one. According to dependency theory, it is trade relations involving unequal exchange which provide the momentum of the world system.[21]

Much of the liberation theology which I encountered in Managua expressed the assumptions of dependency theory, sometimes directly. For example Vijil-Icaza suggested, 'Nicaragua is part of that great number of nations who are victims of the global capitalist system which extracts its wealth by unequal terms of trade and through exploitative financial relations.'[22] Jerez spoke of the analysis of foreign and domestic dependence before Vatican II, from the Christian Democrats, becoming more rigorous in the analysis of socialist groups.[23] Of the several liberation theologians whose authority might have been invoked, it was always Gutierrez who was quoted. Gutierrez's classic text of 1971, *A Theology of Liberation*, arose precisely as the engagement of a theologian with the early stages of this thinking. In fact the book started life in 1968–9 as a contribution to a collection of papers on Theology and Development sponsored by SODEPAX. Its core consists of an exposition of dependency theory drawing on Dos Santos, Gundar Frank, Cardoso and others, which is seen as providing a 'new awareness of the Latin American reality' against which the option before the Latin American Church can be assessed. In a brilliant juxtaposition, Gutierrez shows how a dependent church corresponds to a dependent economy.[24] But most theologians seem to have by-passed this central concern, whilst debates about dependency amongst economists and other social scientists have moved on. It seems to me that anxious Christians in Europe and the US, fearful that Gutierrez's theology represents Marxism masquerading as theology, have failed to notice that *A Theology of Liberation* is the result of an early encounter between a humanistic theology and simple dependency theory which is, if you like, merely one branch of neo-Marxism. Indeed some varieties of dependency theory part company with Marxism altogether.

Of course it is not simply an abstract piece of theory which is at stake here. Nicaragauans are only too aware, as they suffer the effects of the US blockade, that their struggle for political independence has been closely connected with conditions of economic dependence. As one economist has put it, a North American who I met in Managua, the Nicaraguans are 'struggling for the right to grow corn and beans to feed their children instead of just coffee and bananas or strawberries and flowers to please consumers in the north.'[25] Since the beginning of this century, their economy has been fundamentally distorted by the pressure to produce a narrow range of agricultural exports for consumption in the USA and Europe. *Campesinos* (or peasants) were squeezed on to smaller plots of land and finally forced to become seasonal wage-labourers on the agroexport plantations. The agroexport boom of the 1950s and 60s intensified the degree of external dependence. Family farms disappeared and the concentration of landownership and wealth increased substantially. The flow of poor *campesinos* from the land into the cities continued, but the urban economy was unable to absorb this new influx. Both rural and urban underemployment became endemic.[26] The analysis which Nicaraguans find most appropriate to these material realities is one which seeks to transform North-South economic and political relations, and is quite distinct from that which is held to underlie the East-West divide, namely orthodox Marxism-Leninism.

In fact, the neo-Marxism of dependency theory is of a kind which allows for real compatibility with the Christian elements in Sandinismo, via liberation theology, and the nationalist elements. The parallel themes of national liberation, the liberation of a dependent church and the liberation of the human personality, signified in the phrase 'faith in the new man', run through the Nicaraguan process. Furthermore the third element of Sandinismo, the Marxism of the FSLN, is itself rooted in dependency theory, providing the connection with liberation theology.

The FSLN was founded in 1961 as the local result of one of several historic disagreements, then taking place across most of Latin America, with the official communist parties. At that time, and indeed since the 1930s, Latin American communists followed the conservative Moscow line that the allegedly backward, feudal economy of the subcontinent ruled out the possibility of successful revolution. Instead, they argued, communists should unite with the local bourgeoisie against the feudal landowners and foreign imperialists in order to achieve limited democratic reforms. The various insurrectionist movements of the time challenged this basic position, and with the success of the Cuban revolution in 1959, the official communist line seemed firmly discredited. The FSLN was partly the product of this confrontation centring on the figure of Carlos Fonseca, but also owed something to the student revolutionary movement of 1959–61. This emerging 'new left' took the view that their societies were not feudal but for the past three centuries or more had exhibited a form of 'dependent capitalism' dominated by the European metropolis. Today, young Sandinista recruits are instructed how sixteenth-century capitalism created an international division of labour which created economic dependency in Africa, Asia and Latin America.[27]

Of course these debates involved more than a dispute about what actually happened in history. Different groups in Nicaragua, as elsewhere, were trying to establish an authentic understanding of their own experience, sufficient to enable themselves to take concerted action. Thus, the neo-Marxism of liberation theology and of the FSLN has permitted the emergence of a common vocabulary for discussing social goals. As the Nicaraguan Minister of Culture puts it, ' . . . common goals for the destiny of a world which changes in order to arrive, whether it be the Parousia of St John, or Teilhard de Chardin's Omega Point, or Karl Marx's Perfect Communism. As in Ernesto Cardenal's poems, all are one and the same thing'. This involves a liberating praxis, he went on to say, in which Christians will need to utilize a 'scientific analysis of their social and economic reality' if outmoded structures are to be changed.[28]

The significance of dependency theory therefore is that it provides precisely the social-scientific analysis necessary to link theology and social praxis. It is central to liberation theology. But certain questions remain. How far can a theology rooted in the oppressions and hopes of the pre-revolutionary period be adapted to the needs of a new society struggling with difficult problems of economic and social reconstruction? Can it incorporate the urgent priorities of political stability and social reconciliation? In other words, what lies on the other side of liberation? That the adaptations will be made is hardly in doubt. Meanwhile, as Nicaraguan Christians struggle with these questions, official Christian circles in Eastern Europe are looking on with special interest.

The impact in Eastern Europe

The notion of a Christian revolution and the assumptions and political context of dependency theory doubtless present a mildly disconcerting prospect to Eastern European communists. During the last twenty years or so, the mainstream churches of Eastern Europe have benefited from the normalization of Church–State relations and general acceptance of the rights of believers. Church leaders have established a new degree of public recognition through official participation in international conferences on peace and disarmament issues. The main vehicle for these discussions has been the Christian Peace Conference, founded in Prague in 1958, and re-established in 1971.[29] However the basis for this rapprochement, and for the work of the CPC, lies not in the extension of the Christian-Marxist dialogue, which is regarded by some as one of the 'problem elements' in the crisis of 1968, but rather in the perceived compatibility between Christian morality and the 'general principles of social ethics in a socialist society'. The adoption of elements of Marxist analysis has

not been a prerequisite for the renewal of church life under socialism. Rather the churches have created for themselves a special
sphere of public activity in the area of international peacemaking.
A fundamental reinterpretation of Christianity has not been deemed
necessary.[30]

By the mid 1970s however, the greatly increased participation of
Third World and non-aligned countries in the work of the Christian
Peace Conference was radically altering that movement's Eurocentric
character. The formation of a Latin American and Caribbean Continental Section (as well as African and Asian Sections) meant that
liberation theology has played an increasing role in the CPC's delib-
erations. At the 1985 Peace Assembly in Prague, special attention
was given to liberation movements and the militarization of the
Central American region. Articles have subsequently appeared in
the CPC Quarterly on the 'church of the poor' in Nicaragua and on
the conservative Christian opposition to liberation theology.[31] The
growth of neo-conservatism has perhaps provided a safer theme
than the implications of liberation theology for Christian politics in
Europe. However in October 1968, Ernesto Cardenal visited Prague
at the invitation of the Czechoslovakian Government, and engaged
in discussions with church leaders and CPC staff. In a much-publi-
cized interview, a number of difficult questions were pursued,
including the specific contribution of Marxism to liberation theology,
the anti-religious character of socialist revolutions in Eastern Europe,
and the atheistic assumptions of much Marxist thinking. On this
last question, Cardenal suggested that atheism is not the cause of
the conflict between Christianity and Marxism, but is rather the link
between them. 'What Marxism calls atheism is basically the negation
of an idol, which sometimes bears the name of God'.[32]

Alongside the activity of the CPC, the second channel by which
the results of the Nicaraguan process are making themselves felt in
Eastern Europe is the rethinking process now taking place in Cuba.
Only a small minority of Christians participated in the Cuban revolution, and the Catholic Church moved quickly to a position of
outright opposition. In the post-Medellin period however, a movement towards reconciliation and in some instances, even solidarity,
has occurred. More recently, as many Cubans have observed the
Nicaraguan process at close quarters, a substantial re-evaluation of
the relationship between religion and Marxism has been taking
place. Its most conspicuous expression has been the series of dialogues between Fidel Castro and the Brazilian Dominican Frei Betto,
in which Castro speaks of 'the coherence that exists between Christian and revolutionary thought'.[33] Over a million copies of *Fidel y la
Religion* have sold in Cuba, and translations are being prepared for
publication in the GDR and in several Eastern European countries,
as well as in the Soviet Union and Vietnam. The Brazilian sociologist

Pedro Ribeiro, who attended some of Frei Betto's meetings with leading Cuban communists, diplomats and church people, describes this new opening towards religion as 'the beginning of a real cultural revolution, a revolution within a revolution'.[34]

Of course these changes represent only the beginnings of what appears to be a slow reassessment of the rôle of Christianity in socialist countries. It may prove to be the case, unexpectedly, that the transition to socialism cannot be achieved without a fundamental readjustment of religious thought and practice on the scale of that which took place in sixteenth and seventeenth century Europe when the transition from feudalism to capitalism began. Certainly, Conor Cruise O'Brien describes Managua as 'the new Geneva', the seedbed of a new Reformation where you can actually feel a 'new kind of faith'. There is, he says, ' . . . something going on that you know can't be switched off, either from Washington or from Rome'.[35] I certainly felt it myself in Nicaragua, as a powerful and vital current, and that is the thought that I would like to leave with you.

Chapter 11
The Contribution of Religion to the Conflict in Northern Ireland

Paul Badham

One of the most widely believed axioms of contemporary politics is that the conflict in Northern Ireland is not really a dispute about religion.[1] True the participants in the dispute identify each other by the labels 'Catholic' and 'Protestant' but it is argued that these terms must be understood simply as convenient ways of identifying two distinct ethnic, cultural and social groups whom the vicissitudes of history have set at loggerheads with one another. As *The Times* puts it 'Religion is the clearest badge of these (two groups), but the conflict is not *about* religion. It is about the self-assertion of two distinct communities, one of which is dominant in the public affairs of the province.'[2] This analysis has been taken further by many scholars who point to the importance of economic, social, political, demographic, racial, national, cultural and psychological factors to understanding the conflict.[3] I have no wish whatever to dispute the relevance of any of these factors to the situation in Northern Ireland. In exploring the motivation of any human action it is undoubtedly the case that a host of such interacting factors are normally at work. My wish in this essay is not to deny such findings, but simply to argue that it is unrealistic to ignore the contribution religion makes to the dispute, a contribution which, both as a matter of history and in the self-perception of leading participants today, has been and is central to the development of the whole conflict.

Let us start by examining some of the reasons which have led scholars to minimize the religious element in the Northern Ireland conflict. To do this I propose to look first at the arguments presented by Professor Michael Macdonald in his recent work *Children of Wrath: Political Violence in Northern Ireland*. Macdonald recognizes of course that 'Protestants and Catholics are locked . . . in conflict.'[4] What he denies however is that these groups are in any real sense fighting about religion, or indeed that the meaning of the terms 'Protestant' and 'Catholic' are defined by religion alone. He gives two reasons for doubting this. 'First, conflict between Protestants and Catholics is scarcely normal in Western Europe, and so must be explained in something other than religious terms when it does occur. And secondly in Northern Ireland people remain members of their 'religious' groups even if they drop their religion (thus ordinary speech recognizes that there are 'Protestant' and 'Catholic' atheists).'[5]

The first argument is clearly fallacious. That denominational differences between Christians do not lead to conflict elsewhere in the modern world is no ground for supposing that therefore they *cannot* lead to conflict in Northern Ireland. Consider, for example, if one had said in 1937 that since persecution of the Jews was scarcely normal in Western Europe what was then happening in Nazi Germany could not really be taking place. I suspect alas that many did indeed say such things, but that certainly did not help the German Jews. In like manner if there are adequate grounds for thinking that a religious conflict may be taking place in Ulster today, it may seriously hinder the finding of a solution to the conflict if its very existence is denied on a priori grounds. Moreover since many observers maintain that popular religion in Northern Ireland remains enmeshed in the disputes of the seventeenth century,[6] it might be more appropriate to consider the likelihood of religious conflict by reference to seventeenth century European standards rather than by those prevailing today in the more secular and pluralistic areas of modern Europe. Once this possibility is considered then religious conflict between Catholic and Protestant ceases to seem so unlikely. Moreover if this line of reasoning is valid, then identification of an individual with a particular religious group will cease to depend solely on his or her personal commitment. For what is characteristic of strongly religious societies is a sense of group identity with the religion as well as of personal identification with that religion. This was certainly true of seventeenth century Europe and may also be true in Ulster today.[7]

However, the fact that Macdonald may have defended his position with two weak arguments does not necessarily rule out his central thesis. This is that the conflict in Ulster must be understood in colonial, rather than religious terms. It is undoubtedly the case that most of the Protestants of Ulster were originally colonizers, sent from Scotland by James I, Cromwell, and William III in order to ensure a loyal community in a hostile island.[8] It is also the case that for three centuries the Protestants of Ulster enjoyed a wide variety of privileges over the Catholics whom they dispossessed of their lands, and that this privileged status was a characteristic feature of the Stormont Government of Northern Ireland from 1922 onwards.[9] In the light of this Macdonald argues that far more important than religion is the legacy of colonialism. Religion merely 'identifies the antagonistic communities that colonialism created.'[10] What matters most Macdonald argues is not religion but colonialism which 'built privilege into the social order and conferred it on Protestants at the expense of Catholics.'[11] Macdonald believes that this is not simply a matter of past history but of present day reality. 'To be Protestant is to be privileged; to be privileged is to require that Catholics be visibly deprived; and to deprive Catholics is to build the social order on overt as well as covert domination . . . Northern Ireland is a colonial society based on invidious and abiding privileges. It is this, far more than religion, that constitutes the key to understanding Northern Ireland's politics.'[12] Macdonald's thesis is one which is shared by many contemporary writers, who argue that religion in Northern Ireland serves the same function as race and colour served in Colonial Africa and America, as a means of distinguishing the original natives from the dominating settlers.[13]

It would be foolish to deny that historically this thesis has a sound foundation. The question that has to be asked is whether it is adequate to explain the present situation. I suggest it is not. For without the contribution of religion it is inconceivable that the animosities of a displacing settlement nearly four hundred years ago could possibly have survived until today. Unlike the situation in other colonial contexts the interchange of population between Ireland and Scotland over previous centuries meant there were no racial barriers between the two communities. As Conor Cruise O'Brien puts it, 'there were no distinguishable physical differences between the natives and the settlers. Genetically they were of the same mixed stock.'[14] There was no linguistic division either since although the Catholics of Northern Ireland have an emotional commitment to Gaelic, this does not go so far as actually speaking it. Hence, without the contribution of religion, the two communities of Northern Ireland would have merged through intermarriage within a hundred and fifty years just as the Anglo-Saxons and Danes merged in ninth and tenth century England, or as the dominating Norman settlers gradually lost their sense of separateness from the conquered English in the eleventh and twelfth centuries.

What has to be asked is not why people of two cultural and ethnic traditions came to co-exist in a small province, but why they have never merged and today remain as apart as ever. No one can question that there are two communities in Northern Ireland, one self-consciously British, the other self-consciously Irish, each with its own perception of history, each with its own culture, each associating almost exclusively with other members of the same group. The factors that keep this separate identity alive are that the Catholic and Protestant populations of Northern Ireland go to different schools with a fundamentally different ethos; they participate in different cultural activities and sports; they support different political parties; and in a culture where church-going and church-related social events remain of great importance they attend different places of worship; they associate only with each other and have a very strong prejudice against intermarriage. Since religious conviction is the reason for the separate school system, the reason for the separate political parties, and the reason for the prejudice against intermarriage, the contribution of religion to the continuation of the divisions in Northern Ireland would appear to be very considerable. If we then take note of the part played by explicitly sectarian political leaders to frustrate the cautious attempts made by more liberal leaders to lessen the cultural apartheid of Northern Ireland we can see that religion is a major factor in the current troubles. Let us therefore look in more detail at each of these points.

Education in Northern Ireland is organized in fact, though not in theory, on strictly religious grounds. Though state schools are officially non-denominational and open to all, they are almost universally recognized to be 'Protestant schools'. At least half the membership of their governing bodies is reserved for Protestant clergymen, and no Catholic, clerical or lay may be a state school governor.[15] All state schools are required to provide 'biblically based religious instruction' and to 'foster in the schools an atmosphere friendly to the (Protestant) Churches'.[16] By contrast all 'maintained' schools (which receive an 80 percent capital and 100 percent maintenance grant from the Government) are 'overtly and avowedly Catholic'. And there is a long-standing Church law requiring Catholic children to attend Catholic schools.[17] The effect of this dual system is that the overwhelming majority of schools are either exclusively Protestant or exclusively Catholic.[18]

It must be stressed that the difference in religion is reflected throughout the schools in all manner of ways. It is no accident that the Union Jack flies over all Protestant schools but over no Catholic ones, nor that in virtually all Catholic schools the colour of the school uniform is green. A study of the syllabuses show that the Protestant 'state schools are English or British orientated, almost to the exclusion of Irish studies' while the maintained Catholic schools 'tend to emphasize an all-Ireland or Nationalist culture.'[19] In the schools very different accounts are learnt of the history of the Christian Church or of the British Empire and Commonwealth and in all manner of ways the teachers make it clear to the pupils their own sense of interest in, or alienation from such things as the British monarchy or the Remembrance of the Second World War, or with important events in the history of the Irish nation. These differences also extend to the sports played in schools. Most Catholic schools support Irish games such as Gaelic Football, Hurling or Camogie and shun British games like Rugby, Cricket or Hockey. By contrast no Protestant school plays any Gaelic games.[20] Other sports appear to be neutral. But the cultural difference is very clear and cricket as the archetypal 'English' game appears to be totally excluded from all Catholic schools.

This radical segregation between the different school systems means that children often grow up knowing no one from the 'rival' religion, and this affects their attitudes throughout life. Perhaps the most disturbing element in Dominic Murray's research into the two systems is that in the absence of any personal knowledge, stereotyped and hostile images of members of the other religion abound, with serious consequences for any future mutual understanding.[21] Significant also is the finding that the schooling almost invariably reflects itself in subsequent voting patterns such that 'it would be almost inconceivable for a Catholic child who attended a maintained school to subsequently vote Unionist, or for a Protestant who has attended a state school to vote for a Republican . . . the broad political affiliation of any individual in Northern Ireland is a function of his religion and consequently of the school which he has attended.'[22]

The evidence I have given above shows clearly that the difference between Catholic and Protestant extends far beyond any specific religious disagreement into two separate cultural and ethnic worlds. But this does not absolve religion from being the prime factor in the continuation of such division. For although the separate school systems offer differing cultural experiences and support differing feelings of where the pupil belongs, they are not defended on such grounds. The *raison d'être* for separate schooling is religious conviction.[23] If religion were not a factor the children would all go to the same schools and the part that education plays in breeding two separate communities would no longer serve to aggravate and continue 'tribal' hostilities.

Turning to the political sphere we note again that religious divisions are central to the political polarization. As Bill McSweeney puts it 'the link between politics and religion runs throughout the entire social system, eliminating at times of general election all the issues which are normally contended between the political parties in other countries and in other regions of the United Kingdom. What matters in Northern Ireland is where the candidate stands on the constitutional question, and what determines that is whether the candidate is a Catholic or a Protestant.'[24] It has sometimes been suggested that political allegiance at this level represents loyalty to the group rather than any specifically religious commitment, and this may well be mainly true on the Roman Catholic side. But it does not appear to be true on the Protestant side where 74.5 percent give 'fear of the power of the Roman Catholic Church' as one of their reasons for being Unionist.[25] It might be argued that this fear of Rome is utterly unreasonable in that, whatever may have been true of the past, the Roman Church since the Second Vatican Council is wholly committed to religious freedom and toleration.[26] But this is not how the situation is perceived in Ulster where some Protestants act as if the Spanish Inquisition or the St Bartholomew's Day Massacre still epitomized official Catholic policy.[27] And as Steve Bruce puts it 'even those Protestants who do not believe that the

Catholic Church would actually sanction a return to the thumbscrews . . . view with profound misgiving the decline of the Protestant population of the Irish Republic from 330,000 in 1911 to 130,000 in 1971.'[28] They see this as evidence of what would await them if Northern Ireland were to be re-united with the Southern Counties and on religious grounds therefore they oppose any such rapprochement.

It is hard for us in our secularized and pluralist society to appreciate the intensity with which fear of Rome is rooted in Ulster Protestantism. Clearly the patrician leadership of the old Unionist Party had no idea that such passions still burned in the 1960s, and the total overthrow of that régime demonstrates more than anything else the danger of any British or Northern Ireland leader ignoring or playing down the religious dimension of Northern Ireland's problems.

The present troubles in Northern Ireland came into being as the product of a backlash of ultra-Protestant working-class opinion against the very modest and tentative steps of Prime Minister O'Neill to help Catholics feel they had a place in Ulster society. Captain O'Neill was a member of one of the old Anglo-Irish families of Ulster, a member of the Anglican Church, and an Eton-educated Guards officer. He had returned to Ulster to fight unopposed one of the seats traditionally associated with his family. Like his cousin and fellow MP Phelim O'Neill, he regarded the months of the Orange Marches as Ulster's 'silly season' and he felt it incumbent on his administration to at least try and reform some of the worst abuses of sectarian discrimination against the Roman Catholics, and show the common courtesies of a civilized society to the minority community. Accordingly O'Neill accepted an invitation to open a Catholic school and was photographed chatting amiably with a cardinal. Then in 1963, when Pope John XXIII died, O'Neill sent a telegram of condolence to Cardinal Conway. In 1965 he invited the Prime Minister of the Irish Republic to Stormont to talk over the economic problems facing their two countries, and the new possibilities that might open up if they were both to join the European Economic Community.[29] O'Neill also sought to take action to remedy the legitimate grievances of the Catholic community which were being highlighted by the vigorous activities of the Northern Ireland Civil Rights Association. Accordingly O'Neill appointed an ombudsman to look into complaints of prejudice against Catholics in the allocation of housing. He abolished plurality of votes in Council elections, promised a review of the powers given to the Ulster Constabulary under the Special Powers Act, and established the Londonderry Development Corporation to help alleviate unemployment and hardship in that largely Catholic area.[30] Yet this combination of mild and long-overdue reform with acts of common politeness provoked an impassioned outburst of ultra-Protestant fury spear-headed by the Rev Ian Paisley.

For Ian Paisley the willingness of a Protestant Prime Minister to open a Catholic school or send a telegram of condolence on the death of a Pope were quite literally acts of 'apostasy', while to meet with the Irish Prime Minister implied a 'horrendous betrayal of the history and sacrifice of Ulster Protestants.'[31] Paisley's 'O'Neill must go campaign' stimulated an outburst of Protestant violence against Catholics in the late 1960s. This in turn led to a dramatic revival of the almost defunct IRA and in particular to the formation of the Provisional IRA in January 1970, which broke away from its increasingly Marxist parent body partly on political grounds but more importantly in order to take up once more a campaign of terror in the face of the assaults of Protestant paramilitary groups against the Catholic community.

From 1969 onwards violence and tension followed and in the increasing unrest O'Neill was forced to resign, being followed first by his cousin Major Chichester Clarke, then by Brian Faulkner, and then by direct rule from London. In December 1973 an agreement appeared to be reached at Sunningdale which it was hoped would solve the Irish problem. A Council for Ireland embracing North and South was established together with a power-sharing executive in Belfast in which the Catholic SDLP, the Alliance Party and those members of the Unionist Party who still supported Brian Faulkner would seek to unite the legitimate aspirations of both Catholic and Protestant within Northern Ireland. But this historic agreement was undermined almost at once by two factors. First the General Election of 1974 which saw the total rout of every Unionist who supported the agreement and secondly a strike organized by the Ulster Workers Council under the leadership of Ian Paisley to defeat the Sunningdale settlement. Once the Labour Government conceded to the strikers the Sunningdale agreement was finished and no viable alternative has yet emerged.

What appears to me clear from this history is that, although the present situation in Northern Ireland is immensely complex, and although both communities have contributed to the tragedy, one key element in the present dispute is the fact that ultra-Protestant opinion forced the resignation of the last three Prime Ministers of Northern Ireland, destroyed the Sunningdale agreement, and is now seeking to undermine the very limited agreement on security arranged with the Dublin Government.[32] What is also clear is that whatever other motives may influence some of today's leaders, Ian Paisley, who is by far the most influential,[33] is motivated primarily by religious concerns, and his popularity is a demonstration of the fact that a large proportion of the people of Northern Ireland share his concerns.

It is impossible to read Ian Paisley's speeches, sermons, appeals or broadcasts without realizing that his fundamental conviction is that the Roman Catholic Church is deeply and profoundly wrong in its teaching, and pernicious in its influence. For him the controversies of the Reformation are living issues today. He believes passionately that man's eternal destiny depends on belief in justification by faith alone. Believing that Rome denies this, he sees the Pope as the Antichrist, a force for evil which is to be fought at all points. For Paisley it is axiomatic that Christ is the one mediator between God and Man, and hence any religion which teaches the existence of a mediating priesthood, and still more of a priesthood which he thinks claims to repeat Christ's one and only sacrifice is to be utterly opposed. Moreover Paisley is a Biblical fundamentalist who thinks that Rome is opposed to the open Bible, and puts Church tradition on a par with it. He takes the doctrine of transubstantiation to imply belief that the wafer literally becomes the sinews flesh and blood of Christ, and he sees the adoration of the sacred elements as a form of idolatry.[34] For Paisley the Church of Rome is a monolithic organization with political as well as religious goals which it seeks to realize throughout Ireland, throughout Europe, and throughout the world.[35] Believing as he does, he sees himself as called by God to thwart in every way he can this hydra-headed monster, and in particular to ensure that Ulster is never betrayed into an enforced union with a papist Eire.

Dr Paisley takes no account of the fact that Lutheran/Roman, Anglican/Roman and Reformed/Roman theological commissions have established a wide measure of agreement on almost all the disputed doctrines of the Reformation, or that the Documents of the Second Vatican Council present a very different understanding of Catholic teaching from that assumed by Dr Paisley. For he sees the ecumenical movement as a papal plot to subvert the teaching of other churches and he regards all attempts to reinterpret any of the traditional formulae of religion as a betrayal of historic Protestant Christianity. Dr Paisley is first and foremost a defender of what he believes is the pure Gospel from any attack, and above all to defend this Gospel from the Church of Rome. One may disagree totally and profoundly with Dr Paisley. What I submit one cannot do is to suggest that his primary motivation is anything other than religious. What he preaches now is no opportunist attempt to use religion for political advantage, for his preaching today is essentially the same as what he preached as an unknown young minister and indeed what his father preached before him.[36]

What is true of Dr Paisley is also true of those who follow him, and indeed of the mainstream of religious and political thought in contemporary Ulster. For Paisley is not a religious maverick out on a limb of his own. True, his Free Presbyterian Church is more extreme and uncompromising in its style than the other churches of Ulster, yet as Bill McSweeney points out, 'The central doctrines of the main Presbyterian Church in Northern Ireland differ from those of Paisleyism only in the intensity with which they are held.'[37] And with regard to his attacks on Rome the central thrust of his teaching is and always has been the dominant viewpoint of the Orange tradition in Ulster. Consider this definition of an Orangeman's duty as set out in one of their own documents in 1970: 'An Orangeman should strenuously oppose the fatal errors and doctrines of the Church of Rome and scrupulously avoid countenancing (by his presence or otherwise) any act or ceremony of Popish worship; he should, by all lawful means, resist the ascendancy of that Church, its encroachments and the extension of its powers.'[38] The tone is certainly different from that of Paisley, but the underlying message remains the same. When Northern Irishmen vote, demonstrate, and protest against what they see as capitulation to the pressures of a Romeward movement they are not rationalizing social or economic needs, they are as McSweeney puts it, 'Christians fighting for their beliefs, whatever else they may be doing, and however quaint or repugnant their beliefs may seem to others around the world.'[39]

The greatest error we can make regarding Ulster is to look at its problems in the ways we are accustomed to look at our own. In the rest of Britain religion is not a central concern. Churchgoing is very much a minority taste, and both in the churches and in the wider life of society a pluralist, ecumenical toleration is taken for granted by almost everyone. This is just not true of Northern Ireland where we face a culture with one of the highest rates of religious commitment in the world and where no aspect of life is immune from its influence. According to the 1985/86 UK Christian Handbook 13 percent of the people of England are church members contrasted with 80 percent of the people of Northern Ireland.[40] If we turn to church attendance we find that among Ulster Catholics 90 percent attend mass each Sunday, while among Ulster Protestants 39 percent attend weekly, 20 percent more than once a month, and 30 percent attend occasionally.[41] Such figures represent a level of commitment higher than anywhere else in Europe except perhaps the Irish Republic. Hence it is not surprising that in such a context religious identification and commitment has far greater implications in the life of society than in more secular societies.

The tragedy of Ulster is that it remains imprisoned by its past. Its two rival communities are weighed down by the sad history of centuries of communal strife, and in this context religion has done little but strengthen the barriers between the other two communities. In almost all other countries of the world an ecumenical spirit of goodwill and brotherhood has transformed the relationship between Christian communities. In Northern Ireland where such a spirit might do the greatest good it has been the most lacking.[42] This presents a real challenge to the leaders and religious thinkers of the main Christian churches in Northern Ireland to overcome the theological conservatism and narrowness of outlook which still characterize their churches, and help to bring the good news of a Gospel of Reconciliation to a people who profess profound belief in its reality and yet have so far failed to translate their belief into the reality of their human experience.

Chapter 12

Christianity and Religious Pluralism: the Ethics of Interfaith Relations

Kenneth Cracknell

Whether on the global scale or just within the confines of these islands off the shore of Western Europe, Christians have to live with religious pluralism. They have to acknowledge that they are just one more religious minority, along with other religious minorities, within the total population of the world. Even their proportion to the rest diminishes with every year that passes.[1] Equally surely the religious map of the world has altered. Over a million Muslims now live in the United Kingdom, along with countless thousands of Jews, Hindus, Sikhs, Buddhists, Zoroastrians, Jains, Baha'is as well as followers of new religious movements.[2] Like most of the other countries of the old Christian 'heartlands' Britain is now a 'multi-faith society'.

But Christians are ill-equipped to deal with this situation. For they have entered into various kinds of inheritances from the past which operate against their being wholly at ease with religious pluralism. Elsewhere I have called these 'entails' upon each of the various heritages.[3] So the Catholic community has to live with the long tradition of 'extra ecclesiam nulla salus', outside the church no salvation.[4] Reformed tradition, from Calvin to Karl Barth, has always seen other religions as 'giddy imagination' or as 'unbelief'.[5] Lutherans, Methodists, and all sorts of Pietists have been clear that, 'apart from Christ there is nothing except mere idolatry'.[6] In many and diverse ways the Christian traditions affirm that 'Jesus Christ is the only way', and that 'there is no other name given by which we may be saved'.

I, like many others, have sought to show elsewhere that this exclusivism is not the sum total of past Christian responses to the religious convictions of humankind.[7] There is undoubtedly another tradition, stemming from within the New Testament itself, and leading through Justin Martyr and Clement of Alexandria, Zwingli and the Cambridge Platonists, Schleiermacher and F D Maurice, and now being re-asserted in our own day by many of our contemporaries. Another kind of essay could take us deep into the present-day theological wrestlings as Christians come to terms with religious pluralism. Alan Race of the Southwark Ordination Course has dealt with this elsewhere.[8]

I want to concentrate on the practical and ethical considerations that arise for Christians (as indeed for others) as we respond to religious pluralism. I propose to do this by looming at the 'guidelines for dialogue' that are already available from within Christian circles: guidelines for Christians living in religious pluralism.

Guidelines on dialogue between people of different faiths now come from all around the world and often reflect quite different situations. Very often they are what is called 'bilateral' in their scope, referring to what should happen between Christians and Jews or Christians and Muslims, or Muslims and Jews. We must hope that somewhere some scholar is monitoring all this material.[9] Other sets of guidelines are 'multi-lateral' and refer rather more to the general principles involved in interreligious encounter. For our purposes we may choose three sets of guidelines of the multi-lateral type: the *Guidelines on Dialogue with People of Living Faiths and Ideologies*, of the World Council of Churches (1979); the British Council of Churches' *Relations with People of Other Faiths: Guidelines on Dialogue in Britain* (1981); and, from the hands of one individual, 'The Rules of the Game' in Raimundo Panikkar's, *The Intra-religious Dialogue* (1978).

We choose Panikkar's 'The Rules of the Game' for two reasons. Panikkar himself is a figure of extraordinary stature in contemporary interreligious encounter. For him much of this encounter is within his own being, for he was born into two of the major traditions, the Roman Catholic and the Hindu. He is reputed to be a difficult writer and indeed he does think in a most condensed way. But the major cause of the difficulty often seems his ability to think in no less than (and probably more than) four languages, and therefore through language to live at home in the religious traditions and cultures of which these langauge are the vehicles. Out of this range of experience he has written some thirty books on interfaith relations, or as he would prefer 'intrareligious dialogue', most of which are not translated into English.[10] The first reason is therefore his personal authority. Alongside this we set his being a Roman Catholic. We have not yet so far a document from the Vatican which is equivalent to the WCC *Guidelines*, but it would be grossly misleading to treat the ethics of interreligious relationships as though the Roman Catholic Church had not made some decisive contributions in interfaith activity. The great Vatican II statements *Nostra Aetate* and *Lumen Gentium* are not however formal guidelines for interfaith relationships, but Panikkar's 'Rules' serve to make explicit what is often implicit. Panikkar's statement (despite his alleged 'difficulty') offers powerful descriptive and proscriptive ethics which deserves close attention.

The WCC *Guidelines* on the other hand bear all the marks of corporate thinking, the 'camel a horse designed by a committee' syndrome. A word about their provenance is therefore necessary.

The WCC has had a Sub Unit in Dialogue with People of Living Faiths and Ideologies since 1971. In its earliest years this Sub Unit (the DFI) was much extended in the organization of high-level international encounters between leaders of world faith communities. No doubt these early ventures were open to the charge of élitism, and in fact they aroused a good deal of suspicion about the purposes of such dialogue. Was it to shape a new world religion? To eliminate religious differences? To engage in conscious or unconscious syncretism? To offer a substitute for mission and evangelism? The Nairobi 1975 Assembly of the WCC had an unsatisfactory and inconclusive debate on these matters and at this point the DFI programme nearly foundered altogether. It was therefore with a renewed sense of purpose that member churches sent their representatives to the DFI Consultation at Chiang Mai, Thailand in 1977. This gathering produced a new statement entitled *Dialogue in Community*, and much of this material is incorporated into the WCC *Guidelines*. While one can take *Dialogue in Community* as representing an advance in ecumenical understanding of interfaith dialogue across several fronts, for our purpose it is sufficient to note the new emphasis in the title: dialogue is 'in community', that is, where there are existing interreligious or pluralist communities, and that these specific encounters take place in a world which is made up of communities, 'a community of communities'. This focus is ethical rather than theological, or, to be more precise, the concerns expressed are those of theological ethics rather than of systematic theology. It is this strand in the WCC *Guidelines* that we concentrate on, rather than such matters as 'syncretism' which also gets treated in Section E.[11]

The BCC Guidelines, *Relations with People of Other Faiths*, are dependent upon the WCC *Guidelines* in the sense that they are a deliberate working out for a national context of the WCC themes,[12] in fact the BCC Committee for Relations with People of Other Faiths distilled from the disparate WCC material what are now called the Four Principles of Dialogue:

I   Dialogue begins when people meet each other
II Dialogue depends upon mutual understanding and mutual trust
III Dialogue makes it possible to share in service to the community
IV Dialogue becomes the medium of authentic witness

In the pages which followed the BCC Committee showed itself concerned with prescriptive ethics for the Christian churches in Britain, treating such areas as community relations, pastoral care, religious education, denominational schools, and such issues as interfaith worship and the sale of and the use of Christian premises to and by people of other faiths.

Since these Four Principles of Dialogue were first published in June, 1981 they have been widely studied and in many cases whole-heartedly accepted by church decision-making bodies.[13] At the same time they have been expounded to people of other faiths in Britain who have affirmed that they too can accept them in the light of their own convictions or theologies. This unexpected development is felt to be extraordinarily encouraging, indicating that the 'Four Principles' have a general validity.

It is not therefore a matter of mere convenience if we use the Four Principles to give structure to the following exposition of the ethics of interreligious dialogue.

I   Dialogue begins when people meet each other

This principle was derived from the statement in the WCC *Guidelines*: 'Dialogue should proceed in terms of people of other faiths rather than of theoretical impersonal systems.' (Para. 20). Such a formulation reflects the consensus of people everywhere involved in constructive interreligious relationships. This widespread agreement has, however, come to be expressed with varying emphases and we consider these now.

Firstly, there is often a strongly proscriptive element: 'dialogue', i.e., creative interreligious encounter is not to be conducted in terms of religious or ideological systems, and this for two reasons.

On the one hand the practice of dialogue has led again to the discovery that no one person anywhere is the embodiment or personification of ideas and beliefs that are set out systematically in text books for the convenience of students and other interested 'outsiders'. We are learning not to say to one another: 'as a Marxist you must believe in x', or 'you Hindus believe in the doctrine of y, Zaehner says so', or even 'The Holy Qur'an says you Muslims believe in z'. As we meet any given Marxist, or Muslim or Hindu, we discover that he or she may or may not, for whatever reason, believe x or y or z. Deep learning in the history and comparative study of religions is as much a hindrance as a help in meeting and listening to actual men and women. The label of the faith or ideology in which they have been brought up or which they profess is only a first clue to discerning their rich individuality. It is sound ethical practice to approach another person with as few presuppositions as possible, and not to label or stereotype him or her.[14]

Alongside this we must put the experience of practitioners of interreligious understanding that to proceed in terms of systems rather than of individuals is inevitably to enter a *cul-de-sac*. The propositions of, say, Christian faith and the Islamic revelation are mutually exclusive. Jesus Christ may not be confessed as Risen Lord if he was taken up from the Cross before he died.[15] Ultimate Reality cannot be at one and the same time the impersonal Brahman and the God and Father of our Lord Jesus Christ. Dialectical Materialism is incompatible with theistic belief and so on. World views and religious systems exclude each other but human beings with their common, everyday concerns do not. In the words of the BCC *Guidelines*: 'What makes dialogue between us possible is our common humanity, created in the image of God. We all experience the joys and sorrows of human life, we are citizens of one country, we face the same problems, we all live in God's presence.' The right order of going, therefore, is to enable ordinary people (including ordinary theologians) to meet each other. It is almost instantaneously disastrous for future interreligious activity to invite the local bishop, the rabbi, the imam and the Hindu pundit to share the same platform and to discuss religious questions. This will almost certainly be a debate, not a dialogue. It will close doors rather than open them.

These two practical considerations are given positive theological and philsophical grounding in the positions advanced by writers such as Raimundo Panikkar and Wilfred Cantwell Smith.

Panikkar's 'The Rules of the Game' make clear general theoretical positions discussed in his longer works, notably *Myth, Faith and Hermeneutics* (New York, 1979). Summarizing himself, Panikkar insists: *'The Religious encounter must be a truly religious one.* Anything short of this simply will not do.' (The italics are his).[16] He sets out some of the consequences of this prescription of a genuinely religious encounter: 'It must be free from Particular Apologetics,' for 'if the Christian or Buddhist approaches another religious person with the a priori idea of defending his own religion by all (obviously honest) means, we shall have a valuable defence of that religion and undoubtedly exciting discussion, but no religious dialogue, no encounter, much less a mutual enrichment and fecundation.' Apologetics has, he says, its proper place but 'we must eliminate any apologetics if we want to meet a person from another religious tradition'. As a corollary to this Panikkar goes on: 'It must be free from General Apologetics,' when this would imply some kind of intention to enlist the other person into a religious league against 'un-religion' or irreligion. 'If to forget the first corollary would be to indicate a lack of confidence in our partner . . . to neglect the second point would betray a lack of confidence in the truth of religion itself, and present an indiscrimate accusation against "modern" Man.' This, he says, may be understandable but it is not in his terms 'a religious attitude', or in our terms ethically good practice.

Myth, Faith and Hermeneutics contains, as has been indicated, the theoretical hermeneutical basis for such encounter of free persons. He argues there that we must be freed from what he sees as the enslaving Western Myth, the myth of history, into a Myth of tolerance and communion, in which faith is understood as the constitutive human dimension.[17] In this we are taken beyond the mere awareness of plurality into an acceptance of *pluralism*. This cannot belong within what he calls the 'order of the *logos*': 'pluralism cannot be accepted within an ideology. On the ideological level you cannot compromise with error.'[18] Just so, two contradictory conceptual statements cannot be both true at the same level, or according to a single, homogenous cultural framework but rendered inoperable in encounters between cultures that have arisen from fundamentally different pre-suppositions. 'To assume a priori that a given conceptual form can serve as a framework for an encounter of cultures represents, from a philosophical point of view, an unacceptable, uncritical extrapolation. Sociologically speaking, it represents yet another vestige of a cultural colonialism that supposes that a single culture can formulate the rules of the game for an authentic encounter between cultures.'[19] So we have this formulation: 'Pluralism is grounded in the belief that no single group embraces the totality of human experience. It is based on trust in the other, even though I do not understand him and from my point of view I will have to say that is quite wrong. Pluralism does not absolutize error because it does not absolutize truth either.'[20]

Wilfred Cantwell Smith of Harvard understands faith 'as a characteristic quality or potentiality of human life: that propensity of man that across the centuries and across the world has given rise to and has been nurtured by a prodigious variety of religious forms, and yet has remained elusive and personal, prior to and beyond the forms'.[21] Because faith is this primary constitutive human reality, we meet other persons as people of faith and not primarily as Hindus and Buddhists. Indeed it was Smith himself who taught us in his earlier, and now classic, *The Meaning and the End of Religion* (New York, 1962) to set fundamental question marks against the unthinking use of the concept 'a religion' or 'a faith' and against the usage of the terms 'religions' and 'faiths' to indicate contraposed socio-theological communities.[22] He affirms throughout his writings that we are not to talk blandly of the religions to which people belong, insisting that we ought to ask rather about the religion which belongs to them. 'God is interested in persons and not in types', he remarked in 1967.[23]

In his latest book, *Towards a World Theology* (London, 1981), he returns to these issues as they confront the academic community, and especially those professionally involved in humane sciences. In a chapter entitled 'Objectivity and the Humane Sciences', he writes: 'my contention is that objective knowledge in the humane realm is an inherently immoral concept. Many practitioners of this brand of knowledge are, of course, better than their theories; many are better men and women personally than individual scholars with more humane ideas. The goal of an objective scientific knowledge of man, however, is wrong. One element in this inadequacy, shall we say, is its moral wrongness.'[24] Writing primarily as a comparative religionist, his further remarks chime in with Panikkar's as he reflects on cultural superiority: 'Such learning requires, of course, a certain humility and a respect *vis-à-vis* men and women of other cultures, a humility that neither Christians nor Western secularists regularly had. Sceptic and believer, at loggerheads at home, joined company to feel superior when they looked abroad: the one presuming that the religious faith of all humankind was superstitious error, the other that that of non-Christians was; at the very least, both for a time lacked that humility that recognizes that one can learn about oneself and about one's own world from other civilizations.'[25]

He continues, a few sentences later, and now perhaps more overtly as a Christian theologian: 'Man cannot know man except in mutuality; in respect, trust and equality, if not ultimately love . . . One must be ready not only to receive the other but to give oneself. In humane knowledge, at stake is one's own humanity, as well as another person's or another community's. At issue is humanity itself.'[26]

In all this Smith is concerned about how we know another person, and about our not being caught up in 'objectivist ideology'. As in Panikkar, and both WCC and BCC *Guidelines*; the ethic is 'personalist' through and through. How strikingly this all reflects what we learnt in a previous generation from a Jewish theologian who taught us to distinguish between I-it and I-thou relationships. I refer, of course, to Martin Buber, who also wrote on 'Dialogue' (*Zwiesprach*) as 'speech from certainty to certainty . . . from one open-hearted person to another open-hearted person. Only then will common life appear, not of an identical content of faith which is alleged to be found in all religions, but that of the situation, of anguish and expectation.'[27]

II Dialogue depends upon mutual understanding and mutual trust

Put in ethically prescriptive terms engagement in dialogue is in order to remove misunderstanding and to build up friendship. The BCC *Guidelines* see this happening, in so far as Christians are concerned by the deliberate avoidance of misleading and hurtful terminology about other people, in the refusal to dismiss other religions as human attempts to reach God with nothing of His grace in them, by allowing other people to define themselves in their own terms, and lastly by accepting responsibility to help other people to clear away misconceptions about what Christians themselves believe and teach. About such a programme, the WCC *Guidelines* says: 'Dialogue can be recognized as a welcome way of obedience to the commandment of the Decalogue: 'You shall not bear false witness against your neighbour.' Dialogue helps us not to disfigure the image of our neighbours of other faiths and ideologies.' (Para. 17).

Such propositions clearly belong to the realm of axioms in theological ethics, because both truth and love are involved here. They are to be tested by applications in particular contexts, and we content ourselves in this section by indicating some of the considerations that affect each context in which the search for mutual trust and mutual understanding takes place.

First, from Panikkar's 'The Rules of the Game', concerning the avoidance of false witness: ' . . . the golden rule of any hermeneutic is that the interpreted thing can recognize itself in the interpretation. In other words, any interpretation from outside has to coincide, at least phenomenologically, with an interpretation from within, i.e., with the believer's viewpoint. To label a *murtipujaka* an idol worshipper, using idol as it is commonly understood in the Judaeo-Christian-Muslim context rather than beginning with what the worshipper affirms of himself is to transgress this rule. An entire philosophical and religious context underpins the notion of *murti*; we cannot impose alien categories upon it.'

And sometimes it is even less forgivable because the misinterpretation, the false witness, happens within the Judaeo-Christian-Muslim tradition. Since in a moment I shall write of other people's failures let me record a characteristic Christian error, but one of my own. I had for several months been telling the story of the conversion of a well-known American black entertainer to Judaism. He is reputed to have replied to the question, 'Why Judaism rather than Christianity?' by saying, 'Because the Christians talk about love, but the Jews about justice'. This I had been doing in good faith, to illustrate the individualism and privatization of Christian ethics, compared with Jewish concern for how people live together, *Torah*, *Talmud*, *Halachah*, and so on. I mentioned this story to a rabbi, a friend of mine. 'But, he said, 'we Jews also believe in love.' I could tell that he felt I had simply been reinforcing the stereotype of legalism that Christians lay upon the Jews. I apologized then, and I apologize now, for that is indeed what I had been doing, however unintentionally.

Secondly, there is the need to avoid language which is dismissive of other religious traditions. Stanley Samartha, the first Director of the WCC Sub Unit on Dialogue, has reported on the reactions of the guests of other faiths at the Nairobi WCC Assembly in 1975: 'they were,' he writes, 'not sure why dialogue should be suspect to some Christians and attacked by others. They were disappointed that the question of seeking community in the contemporary world was not taken up with greater urgency. They felt uneasy to discover that they were part of the statistics that made up the 2.7 billion who were the objects of the proclamation of the gospel.

'The missiologist who described all non-Christian religions as demonic missed the chance of personally meeting these "non-Christian" guests to discover and perhaps to do battle with "demonic" elements in them. At least one of these guests expressed disappointment that no one among those who talked loudest about proclamation actually came to him or others personally to proclaim the love of God in Jesus Christ.'[28]

The question raised in this last paragraph is not, I think, so much about theological ethics as the ethics of theologians, and you may like to be reminded of a story concerning one of the greatest of Protestant theologians with one of the greatest of Protestant evangelists of our century. D T Niles of Sri Lanka met Karl Barth for the first time in 1935. In the course of conversation Barth said, 'Other religions are just unbelief'. Niles asked, 'How many Hindus, Dr Barth, have you met?' Barth answered, 'No one'. Niles said, 'How then do you know that Hinduism is unbelief?' Barth replied 'A priori.' Niles concluded, 'I simply shook my head and smiled.'[29]

Part of the problem for the Christian theologians, and especially for those who see their first task as the articulation and explication of the faith of the Church, the formulation of 'Church Dogmatics',[30] is that they are driven by circumstances to use the third person plural as an exclusive: there is 'us' and there is 'them'! The 'we' form articulates subjective, firsthand knowledge, and the 'they' form necessarily suggests objective knowledge. Here is Wilfred Cantwell Smith again: '(Objective knowledge) . . . does not yield personal understanding, or the kind of knowledge on which to found friendship. One may remark that last century's missionaries, who were objective in another fashion (individually very friendly, but in their group's theoretical relation to the "other" religion, and in their writings, objectivist, alienist) were victims essentially of the same we-they fallacy . . . Mutual understanding between groups is part of the truth, in this realm; it provides a criterion, a verification principle.'[31]

It would go far beyond the limits of this essay, and way beyond my own competence, to discuss the philosophical and theological issues involved here, but I may be permitted to refer to John Macmurray's first volume of his Gifford Lectures, *The Self as Agent*, whose declared intention was to construct and illustrate in application the 'form of the personal', that 'personal existence is *constituted* by the relation of persons'. You will recall the words of his introductory preface 'The simplest expression I can find for the thesis I have tried to maintain is this: All meaningful knowledge is for the sake of action, and all meaningful action is for the sake of friendship.'[32]

III   Dialogue makes it possible to share in service to the community

The guests from other faiths at the Nairobi Assembly of the WCC in 1975 were, we learnt from Dr Samartha, disappointed that the question of seeking community in the contemporary world was not taken up with a greater sense of urgency. A number of hypotheses might be advanced as to why this may have been so, and some of them need extended consideration and indeed condemnation from within the Christian ethical tradition. David E Jenkins, writing out of his experience in the *Humanum* programme of the WCC, discusses some of the factors involved in the first chapter of *The Contradiction of Christianity* in which he refers to the tribalism of Christian traditions. He quotes Niebuhr's remark in *Man's Nature and his Communities*, 'The chief source of man's inhumanity to man seems to be the tribal limits of his sense of obligation to other men.'[33]

This is painfully true, and yet there may also be for some Christians deeply held theologicial beliefs which are not necessarily epiphenomenological to the preservation of cultural identity. For it may be, for example, that the Church, 'the people of God in world-occurrence', is qualitatively different from all other communities. So Karl Barth, in the very act of arguing eloquently and persuasively that the Church is 'the community for the world', seeing and finding its own cause in that of the world, and that of other men in its own, remarks, 'Now there can be no doubt that in the discharge of its mission to them the community has in a sense to keep its distance, and even to contradict and oppose them. Without saying No it cannot really say Yes to them.'[34] He speaks of this withdrawal as 'well-founded and solemn', this contradiction and opposition as 'well-meaning and justifiable' even at the same time as it proceeds from the 'profoundest commitment to the whole of humanity and each individual man'.[35]

Here is another instance. The Nairobi 1975 Assembly took place within the context of the whole 'humanization' debate begun in the late sixties, and still reflected in internal Christian discussion in various ways even now. Peter Beyerhaus, Professor of Missions and Ecumenics at Tubingen, is one of the architects of the 1970 'Frankfurt Declaration on the Fundamental Crisis in Christian Mission.' About such propositions as 'we have lifted up humanization as the goal of mission' Beyerhaus says: 'here, it seems to me, we are encountering nothing less than the bankruptcy of responsible mission theology . . . In former ages people were religious and asked for the true God, and Christian missions directed them to Him. Today people do not care for gods any more, but for better human relations. Thus mission does not speak of God but directs them to the humanity in Christ as the goal of history.

'True all this is done in the concern of missionary accommodation. By confining ourselves to the concept of humanization we hope to find a field of common concern with Hindus, Muslims, Marxists and Humanists. For according to the concept of the anonymous Christ *extra muros Ecclesiae*, we are already sharing in Christ if we work together with them for the humanization of mankind. Perhaps by means of dialogue if the others ask us for the motives of our actions, they might even become disposed to accept Christ and integrate him into their present faiths.'[36]

I have given these rather extended quotations for fear lest I caricature or misrepresent either Barth or Beyerhaus and those of Christian traditions who responsibly feel the force of these or similar arguments. There are also, of course, many other Christians who would not even be concerned to enter this discussion, for it is foreclosed by the very nature of the views of salvation which they hold.[37] But we have sufficiently established the point that the BCC's third Principle: 'dialogue makes it possible to share in service to the community' is affected by prior theological understandings.

We take notice, therefore, that Paragraph 18 of the WCC *Guidelines* is deliberately and consciously 'ethical' when it states: 'Dialogue is a fundamental part of service within community. In dialogue Christians actively respond to the command to "love God and your neighbour as yourself". As an expression of love, engagement in dialogue testifies to the love experienced in Christ. It is a joyful affirmation of life against chaos, and a participation with all who are allies of life in seeking the provisional goal of a better human community. Thus "dialogue in community" is not a secret weapon in the armoury of aggressive Christian militancy. Rather it is the means of living our faith in Christ in service of our neighbours.'

Yet, because of the issues we are raising by citing Barth and Beyerhaus, i.e. that for many within the Christian community theological presuppositions govern the way in which they may behave towards people of other faiths, these statements are still likely to be seriously questioned: what is meant by 'provisional goal?' what is meant by 'a better human community?' what is this 'life' which is to be affirmed over against chaos? How does all this fit in with traditional understandings of e.g. 'the Church', 'the World' and 'the End'?[38]

If we have spent so much time on the Christian theological considerations anteceding the ethics of co-operating with people of other faiths, this is only because such considerations are the nearest home for most of us. With the necessary changes in terminology or patterns of thinking, similar issues affect other communities of faith. For example, many Muslims might have the gravest reservations about working with non-Muslims for 'the provisional goals of a better human community'. For non-Muslims traditionally belong to the *dar ul harb*, literally the 'house of war': a better human community could only come into being as the house of war becomes the *dar ul islam*, the house of peace wherein Muslim *mores* are normative. For such Muslims their concept of *jihad*, striving for God, would be seriously jeopardized by co-operation with those who do not believe. The same could be said about many other religious groupings, bearing in mind that the force of Niebuhr's comment about 'tribal limits' applies across the board. Questions of cultural identity and absolute religious truth are inextricably intertwined for them as for Christians.

In this context the WCC *Guidelines* are right to locate their ethical imperative not so much in romanticized (or even realistic) ideas of 'community' or 'humanization' as in the love of God and the love of neighbour, two axioms of theological ethics neither of which is peculiar to Christianity.

So it is no surprise that my own experience of expounding these 'four principles of dialogue' to interfaith gatherings has often found the greatest response at this point. One could, if space permitted, firstly indicate the ways in which the several traditions echo the command to love the neighbour; secondly the ways in which the old exclusivenesses are being re-interpreted; and thirdly, some of the areas which are already being tackled in this kind of interreligious co-operation.[39]

IV   Dialogue becomes the medium of authentic witness

We have seen how insistent Raimundo Panikkar is in his 'The Rules of the Game' that *'the Religious encounter must be a truly religious one'*, or in his other words, it is more than 'just a congress of philosophy', more than 'merely an ecclesiastical endeavour'. In his discussion Panikkar touches on many of the themes covered in the first three of our 'Four Principles' and here we highlight those that belong specifically to the areas of 'authentic witness'. Panikkar is clear, as are the WCC and BCC *Guidelines* that, 'one must face the challenge of conversion': 'to enter the new field of religious encounter is a challenge and a risk. The religious person enters this arena without prejudices and preconceived solutions, knowing full well that he may have to lose his life – he may also be born again'.[40]

Here is one of the clearest statements of the openness and vulnerability that can be expected of participants in the deepest forms of 'dialogue'. This should not, however, be set out as the *sine qua non* or absolute condition for earlier stages in interreligious encounter represented in some part by the first three Principles. It is certainly possible, for example, to work in a dialogical relationship with people of other religious commitments for a better human community without this form of openness and vulnerability.[41] It is equally possible for people utterly committed to their own faith-understandings to explain themselves to each other without expecting that they should be, in Panikkar's expression, 'without prejudices and preconceived solutions'. If this were the necessary condition, almost every possibility of discourse in this area would be foreclosed, and few of any of the world religious traditions would ever set out on this path.[42]

And yet vital ethical issues here are at stake. The WCC *Guidelines* wrestle with the problem of 'integrity' in commending the way of interfaith dialogue to Christians, recognizing that Christians (no more or less than Hindus, Buddhists, Muslims and everyone else) enter into such dialogue with prior commitment, in the Christian case commitment to Jesus Christ. As an attempt to deal with this, the WCC formulation runs like this: 'In dialogue Christians seek to "speak the truth in a spirit of love", not naively "to be tossed to and fro, and carried about by every wind of doctrine." (Eph. 4:14–15). In giving their witness they recognize that in most circumstances today the spirit of dialogue is necessary. For this reason we do not see dialogue and the giving of witness as standing in any contradiction to one another. Indeed, as Christians enter into dialogue with their commitment to Jesus Christ, time and again the relation of dialogue gives opportunity for authentic witness. Thus to member churches of the WCC we feel able with integrity to commend the way of dialogue as one in which Jesus Christ can be confessed in the world today; at the same time we feel able to assure our partners in dialogue that we come not as manipulators, but as genuine fellow-pilgrims, to speak with them of what we believe God to have done in Jesus Christ who has gone before us, but whom we seek to meet anew in dialogue.' (Para. 19)

We may note, but refrain from commenting on at this moment, the Christological proposition embedded in the last fourteen words of this passage – we shall take them up in the last paragraphs of this essay. Here let us concentrate on the phrase 'not as manipulators but as genuine fellow-pilgrims', as pointing to the major ethical issue here.

Stanley Samartha's invaluable collection of essays *Courage for Dialogue* contains more than one reference to the reactions of people of other faiths to new-found Christian enthusiasm for dialogue. Here is one such: 'Do not think I am against dialogue . . . on the contrary, I am fully convinced that dialogue is an essential part of human life, and therefore of religious life itself . . . Yet to be frank with you, there is something that makes me uneasy in the way in which you

Christians are now trying so easily to enter into official and formal dialogue with us. Have you already forgotten that what you call "inter-faith dialogue" is quite a new feature in your understanding and practice of Christianity? Until a few years ago, and often still today, your relations with us were confined, either merely to the social plane, or preaching in order to convert us to your *dharma* . . . For all matters of *dharma* you were deadly against us, violently or stealthily according to cases . . . '[43]

This Hindu from North India was politely declining to take part in a dialogue instigated by Christians: the memory of past attacks and derogatory remarks was too fresh in his mind. What also, perhaps, he was too polite actually to express in words was the fear that others have made explicit, that in this context dialogue remains a disguised form of mission: 'you have failed to convert us by direct methods, now you will try to manipulate us by dialogue'.

Many on the Christian side hear this charge with too great an arousal of guilt feelings, for it often goes along with other indictments like 'cultural imperialism', 'Western feelings of superiority' and so on. At this point certain strategies are adopted, sometimes consciously but more often in an unreflecting and unaware manner. We must spend a little time on such moves, for they are quite simply *unethical* or, in Panikkar's terminology, *irreligious*.

One such move is to relativize the concept of truth itself, and to describe it in cultural terms. Christopher Lamb describes it thus ' . . . one strong defensive tendency among British Christians is to adopt a "cultural-bound" interpretation of faiths, saying in effect "Jesus is the way for me because other religious traditions are culturally inaccessible to me. My Western upbringing makes them opaque to me, and I presume that Christian tradition is equally opaque to their followers".'[44] Paradoxically there are many who are willing with this understanding to engage in a dialogue of a kind, though such a position would at first sight suggest that interreligious understanding is impossible from the start. My own work takes me constantly to local groups in Britain who desire to have closer relationships with, say, the local mosque, and who are startled when I suggest that they should want to talk to Muslims as it were 'from faith to faith'. To meet, yes; to build up trust and friendship, yes; to work together on city and neighbourhood issues, yes . . . but to witness to Christ . . . ? that is a much more doubtful proposition.

And so it often comes about that 'truth-claims' are excluded from the agenda of interfaith dialogue. Let another Hindu hold the mirror up for us here. Lesslie Newbigin tells us of the comments of Dr R Sundara Rajan of Madras: 'the emphasis on a self-critical attitude, the demand that each party should try to see things from within the mind of the other, and the disavowal of any attempt by either side to question the faith of others, can easily mean that dialogue is simply an exercise in the mutual confirmation of different beliefs with all the really critical questions excluded. 'If it is impossible to lose one's faith as a result of an encounter with another faith, then I feel that the dialogue has been made safe from all possible risks.'[45] Newbigin adds 'A dialogue which is safe from all possible risks is no true dialogue.'[46]

It is on grounds such as these that Panikkar and both WCC and BCC *Guidelines* reject explicitly or implicitly the 'congress of philosophy' or 'parliament of religions' approach to dialogue. It is vitally necessary in serious dialogue that the partners come with open commitments, not 'hidden agendas' or worse 'concealed ideologies'. So the WCC *Guidelines* believe that 'we must come as partners, genuine fellow-pilgrims, to speak of what we believe God to have done in Jesus Christ . . . ' The BCC *Guidelines*: 'If we are concerned with religion we cannot avoid being concerned with truth — otherwise we are playing games, and dangerous games at that,' and: 'Christians will wish to be sensitive to their partners' religious integrity and also to witness to Christ as Lord of all.'[47] And Panikkar 'If the encounter is to be authentically religious, it must be totally loyal to truth and open to reality.' The last word to Samartha: 'The freedom to be committed and to be open is the prerequisite of genuine dialogue.'[48]

Once again we have approached the ethical and religious issues from a viewpoint within the Christian tradition. Strictures against less worthy forms of behaviour in dialogue have been charged to the account of Christians: positive precepts and prescriptions have been couched in Christian terms and Christian language. But it is reassuring that the fundamental positions and commitments are susceptible to interpretation in the terms of the other religious traditions of humankind, and indeed that from time to time it is possible to hear people within those traditions expounding them for their communities. Just as we Christians have to hear, mark and inwardly digest comments like those of the two Hindu scholars quoted in this section, so there are comments made by Christians to, say, Muslims or Hindus that have to be heard on their side, for we, too, sometimes find ourselves 'manipulated', and not treated as 'fellow-pilgrims'.[49] Part of truth-seeking dialogue is to help one another in this process, so that all of us become as 'the disciples of Aaron, loving peace and pursuing peace', loving our fellows and drawing them nearer to God.[50]

Chapter 13

The Multi-Faith Dimensions of Sanctuary in the United Kingdom

Paul Weller

Introduction

On 8 January 1989, the *Observer* newspaper carried an article[1] on the activities of the so-called 'underground railroad' of sanctuaries organized by members and sympathizers of the Refugee Forum[2], a federation of self-organized refugee groups operating in various parts of Britain and Western Europe. The report, based on an interview with Ronnie Moodley, the Chair of the Refugee Forum, notes that there are 100 'stations' on the 'railroad' where people are prepared to help shelter and sustain migrants, immigrants and refugees under threat of deportation. At the time when this article was written, there were 52 people living in these underground 'stations', and in total the railroad had helped 125 people. Out of a sample of 23 recent cases, all but one were eventually given leave to remain in Britain.

At dawn on Wednesday 18 January 1989 around 50 police and immigration officers took part in an operation which used sledgehammers and hydraulic equipment to break down the door of the sacristy of the Church of the Ascension in Hulme, Manchester, where Viraj Mendis, a Sinhalese Sri Lankan, had been living for the past two years. They dragged him out in his pyjamas to a waiting police van and drove him at high speed to Pentonville Prison in London where he was detained, still in his pyjamas, pending a projected date of deportation to Sri Lanka on Friday 20 January.[3]

Viraj Mendis and those who had supported him believed that as a Sinhalese supporter of Tamil rights he had a 'well-founded fear of persecution' in that country.[4] The deportation was carried out at a time when the Bishop of Manchester and other Church personnel were involved, with the Home Office's knowledge, in trying to find an alternative country of destination. These efforts continued over the two days after Mr Mendis's arrest, but although the Home Office had received an offer to accept Mr Mendis from one of the states of the Federal Republic of Germany, the deportation went ahead as planned, at around midday on 20 January.

The events of these three days, coming just a week after the breaking of the *Observer* story on the underground railroad, gave birth to an immediate and high-profile political and public debate on sanctuary, with lead stories and editorials in almost every national newspaper,[5] and bulletins on television and radio news programmes. There could be few people in Britain who were no longer aware of sanctuary as a political and religious issue.

Viraj Mendis is a friend of mine and I was involved in setting up his sanctuary whilst working for the Greater Manchester Ecumenical Council as its Community Relations Officer. For this and other reasons somewhere near the beginning of this essay I must, as they say, 'come clean' and acknowledge that I am not a detached observer of the development of the sanctuary movement and of its multi-faith dimensions, but rather, am a committed and engaged participant. I hope, in fact, that what I have to say will actually gain in critical depth precisely through the practical knowledge of this subject which my engagement brings and that dimensions and perspectives will thereby be included which would not perhaps be available to a more detached observer.

The meaning, tradition and law of sanctuary

Sanctuary is a word which finds a resonance within many religions traditions. Its English dictionary definition embraces both the meaning of a 'sacred place' and a 'place of safety'. In contemporary terms the word has also come to be connected with that part of a worldwide movement to uphold the rights of immigrants, migrants and refugees in which Christian churches, Hindu mandirs, Jewish synagogues, Muslim mosques and Sikh gurdwaras have all been offered as places of refuge for people under threat of deportation. These 'sanctuaries' have been dynamic and symbolic actions which have welded together the two meanings of the word sanctuary in a multireligious pattern of response to human need.

In the Western world, the practice of sanctuary is rooted in the Jewish tradition recorded in the Hebrew Scriptures where cities of refuge were designated in the Promised Land as places where the manslayer, as distinct from the murderer, could flee to escape from the arbitrary punishment of blood revenge. In the Book of Joshua, it is recorded that:

> Then the Lord told Joshua to say to the people of Israel, Choose the cities of refuge that I commanded Moses to tell you about. A person who kills someone accidentally can go there and escape the man who is looking for revenge. He can run away to one of these cities, go to the place of judgement at the entrance of the city, and explain to the leaders what has happened. They will let him into the city and give him a place to live in, so that he can stay there. If a man looking for revenge follows him there, the people of the city must not hand him over to him. They

must protect him because he has killed a person accidentally and not out of anger. He may still in the city until he has received a public trial and until the death of the man who is then the High Priest. The man may then go back to his home town, from which he had run away . . . These were the cities of refuge chosen for all the people of Israel and for any foreigner living among them. Anyone who killed a person accidentally could find protection there from the man looking for revenge: he could not be killed unless he had first received a public trial.[6]

There were, however, places of sanctuary which pre-dated the Hebrew sanctuaries. From the earliest times in Egypt:

Every shrine . . . royal altars, pictures and statues of the ruler, or sites used for the taking of oaths, was a protected region sought out by the persecuted, by mistreated slaves, oppressed debtors and political offenders.[7]

With the adoption of Christianity by the Emperor Constantine, the long history of the connection between and dispute over the spheres of Church and State authority began. During the fourth and fifth centuries, the main conflict over the use of sanctuary was not so much between Church and State as between the Church and slave-owners, since sanctuary was often claimed by fleeing slaves. However, by the eighth-ninth century sanctuary became part of the contested ground in the struggle between Church and State:

The law of ecclesiastical sanctuary was conditioned by the struggle between State and Church which dominated the entire Middle Ages. Contractions and expansions of the privilege depended upon whether power lay in the spiritual or in the secular authority. For a time the Church was able to use the law of sanctuary to advance its secular power. It extended the protective quality of sanctuary to all grounds connected with the Church; these comprised episcopal dwellings and a specific area of surrounding territory, oratories for public divine services including those located in private residences, cloisters, abbeys, ecclesiastical hospitals and other religious institutions.[8]

In addition to these religious sanctuaries there were also purely secular sanctuaries where the local lord had full rights and the king's writ did not run. In addition, there were chartered sanctuaries, deriving their authority from royal grant. However, as sanctuary developed in this more secularized direction an important, and from the perspective of the contemporary use of sanctuary, an ironic change occurred. From being something primarily concerned with the prevention of private revenge and affording the possibility of intercession and mediation, sanctuary became institutionalized as part of the system of 'outlawry' and 'abjuration of the realm'. Abuses of sanctuary also developed, and then, with the escalating conflict between King Henry VIII and the Papacy, restrictions on sanctuary were introduced. By an Act of 1540, all privileges of chartered sanctuary were revoked and all sanctuary protection was abolished for the crimes of murder, rape, burglary, arson, robbery and sacrilege. The final abolition of sanctuary was enacted in 1623, although it appears that its remnants did not finally die out until as late as the mid-eighteenth century when several royal decrees repudiated all remaining claims to sanctuary in the area of the Strand.

With regard to the current practice of sanctuary in religious buildings, there is no legal basis for the recognition of sanctuary rights. Indeed, under immigration legislation there is a legal offence of 'harbouring' which carries a penalty of a £2,000 fine or up to six months imprisonment. Whilst this offence could clearly be applied to people offering so-called 'underground sanctuary', the basis of its application to people offering public sanctuary in religious buildings is not so clear since unlike 'underground sanctuary' public sanctuary, by definition, is not concerned with concealing people from the authorities. But, as Grant and Martin's handbook on *Immigration Law and Practice*[9] points out, in the case of R v. Asare the Court of Appeal held that proving the offence of 'harbouring' does not necessarily imply a need to prove an intention to impede the authorities in taking action against the person harboured, but simply a necessity to show that the person concerned has been sheltered whilst it was known that they were illegally present in the country. However, this has not, as yet, been tested in the courts with regard to public sanctuary.

The sanctuary movement in the USA

The best known contemporary expression of the idea and practice of sanctury movement is in the USA where both Christian churches and Jewish synagogues have offered refuge to people fleeing from the conflicts of Central America.[10] In the USA, however, it is noteworthy that the community of sanctuary rather than the place of sanctuary has been the main focus of sanctuary activity which builds on the historical traditions of the 'underground railroad' for the black slaves who escaped to the North from the Southern States. During the early 1980s, the churches of the border states with Mexico became increasingly involved in providing pastoral and legal help to people claiming refugee status who were being returned across the Mexican border by the Immigration and Nationality Service of the Federal Government. Eventually, frustration grew as it proved more and more difficult to be of real practical help to these people and it was at this time that Jim Corbett, a Quaker Christian, began to guide refugees to safety by illegally crossing the Mexican border with them. Whole congregations soon became involved, beginning with the Southside Presbyterian Church in Tucson, Arizona, where

Rev John Fife led his congregation in covenanting to be a sanctuary congregation. The movement then grew and spread throughout the border states and other parts of the USA until more than 300 churches and synagogues were directly involved in its activities, with many others offering various kinds of support. By January 1985, several sanctuary workers were indicted and after a trial lasting seven months eight people were convicted with most being placed on probation. During this past year, the Federal authorities have unleashed another legal assault on the movement in an attempt to break it.

The sanctuary movement in continental Europe

Whilst the USA represents the most developed example of the phenomenon, sanctuary actions have also begun to appear in Western Europe, although in this context sanctuary has more often focused on the role of religious buildings in providing a haven for deportees, in addition to the rôle of the congregation or religious community. In West Berlin the Heilige-Kreuz Lutheran Church became involved in the safehousing of refugees.[11] In Denmark, Rev Inge Tanholm-Mikkelson of Vodskov in Denmark gave sanctuary in her family to some Syrian Orthodox Turks. She was fined by the authorities, but many people contributed to the cost of her fine and the refugees finally got asylum in Sweden.[12] In Sweden, Sister Marianne of the Alsike convent near Uppsala has used her convent as a sanctuary for refugees.[13] In Switzerland, sanctuaries began in 1981 with the occupation of the Paroisses des Eaux-Vives when 40 Turks occupied the church building.[14] In the Netherlands, the Mozes and Aaron Kerk in Amsterdam was sanctuary to 180 Moroccans.[15] In the Netherlands, in fact, sanctuary in religious buildings has a strong legal instrument for use in its defence in so far as there is a Dutch law which prohibits the police from entering a church building whilst a religious service is in progress. Congregations have therefore organized continuous vigils at times of danger from the authorities. Out of the Dutch experience of sanctuary, and especially from the experience gained in the northern town of Groningen, the Charter of Groningen has been drawn up.[16] The Charter is supported by a network of around 600 faith communities and basic groups throughout Western Europe who have covenanted to work together within the framework of the International Network for Local Initiatives on Asylum for the protection of refugees. As point 3 of the Groningen Charter declares:

> When we have good reason to assume that a refugee or asylum seeker, threatened with deportation, is not being given humanitarian treatment, or that decisions are being taken that may seriously affect the quality of

his or her existence, we pledge ourselves to take in and protect him or her until a solution has been found that is acceptable to all parties concerned. We will not avoid open confrontation with our governments or direct actions of solidarity and protest when in our opinion the situation requires it.[17]

In continental Europe no case has as yet come to light of a public sanctuary that has taken place in the building of a community of faith which is other than Christian. However, it is perhaps significant that the Groningen Charter is at least open to the development of an alliance between Christian congregations and other local faith communities since it includes the formulations of 'faith community' and 'basic group' alongside the word 'church'. As point 5 of the Charter says:

Regarding ourselves as partners in a covenant of local faith communities and other groups that take sides with refugees and asylum seekers, we promise each other support and solidarity, and we endeavour to encourage many other churches, faith communities and basic groups to also join us in this covenant.[18]

The beginnings of sanctuary in the UK

In 1987 I wrote a Runnymede Trust booklet entitled *Sanctuary: The Beginning of a Movement?*[19] The use of a question mark at the end of the title was very deliberate, as was the inclusion in the title of the words 'the Beginning'. At that time, although the United Kingdom had already experienced a number of instances of public sanctuary being offered in buildings used for worship by faith communities, these instances had not yet become a movement in the sense of what was happening in the USA or even in comparision with the activities associated with the Groningen Charter. However, there were signs that these stirrings might yet develop into a movement in the full sense of the word.

One of the remarkable features of public sanctuary in Britain is that it has not been restricted to the Christian churches alone. It has taken on a multi-faith dimension unique in Europe and paralleled in the USA only by the involvement of Jewish synagogues alongside Christian churches. There have been sanctuaries in Muslim mosques, Sikh gurdwaras and Hindu mandirs, and these sanctuaries have been backed up by supportive statements from Muslim, Sikh and Hindu religious leaders.

Some of the earliest sanctuaries in the UK were, in fact, in mosques,[20] although these received very little publicity in comparison with those which began to occur in Christian churches towards the middle of the 1980s. The first amongst these Christian sanctuaries was a highly publicised but very short act of a 'Sanctuary Fast'.[21]

This was undertaken in November of 1984 in the Welbeck Street Baptist Church in Ashton-under-Lyne, Greater Manchester, on behalf of Vinod Chauhan, an Indian Hindu whom the Home Office were seeking to deport after the breakdown of his marriage to a British citizen. At the time, I was Chairperson of his defence campaign and a minister in the group of churches of which the Welbeck Street Baptist Church was a part. A crisis was reached in Vinod Chauhan's long legal and political fight to remain in Britain[22] when he received a letter from the Home Office giving notice of a date by which he should have departed from the country or else steps would be taken to enforce his departure.

Just around that time I happened to see a television programme on the sanctuary movement in the USA and asked myself the question of whether the same could be done here in Britain. The Defence Campaign discussed the idea and felt that some such act should be attempted, although only as a short-term and symbolic act, since we didn't feel that we had the experience, strength, or organizational capability to sustain a long-term sanctuary. We therefore decided, and the Welbeck Street Baptist Church congregation agreed, to organize a 'sanctuary fast' over a long weekend from a Friday to a Monday, in order to draw attention to Vinod's plight. The sanctuary fast had an impact on the Home Office, since soon after it took place the Minister responsible for deportations, Mr David Waddington MP, agreed to meet a delegation consisting of myself, the local Member of Parliament and the Mayor of the Tameside Metropolitan Borough. This in itself was a major step forward and certainly delayed the deportation. However, in the Spring of the following year Vinod was finally deported from Britain when, having decided not to go 'underground' into hiding he was snatched from work and put on a plane to India.

The first longer-term sanctuary in a Christan church in the UK began on 26 February 1985, when two Cypriot refugees, Katerina and Vassilis Nicola went into sanctuary in the Anglican Church of St Mary's, Eversholt Street, London. The sanctuary went on until 12 July when the couple finally conceded and left Britain due to the pressures of living in a confined space.[23] Although this outcome did not perhaps seem very propitious for the spread of sanctuary a seed had been planted. In fact, on 15 March of the same year, Phillipina Pina Manuel and her son Arman had taken refuge in St Aloysius Catholic Church and by August of the same year they had won their right to remain in Britain.

The best-known and longest running of all public sanctuaries in Britain has been that of Viraj Mendis. His sanctuary began on 16 December 1986, but his defence campaign had been set up long before this.[24] However, unlike many anti-deportation defence campaigns, Viraj's campaign achieved a national profile and this was largely thanks to the groundwork laid for the sanctuary by the march from Manchester to London which the campaign organized between 5–26 July 1986. This march ensured that there were groups of active supporters at many different places along the route, with the result that when the sanctuary was launched not only did it have a strong base of local support in Manchester, but there were also other support groups all over the country ready to build the campaign into a national force. Although ultimately unsuccessful in terms of finally stopping Viraj's deportation, the sanctuary did prevent it from happening for two years and during this time many others were inspired in their resistance to racism in the immigration and nationality laws and in the treatment of refugees, and direct links of mutual solidarity were established between the Mendis sanctuary and the successful sanctuaries of Rajwinder Singh, Renouka Lakhani, and Salema Begum.

Sanctuary post-Mendis

Following the first use of forcible entry into a church in modern British history, it is clear that questions have to be asked about the continued usefulness of sanctuary in religious buildings as a means of defending those who are under threat of deportation. However, whilst this debate must continue it should be noted that during the first week of January 1989, Amir Kabul Khan and his family were given sanctuary in Birmingham's Central Mosque.[25] The Home Office had refused Mr Khan permission to remain in the UK because they claimed that his marriage was only a so-called 'marriage of convenience', contracted with the primary purpose of securing settlement in Britain.[26] Despite the forcible entry into Viraj Mendis's sanctuary in January, during February Amir Kabul Khan and his family were able to leave the mosque with an undertaking from the Home Office that his case would be reviewed.

The outcome of the Khan sanctuary might suggest that public sanctuary in religious buildings is still a viable option for people struggling to avoid deportation, even after the deportation of Viraj Mendis. However, it should be noted that there were some special circumstances which contributed to a positive outcome in this case. Perhaps not least of these was the anger which was raging among the Muslim communities of Britain over the Government's refusal to ban or take other action against Salman Rushdie's book, *The Satanic Verses*. In an atmosphere which had been highly charged by the public burning of a copy of the book in Bradford; by the Ayatollah Khomeini's pronouncement of a death penalty against Salman Rushdie; and by Muslim demonstrations in many towns and cities up and down the country, it would have been inviting an escalation of trouble for the Government to have sent police and immigration officials to forcibly break into a mosque.

The then Home Secretary, Douglas Hurd, was also due to speak at the mosque in March, when he used the occasion to appeal for calm among the Muslim community in the face of the debate around *The Satanic Verses*.[27] It would, to say the least, have been highly unusual for a Home Secretary to speak in a building where a family were sheltering in direct defiance of the immigration laws. Perhaps it was partly as a result of these factors that the family were promised a review of their case and were therefore able to leave the mosque. At this particular moment in time it was possibly safer to take sanctuary in a mosque than in a building of the Established Church of England!

Muslims and sanctuary

Since the Muslim community in the United Kingdom contains a large proportion of people who have been migrants, immigrants or refugees, they have an intimate knowledge of the harsh realities of immigration controls from their own community in their critique of the law. For example, Imam Abduljalil Sajid of the Brighton Islamic Centre has declared that:

> We, the Muslims of the United Kingdom . . . are closely monitoring the present policies and practices with regard to immigration control in the UK. We feel that current immigration and nationality rules are unjust, unfair and arbitrary. The current immigration rules cause a serious erosion of human rights due to severe restrictions on the right of appeal, and they undermine family life further because they remove the only absolute right to family unity in British immigration law.[28]

On this basis Imam Sajid has outlined his Islamic perspective on sanctuary as follows:

> From the Islamic point of view, Houses of God (Mosque, Church, Temple, Gurdwara, Synagogue, etc.) are symbols of peace for all mankind. The Holy Qur'an (3:96) declares that the first House of God ever set up on earth for the worship of the Divine being is a sanctuary, for all living beings. The Arabic words 'amn' (literally 'security and safety') implies 'ease of mind and freedom from fear'. That is why all hunting and fighting is strictly prohibited in the near vicinity of places of worship in Islam. In another verse (2:125) the Holy Qur'an speaks about the ancient and inviolable House of worship (i.e. the Kaabah in Maakah, Saudi Arabia) which has been rebuilt by the prophet Abraham and his son Ishmael. Its sacredness was respected even before Prophet Muhammed was born. Even arms were not allowed to be carried. It was just like the cities of Refuge under the Mosaic Dispensation to which slaves could flee, or as the sanctuaries in medieval Europe into which

criminals could not be pursued. Makkah was recognized as inviolable from pursuit, revenge or violence.[29]

Hindus and sanctuary

Among Hindus Vinod Chauhan, as has already been referred to, took sanctuary in a Christian church. However, Hindus have also given as well as sought refuge. When Tamils fled to Britain from the ethnic conflicts of Sri Lanka before the new visa restrictions were imposed against them, around 60 of them took refuge in the Ghandapathy Hindu Temple in Wimbledon. The temple supplied food and mattresses to the refugees and eventually, when the local authority pressurized the temple authorities into ending the action on the grounds that there was no planning permission for such a use of the temple building, the temple community gave help with accommodation in private homes.

Between 8 July and 11 September 1987, a successful sanctuary took place in the Shree Sanatan Mandir in Leicester, where Renoukaben Lakhani and her daughter sought refuge after coming under threat of a deportation as a result of a Home Office refusal to accept the genuineness of her marriage.[30] In July of 1988, the National Council of Hindu Temples issued a statement actually seeking the re-establishment of a recognized right of sanctuary.

> In former times, both in India and England, a place of God was considered to be beyond the laws of the State. However, at present, the society expects places of religion to conform with the laws of the State, and therefore does not recognize places of worship such as temples, mosques, churches and synagogues as transcendental places of shelter. We strongly feel that religious places should be recognized, as in the past, for sanctuary. Steps should be taken jointly by religious leaders to re-establish this so that religious centres can give shelter to just cases. That is, after having tried all possible channels, one should be able, as a last resort, to turn to God for shelter.[31]
>
> (*The President of the Council Mr O P Sharma and the Secretary, Mr Trikalajana Das.*)

This plea is all the more remarkable when it is seen against the background of a recent Indian Government decision, in the wake of the conflict at the Golden Temple in Amritsar, to finally abolish any secular recognition of religious places as sanctuaries. Whilst there is no religious consensus on the idea of seeking the legal restoration of sanctuary, in November of 1988 the Faith Alliance for Human Rights and Racial Justice did request a meeting between leaders of various religious communities and the Home Secretary to discuss the issue of sanctuary and to urge that force should not be used against the sanctuary in the Church of the Ascension in Manchester.

No reply or even acknowledgement of the letter was received before Viraj Mendis's deportation. As a result, a further letter was sent to the Home Secretary on 24 February 1989. At the time of writing no reply had been received to this letter either.

Sikhs and sanctuary

On 6 February 1987, Rajwinder Singh, a handicapped young Sikh whom the Home Office claimed was not related as claimed to his Bradford parents, took sanctuary in a Sikh gurdwara in Bradford, where he remained for several months until the Home Office eventually gave him leave to remain in the UK.[32] A number of leading Sikhs in Britain have spoken out on the issue of sanctuary:

> Sikhs share with alarm the adverse impact of immigration law upon innocent families and innocent lives. The above verse from the Guru Granth Sahib, the Sikh holy Scriptures, makes clear the emphasis contained in Sikh teachings on a higher vision of justice; a vision that encompasses a belief that all men and women are children of one father with equal rights of dignity . . . The Sikh view of equality is the quality of all regardless of race, class, creed, or sex. Particular emphasis is placed on the equality of opportunity and this includes the right to move about this planet in legitimate search of better opportunities, and, all to often, freedom from persecution.
>
> Sikhs are duty bound to assist in all possible ways those denied the basic human right of freedom of expression and those fleeing persecution, providing they are otherwise innocent of criminal actions. It is the clear duty of every Sikh home and every Sikh institution to provide such people with food, shelter and sanctuary.[33]
>
> (*Mr Indarjit Singh, the Editor of the Sikh Messenger, Mr G S Sahni, the President of the Central Gurdwara in London, Mr S S Kandola, the General Secretary of the Gurdwara Singh Sabha in East London.*)

Jews, Buddhists, others and sanctuary

In the United States the Jewish community has been quite extensively involved in sanctuary work. Many Jewish organizations have passed resolutions in support of sanctuary and the Union of American Hebrew Congregations has published a practical handbook on sanctuary.[34] In the United Kingdom, however, whilst a significant number of Jewish individuals have been involved in sanctuary work, there has been little corporate response, and as yet no synagogue has been used for public sanctuary. Some of the reasons for this have been discussed by the Jewish immigration lawyer Steve Cohen in his recent article in the journal *The Jewish Socialist*. Cohen argues that:

The Jewish community in the UK is far less politically and socially secure than in the US. It is therefore more timid. It is also moving towards the right.[35]

Whilst the Jewish community obviously has a deep historical under-standing and continuing experience of the realities of racism, its members do not always make the connection between their experi-ence and that of black people suffering from racism. Whilst Cohen is undoubtedly right that the Jewish community in the UK is much less secure than in the US, the Sikhs, Hindus and Muslims in the UK also have grounds for insecurity and yet their religious com-munities have offered sanctuary. The lack of Jewish corporate response perhaps lies more in the fact that there are very few black members of the UK Jewish community, with the result that contem-porary experience of discrimination in immigration, nationality and refugee law (an experience largely based upon skin colour) cannot directly challenge the Jewish community from within in the way in which this can happen in the predominantly black Muslim, Hindu, and Sikh communities and in those sections of the Christian com-munity in which there is a significant black presence. There have, nevertheless, been a number of recent developments. The 1988 annual Conference of the Reform Synagogues of Great Britain passed a motion which specifically criticized the new Immigration Act and called upon member shuls to 'be active locally in their concern for individuals' subjected to racism. In the same year, the Manchester Jewish Museum hosted a joint public meeting between Jewish refugees of the 1930s and Tamil refugees of today, and at the end of 1988, the Viraj Mendis Defence Campaign organized a national tour of Britain by two US sanctuary workers one of whom was Jewish, and part of his brief was to make contacts on this issue among Jewish organizations.

With regard to Buddhists and to members of other smaller religious minorities in the UK such as the Baha'is, the Zoroastrians, and the New Religious Movements, as far as I have been able to ascertain there have been no actions taken or statements issued in regard to sanctuary.

Christians and sanctuary

There have now been a substantial number of sanctuary actions on behalf of Christians and people of other faiths or none which have taken place in Christian churches. There have also been a significant number of cases in which the threat of sanctuary has actually brought about a change in the Home Office's position.[36] Throughout this whole period, the debate on sanctuary has been growing within the churches. In November of 1987, a major conference sponsored by the Community and Race Relations Unit (CRRU) of the British Council of Churches (BCC) and the Programme to Combat Racism (PCR) of the World Council of Churches (WCC) called on the British churches to:

> provide accommodation and bail for refugees and asylum-seekers, to oppose deportations wherever appropriate and to support those seeking sanctuary in the churches and other places of worship.[37]

In January of 1988, a Working Party of the Community Relations Committee of the Roman Catholic Bishops' Conference of England and Wales issued a report entitled *Towards the Rights of Migrants and Settlers*, in which they concluded that:

> Because the right of free movement and other rights are not sufficiently recognized in the immigration policies of states, illegal immigrants may often be victims of unjust law. They may be morally justified in evading the repercussion of their illegality and others may be morally justified, or even obliged, to assist them. In such a context, the increasing phenomenon of sanctuary can be understood as an authentic expression of morality and Christian principle.[38]

This endorsement of sanctuary was followed by an Issues Paper published by the Community and Race Relations Unit of the British Council of Churches, in which it was stated that:

> . . . given the frequently restated position of the churches on present immigration and nationality law and practice, and that the churches have offered support on occasion to those who oppose the law for conscience's sake, if unjust law is no law and if indeed immigration law and practice have become unjust, and if human rights are being diminished, it may be a requirement of contemporary Christian discipleship to grant sanctuary when it is sought.[39]

Following the circulation of this paper, a discussion pack was prepared on sanctuary in religious buildings, the aim of which is to help Christian congregations to examine the legal, political and theological issues involved in sanctuary. This pack was almost ready for publication at the time of Viraj Mendis's deportation. But in the light of the deportation and the newspaper stories about the 'underground railroad', the BCC Executive Committee entered into extensive discussions on sanctuary, as a result of which it was felt desirable to produce a substantial booklet to be included in the proposed sanctuary study pack. The outcome of this proposal was the writing of the booklet *Why Sanctuary?* The March meeting of the BCC Executive Committee discussed the issue again in the light of the draft of the *Why Sanctuary?* booklet and produced a *Policy Statement*,[40] which is now contained within the booklet. This statement was debated at the April meeting of the BCC Assembly and was commended to the member churches for study and action along with the *Why Sanctuary?* study pack.[41] In its *Policy Statement* the BCC Executive says:

> In earlier centuries the practice of sanctuary provided a space so that action on what was perceived as injustice could be delayed in order for cases to be re-examined, and where appropriate, an alternative form of action taken. The Council believes that such opportunities should exist in legal and administrative systems but that in present UK immigration law and practice they do not exist to a sufficient extent.[42]

It then called for 'a fundamental review of UK immigration policy, law and practice', including an end to deportations which divide families; the granting of effective appeal rights before removal takes place; an end to deportation to countries with oppression or civil unrest; and a call for a comprehensive, well-publicized amnesty for illegal immigrants who have made their homes in the UK. The *Policy Statement* then continues:

> Failing measures such as these to overcome the current difficulties, sanctuary movements and other efforts to protect threatened individuals and families are likely to increase. The Council believes that it is inappropriate that it should give support to evasion of the UK immigration laws. Where, after a full exploration of an impending deportation, Christians believe that fear of persecution is well-founded, there is a serious threat to family life and/or there is the possibility of gross injustice, and decide to challenge the law, the Council is clear that they can claim no special privileges with regard to the consequences of their action. The Council nevertheless fully understands the dilemmas involved and respects the courage and integrity of those who stand with and support vulnerable and fearful people and their families in their search for a safe and secure future.[43]

The *Policy Statement* therefore takes a middle way between respect for those who engage in sanctuary and an acceptance that such actions can claim no legal privileges. It is not, however, only the National Council of Hindu Temples which argues that forms of sanctuary should once again be recognized. From within the Western legal tradition Hermann Bianchi, a Dutch criminologist, argues that a dual system of law of a kind which was represented in the practice of sanctuary during the Middle Ages has the best chance of bringing about the goals of justice and reconciliation within the legal framework of human and social relations. He sees a dialectical relationship between Church and State, canon law and secular law, divine law and human law as being positive, and argues for a revival of some of the structures of the medieval idea of sanctuary, adapted to modern conditions.[44]

Sanctuary and law: national, international and moral?

Of course, sanctuary cannot substitute for changes in law and practice. However, immigration lawyers used to struggling with the complicated web of immigration law and to seeing its effects in terms of shattered dreams and broken families have affirmed the value of the developing sanctuary movement. A statement by 27 immigration laywers affirmed that:

> As lawyers active in the fields of immigration and refugee law, we are well aware of their fundamentally racist and sexist nature and application. We understand that many individuals and families cannot secure justice through formal legal channels. We therefore welcome the increasing involvement of members of this country's different religious communities on behalf of victims of the State.
>
> Against this oppressive background, sanctuary is increasingly sought. It is a source of strength. It is also a statement of moral principle – something sadly lacking in the immigration laws themselves. It gives time for officials to reflect. Above all, it provides an opportunity for a consideration of an individual's true claim to live here freed from the distorted demands which the immigration laws impose.
>
> We confirm our continuing commitment to those who have suffered under immigration control. We offer such skills as we have in support of their struggle in sanctuary and elsewhere.[45]

Government spokespeople, however, have argued that in a democratic society it is quite wrong for religious institutions directly to challenge the law in this way. And despite the impressive array of religious arguments in favour of sanctuary which have already been referred to, there are indeed also concerns of this nature within the religious communities. As we have already seen, a Muslim statement has cautioned on the use of sanctuary. Within the Christian churches there have been those like Claire Disbrey who, in a recent *Third Way* article has argued that whilst Christians should be deeply concerned about racism they need to balance this concern with 'a respect for democratic processes and the rule of law', concluding that Christians should be cautious in resorting to sanctuary which she calls 'such a dubious device'.[46] Others, such as the Presidents of the Greater Manchester Ecumenical Council, whilst supporting the sanctuary of Viraj Mendis have urged that its use be restricted to only certain categories of people under threat of deportation. In a letter to *The Times* they argued that:

> It is our own belief that refuge in a religious building should only be offered in cases of life and death.[47]

The BCC's Community and Race Relations Unit *Issues Paper* statement on sanctuary rejected this restriction and argued that sanctuary might be an appropriate response not only for people for whom there is 'a well-founded fear of persecution', but also where there is 'a serious threat to family life', or where 'gross injustice would ensue'. This position is based on an analysis that the deterioration in the treatment of refugees by the British state is integrally connected with the gradual institutionalization of racism in British immigration law and practice. In this context, the booklet *Why Sanctuary?* draws attention to the international agreements which many feel that our national legislation and practice are contravening, such as the Universal Declaration of Human Rights (1948), the European Convention on Human Rights (1950), the Convention Relating to the Status of Refugees (1951), the Helsinki Final Act (1975), and the Concluding Documents of the Vienna Follow-Up Meeting.[48]

This appeal to international law parallels the legal defence adopted by sections of the US sanctuary movement, which was that citizens are justified in challenging national law and practice where this is deemed to be in violation of international law. However, whilst international law might be appealed to on the basis that it sets the debate about sanctuary in a framework of discourse that Governments can relate to, the final court of appeal for many religious believers who engage in sanctuary actions is not secular law, whether national or international, but a moral imperative which religious believers have always believed must in some cases override observance of the laws of the powers that be. Religious believers can never accept that the State is the final authority, because religions relate to believed realities beyond the boundaries of the present social structures and appeal to visions of reality which act as constant critiques of the present order of things. For this reason, religious people are open to the possibility of being called to civil disobedience out of faithfuless to their transcendent vision. This is not to say that such actions are lightly undertaken, and there will inevitably be disagreements of discernment as to when a particular situation is of a kind which calls for such actions and when it is not. But the possibility of being called to break the law is, for the believer, always present.

Sanctuary as a place of dialogue

The World Council of Churches *Guidelines on Dialogue* declare that:

> It is in the search for a just community of humankind that Christians and their neighbours will be able to help each other to break out of cultural, educational, political and social isolation.[49]

One of the most interesting developments that has arisen out of the multi-faith pattern of sanctuary in the UK is that sanctuary has become a focus of dialogue as well as a symbol of struggle. In the brief sanctuary of Vinod Chauhan, for example, a Christian church was used for sanctuary whilst the weekend which was chosen for it was that of the Hindu Divali festival, and instead of feasting the festival was used for fasting. This reversal of normal conventions and the conjunction between this and the sanctuary action in a Christian church created a powerful active symbol which whilst challenging injustice also stimulated creative dialogue among people of faith. As has already been pointed out, sanctuary is an idea that has a resonance within many religious communities whilst fasting has been recognized as a tool in the struggle against evil through prayer and through social action, and sometimes through both at the same time as seen in the life and work of Mahatma Gandhi. Since the sanctuary fast took place during a Hindu festival it was decided that the Sunday morning worship of the church should take account of Vinod's presence as a Hindu by using the famous words of a Hindu prayer from the Upanishads:

> From the unreal, lead me to the Real,
> From darkness, lead me to Light,
> From death, lead me to Immortality.

This prayer was recited within a service which was framed by the overall theme of 'Am I my Brother's Keeper?' referring to the story of Jacob and Esau as it is told in the Hebrew scriptures. Despite this rather 'unorthodox' worship, when reflecting on the sanctuary fast one of the deacons of the church declared 'This is the most biblical thing we've ever done'. For the congregation the sanctuary fast had been a transformatory event with implications both for its own Christian faith and for its relationships with people of other faiths and none.

If the experience of sanctuary as a place of dialogue was significant in the case of this short weekend action, then all the more significant was the dialogical activity which was stimulated by the longest sanctuary to date in the UK – that of Viraj Mendis. In this sanctuary Christians of all sorts, Jews, people of other faiths, atheists, Marxists, socialists, anarchists, feminists, gays and lesbians were all involved and the mere conjunction of person, place and cause and supporters had a profound impact. As Stephen Cherry says in a recent article:

> The sanctuary of a black, atheist, revolutionary communist in a Church of England building has created a powerful symbol which demands a response from those who perceive it.[50]

In fact, it is actually when a sanctuary is based in a religious building that the dialogical impulse is at its strongest since the public associations of such buildings in themselves bring elements to the dialogue. As Cherry points out:

Church buildings (think of Westminster Abbey or St Paul's or the village church next to the squire's house) cannot fail to confirm to those who are inclined to believe it that God looks favourably on the way things are. For church buildings are the descendants not of the prophetic but of the priestly, cultic, temple-dominated side of our religious heritage . . . Now if this is the significance of church buildings, then it follows that the use of such a building as a sanctuary is bound to be creative.[51]

The creativity of Viraj Mendis's sanctuary is attested to by Sister Judith Watkins of the Viraj Mendis Defence Campaign's Religious Support Group:

We have seen people finding purpose and meaning where they had none; we have seen people flinging away discarded depressions and anxieties; we have seen people coming into faith; and we have seen commitment like we've never seen it before; we've seen new and exciting truths dawning on both lay people and clergy; we've seen barriers being broken down. Nowhere more clearly than here have we seen the eyes of the blind being opened, the ears of the deaf being unstopped, the lame jumping into action, and the tongue of the dumb coming to life; the poor receiving good news, the captives hearing release proclaimed for them, and the oppressed being set at liberty.[52]

Testifying to the impact that sanctuary as a place of dialogical action had upon him as a revolutionary Marxist, Viraj Mendis himself said:

It's good that people talk about socialism, but when it really matters they don't actually take the side of the oppressed. And it says in the Bible 'By your deeds shall they know you', not by your words. I see that what the Christian people here involved in sanctuary have done is actually at the heart of Christianity. Even though I'm not a Christian I feel that's true.[53]

The future of sanctuary

In 1992, the countries of the EC become a single market with the aim of achieving the free movement of capital and labour within the borders of the Community.[54] There are clear indications that the Governments of the EC are concurrently seeking to introduce tighter restrictions at outer borders of the Community and to co-ordinate internal controls within it. The result of this trend, if unchecked, will be the development of a Fortress Europe – in human as well as economic terms. This trend has already been fore-shadowed in the terms of the Schengen Treaty between France, the Federal Republic of Germany, the Netherlands, Belgium and Luxembourg, where co-ordinated monitoring, information-exchange and action on these matters are a significant part of the Treaty. In this context, resistance to immigration controls and deportations will become increasingly difficult to carry out at an isolated national level. Just as the trade unions have begun to realize that to work effectively on behalf of workers' rights in the modern world it is necessary to organize beyond the borders of the nation state, this will also become increasingly true with regard to anti-racist campaigning against deportations and in the developing sanctuary movement.

In the course of this necessary Europeanization of the movement, the experience of the British sanctuary movement has important contributions to offer. First of all, its sanctuaries have largely been undertaken within the framework of an anti-racist struggle which embraces migrants and immigrants as well as refugees. Secondly, the religious diversity of the British sanctuary movement means that it is perhaps more strongly rooted in the black communities than is the case in some countries, since the majority of people from the British minority faith communities (with the exception of the Jews) are not white. What is more, a significant proportion of these minorities are British citizens, and although this formal status is far from being universally translated into social and political practice, such a difference in legal status does provide the British minority faith communities with just that little bit more security than is the case in other EC countries such as the FRG where the Muslim minority is, in the main, composed of 'gastarbeiters' rather than FRG citizens.

The multi-faith dimensions of sanctuary in Britain therefore present some of the minimal conditions necessary for the development of an alliance between organizations of the relatively powerless black Christians, Muslims, Hindus and Sikhs and the more powerful and socially secure white-controlled Christian institutions. And in the course of the Europeanization of the movement this potential for multi-faith alliance could be highly significant since religious communites and institutions provide important trans-national channels of information and networks of solidarity. This is particularly true of the Christian churches with their very widespread geographical dispersion, but it is also true of other faiths and in this context the multi-faith development of the British movement provides a potentially very extensive potential European network of information and co-operation in resistance to racism in the treatment of immigrants, migrants and refugees.

If such a multi-faith dimension is important on a European level then it is all the more important for the internationalization of the movement which will surely eventually prove to be necessary. Western European trends are not isolated from those occurring in other 'white enclaves' around the world. Migration officials from EC countries have already been in discussions with Australian Government representatives on the implications of 1992 for other parts of the world, and there is evidence of a growing number of links on these questions between the white enclaves of Canada, USA, Australia, and the EC. Some tentative steps have been made to provide international links of sanctuary challenge such as the 1985 meeting held in Driebergen in the Netherlands between sanctuary activists in the USA and in Western Europe, but much more remains to be done.

Postscript

As I was finishing the writing of this essay an important development took place in the Netherlands. At the beginning of 1989, 250 Syrian Orthodox Christians came under threat of deportation from the Netherlands. On 2 January, two Syrian Orthodox women were deported, separating them from their husbands and children. The husbands and children were taken into sanctuary in Groningen and a visit was organized to Syria, on the basis of which a report was presented to the Government on the situation in that country and the plight of these refugees. As a result of this report the Government allowed a majority of the 250 Syrians to remain, but said that the rest had to go. In April, 81 families were given notice of deportation and many people in the churches could not accept the seemingly arbitrary nature of this decision. As a result sanctuary was provided in 10 churches in various parts of the country, with 60 additional congregations providing all kinds of support, and all in all with the involvement of a network of over 1,000 volunteer helpers. Some of the refugees stayed in sanctuary for nearly a year, but all were eventually successful in winning the right to stay in the Netherlands, and the success of their sanctuaries represents a new level of activity in the development of sanctuary in Western Europe.

Chapter 14
Jewish Faith and the Holocaust
Dan Cohn-Sherbok

Throughout their long history suffering has been the hallmark of the Jewish people. Driven from their homeland, buffeted from country to country and plagued by persecutions, Jews have been rejected, despised and led as lambs to the slaughter. The Holocaust is the most recent chapter in this tragic record of events. The Third Reich's system of murder squads, concentration camps and killing centres eliminated nearly six million Jews; though Jewish communities had previously been decimated, such large-scale devastation profoundly affected the Jewish religious consciousness. For many Jews it has seemed impossible to reconcile the concept of a loving, compassionate and merciful God with the terrible events of the Nazi régime. A number of important Jewish thinkers have grappled with traditional beliefs about God in the light of such suffering. Yet whatever one makes of such responses, the contemporary Jewish community will need to find some solution to this religious crisis if the Jewish faith is to endure.

Theology of protest

Prominent among modern Jewish writers who have wrestled with the theological implications of the Holocaust is the novelist Elie Wiesel. At the concentration camp Birkenau Wiesel came close to death as he marched toward a pit of flaming bodies only to stop a few feet from the edge. 'Never shall I forget those flames which consumed my faith forever,'[1] he wrote. For Wiesel the Holocaust is inexplicable with God, but also it cannot be understood without Him. Auschwitz made it impossible for Wiesel to trust God's goodness, but it also made questions about God more important. In this regard Wiesel has been heard to remark: 'If I told you I believed in God, I would be lying; if I told you I did not believe in God, I would be lying.'[2] Wiesel is thus at odds with God because the only way he can be for God after Auschwitz is by being against Him – to embrace God without protest would be to vindicate Him and legitimize evil.

This stance is eloquently portrayed in Wiesel's play, *The Trial of*

God which is set in the village of Shamgorod during the season of
Purim. Three Jewish actors have lost their way and arrive at the
village which they discover is not the place for joyous celebration
since it was devastated by a pogrom two years before. Only two
Jews survived: Berish the innkeeper who escaped and his daughter
who was abused on her wedding night and has now lost touch with
the world. In the area of Shamgorod anti-Semitic hatred has flared
up once again and a new pogrom appears imminent. The Festival
of Purim calls for a play which will enact the trial of God. Yet
there is a difficulty. None of the actors wants to speak up for God.
Unnoticed however a stranger whose name is Sam enters the inn
and volunteers to act as a defense attorney for God. It appears that
Berish's housekeeper Maria has seen this person before and she
cautions Berish to have nothing to do with him. But despite this
warning the play commences.

Berish begins his persecution by contending that God could use
his power to save the victim, but He does not. 'So', he asks, 'on
whose side is He? Could the killer kill without His blessing – without
His complicity?'[3] Berish has no sympathy for the defendant: 'If I am
given the choice of feeling sorry for Him or for human beings, I
choose the latter any time. He is big enough, strong enough to
take care of Himself; man is not.'[4] In response Sam answers every
accusation and urges that emotion should not take the place of
evidence. The actors who have formed the court are impressed and
inquire who Sam is. As the play concludes, a violent mob
approaches the inn. Realizing the end is near, the Jewish actors elect
to die wearing their Purim masks. Sam puts a mask on as well, and
Maria's premonition is confirmed – the mask he wears is that of
Samael which signifies Satan. As a final candle is extinguished, the
inn door opens to the sound of a murderous tumult including
Satan's laughter.

Though this play is not directly about the Holocaust since it is set
three centuries previously, it does touch on the central theological
dilemma posed by the death camps. As Wiesel explains in the foreword to the play and elsewhere, he witnessed a trial of God at
Auschwitz where three rabbis who conducted the proceedings
found God guilty and then participated in the daily prayer.[5] The
reason they performed this seemingly inconsistent act is related to
a story Wiesel tells about a Spanish Jewish family that had been
expelled from Spain. Finding no refuge from continual persecution,
the father who was the last to survive prayed:

Master of the Universe, I know what You want – I understand what You
are doing. You want despair to overwhelm me. You want me to cease
invoking Your name to glorify and sanctify it. Well, I tell You! No, no –
a thousand times no! You shall not succeed! In spite of me and in spite

of You, I shall shout the Kaddish, which is a song of faith, for You and against You. The song You shall not still, God of Israel.[6]

In stating his case for and against God, Wiesel emphasizes that there was no need for God to allow the Holocaust to occur – it was an event that produced only death and destruction. Yet Wiesel asserts to be Jewish is 'never to give up – never to yield to despair.'[7] It is in this spirit that Wiesel conducts his dispute with God. As a survivor of the horrors of the death camps, Wiesel refuses to let God go. His struggles serve as a testimony that the religious quest was not incinerated in the gas chambers of the Nazi period.

Although Wiesel's literary works dealing with the Holocaust are not intended to provide a systematic theological response to the death camps, he does struggle with central religious questions. As we have seen, his experiences did not lead him to atheism, yet he repeatedly casts doubts on the traditional Jewish understanding of God. Unfortunately, in these reflections Wiesel does not clarify what position he adopts; his statement that he would be lying if he claimed both to believe in God and not to believe in Him simply highlights his own confusion. Thus for those who are anxious to find a solution to the theological dilemmas posed by the Holocaust, Wiesel's protest against God simply reinforces their religious perplexity and underscores the urgency of discovering a theodicy in which God's silence during World War II can be understood.

A non-theistic response

Unlike Wiesel some Jewish thinkers have found it impossible to sustain a belief in the traditional understanding of God after the Holocaust. According to Richard Rubenstein – the most eloquent spokesman for this viewpoint – Auschwitz is the utter and decisive refutation of the traditional affirmation of a providential God who acts in history and watches over the Jewish people whom he has chosen from all nations. In *After Auschwitz* published in 1966, he writes:

> How can Jews believe in an omnipotent, beneficient God after Auschwitz? Traditional Jewish theology maintains that God is the ultimate, omnipotent actor in historical drama. It has interpreted every major catastrophe in Jewish history as God's punishment of a sinful Israel. I fail to see how this position can be maintained without regarding Hitler and the SS as instruments of God's will . . . To see any purpose in the death camps, the traditional believer is forced to regard the most demonic, anti-human explosion of all history as a meaningful expression of God's purposes.[8]

In this study Rubenstein insists that the Auschwitz experience has resulted in a rejection of the traditional theology of history which must be replaced by a positive affirmation of the value of human life in and for itself without any special theological relationship. Joy and fulfilment are to be sought in this life, rather than in a mystical future or eschaton. Thus he maintains that we should attempt to establish contact with those powers of life and death which engendered the ancient Canaanites' feelings about Baal, Astarte and Anith. This would not mean literally a return to the actual worship of these deities, but simply that earth's fruitfulness, its vicissitudes and its engendering power will once again become the central spiritual realities of Jewish life. According to Rubenstein, God is the ultimate nothing, and it is to this Divine source that man and the world are ultimately to return. There is no hope of salvation for mankind; man's ultimate destiny is to be returned to Divine nothingness. In this context Auschwitz fits into the archaic religious consciousness and observance of the universal cycle of death and rebirth. The Nazi slaughter of European Jewry was followed by the rebirth of the Jewish people in the land of Israel.

Today Rubenstein sees his position as akin to mystical religion. In a recent investigation of the origins of the Holocaust and its consequences on Jewish thought,[9] he notes that his loss of faith and the events of World War II caused him to have a bleak view of the world. But at present he would be more apt to adopt an optimistic stance. Yet what has remained the same is his insistence that the traditional conception of God needs to be rejected. Further he asserts that the Jews are not God's Divinely chosen people; they are a people like any other, whose religion was influenced by cultural and historical events. Some of Rubenstein's critics have asked whether anyone who accepts his view has any reason to remain Jewish since the Jewish heritage is infused with the belief that the Jews are under the obligation to observe Divinely ordained commandments. What reason could there be to keep the Sabbath, observe dietary laws, practice circumcision, or even marry someone Jewish if the God of the Biblical and rabbinic tradition does not exist?

In an early response to such criticism, Rubenstein pointed out that the elimination of the religious framework of the Jewish faith does not undermine the sociological and psychological functions of Judaism. The ethic content of Judaism can persist even in the absence of religious faith. Judaism, he argued, is not simply a belief system – it is constituted of rituals and customs, which enable adherents of the tradition to celebrate life-cycle events and cope with crises. As Rubenstein explained:

> I do not believe that a theistic God is necessary for Jewish religious life . . . I have suggested that Judaism is the way in which we share the decisive times and crises of life through the traditions of our inherited community. The need for that sharing is not diminished in the time of the death of God.[10]

Yet despite this stance, Rubenstein believed it is nevertheless possible to view the cosmos as the expression of a single, unified and
unifying source and ground which we name as God. If human
beings are seen as an integral element of the cosmos, which is an
expression of the Divine ground, then God is capable of thought,
reflection and feeling.

Such a reversion to nature paganism parallels the return of the
Jewish people to the land of Israel. Referring to traditional liturgy,
Rubenstein pointed out that during the period of the diaspora Jews
prayed that they be returned to the Holy Land. When this goal was
attained, Jewish history had in principle come to an end, but since
Rubenstein does not embrace polytheism, he argued that after
Auschwitz and the return to Israel, the Divine manifested in nature
was the God to whom Jews would turn in place of the God of
history, especially in Israel. Rejecting the Biblical view of a providential God, Rubenstein thus subscribed to a form of Canaanite nature
paganism.

Over the years Rubenstein's earlier paganism lost its importance.
He previously argued that when the Jewish people lived in their
own country, they would revert to nature worship. But he eventually came to see that most Jews did not desire to live in Israel and
those who settled there had no interest in nature paganism. Those
who ceased to believe in God simply became secular Jews. But
Rubenstein has parted company with these Jewish secularists; in
mysticism he has found the God whom he can believe after Auschwitz. 'I believe there is a conception of God,' he writes, 'which
remains meaningful after the death of the God-Who-acts-in-history.
It is a very old conception of God with deep roots in both Western
and Oriental mysticism. According to this conception, God is spoken
of as the holy nothingness. When God is thus designated, He is
conceived as the ground and source of all existence . . . God as the
nothing is not absence of being but superfluity of being.'[11] Though
such a view has affinities with other religions such as Buddhism,
Rubenstein's position is far removed from the traditional understanding of God as the compassionate redeemer of Israel who lovingly watches over His chosen people.

Rubenstein's redefinition of God's nature avoids the dilemma of
Divine theodicy, but it is meaningless for Jews who accept the
traditional understanding of God. Rubenstein declares that after
Auschwitz it is an illusion to believe in such a God and that each of
us must accept that the universe is unconcerned with our lives,
prayers and hopes. Yet it is just such a view that the theist rejects;
what he sees instead is a justification for God's ways, and that is
what Rubenstein contends is impossible. To say that God is Divine
nothingness merely confuses the issues. Thus rather than providing

an adequate theodicy in the face of the horrors of the Holocaust, Rubenstein merely plunges the believer deeper into despair.

A deistic alternative

Unlike Wiesel and Rubenstein a number of Jewish thinkers have attempted to adopt a more positive theological stance. In the *Tremendum* published in 1981 Arthur A Cohen addressed the religious dilemmas raised by the Holocaust. Previously he had said nothing about the religious perplexities connected with the destruction of six million Jews in the Nazi era. In *The Natural and the Supernatural Jew* published in 1962 he had constructed a modern theology of Judaism without dealing with evil either in itself or in its horrific manifestation in the concentration camps. But in his later book Cohen uses the term 'tremendum' to designate an event of vast significance. Mindful of Rudolf Otto's characterization of God's holiness as *mysterium tremendum*, Cohen argues that *mysterium tremendum* and *tremendum* convey the aspect of vastness and the resonance of terror. Yet these terms designate different realities. According to Cohen, the Holocaust was the human *tremendum*, the enormity of an infinitized man, who no longer seems to fear death or, more to the point, fears it so completely, denies death so mightily, that the only patent of his refutation and denial is to build a mountain of corpses to the divinity of the dead.'[12] For Cohen the death camps were the *tremendum* since they represent an inversion of life to an orgiastic celebration of death. Like Otto's *mysterium tremendum*, Cohen's notion of the *tremendum* is meant to suggest a sense of unfathomable mystery. Cohen believes that the Holocaust was completely irrational and unique, and he doubts whether historians can understand its nature and significance.

Like Rubenstein, Cohen recognizes that the Holocaust presented insurmountable difficulties for classical theism and for the Jewish understanding of God's relationship with the Jewish people. For Cohen post-Holocaust theology must take account of three central elements: (1) God must abide in a universe in which God's presence and evil are both seen as real; (2) the relationship of God to all creation must be seen as meaningful and valuable; and (3) the reality of God is not isolated from God's involvement with creation. In formulating a theological response which embraces these features, he drew on Lurianic kabbalah as well as the philosophy of Franz Rosenzweig. According to Cohen, initially God was all in all and there was nothing else. But God overflowed absolute self-containment in a moment of love. For Cohen the world is God's created other, lovingly formed by the Divine word without the surrender of human freedom. Humanity is essential because without it the world would be unable to respond to God's love or personality.

Human beings, Cohen asserts, have the capacity to respond to God since they partake of God's speech and freedom. According to Cohen, such freedom was intended to be tempered by reason, but this did not occur and therefore human freedom became the basis of the horrific events of the Holocaust. In advancing this view, Cohen criticizes those who complain that God was silent during the events of the Holocaust. Such an assessment, Cohen notes, is a mistaken yearning for a non-existent interruptive God who is expected to interfere with earthly life. But if there were such a God, the created order would be an extension of the Divine realm, and there would be no opportunity for freedom. 'God is not the strategist of our particularities or our historical condition', he writes, 'but rather mystery of futurity, always our *posse*, never our acts. If we can begin to see God less as the interferer whose insertion is welcome (when it accords with our needs) and more as the immensity whose reality is our prefiguration . . . we shall have won a sense of God whom we may love and honour, but whom we no longer fear and from whom we no longer demand.'[13]

Since Cohen does not believe that God acts in history, he dismisses the view that God was responsible for Auschwitz. Instead he asserts that God acts in the future. The Divine Life is 'a filament within the historical, but never the filament that we can identify and ignite according to our requirements.' Human beings, he believes, have the capacity to 'obscure, eclipse, burn out the Divine filament.'[14] God's rôle is not to act as a direct agent in human affairs, but as a teacher; His intention is to instruct human beings so as to limit their destructive impulses. For Cohen, Divine teaching is manifest in the halachah; in this way human freedom is granted within the framework of Jewish law. Given this conception of Divine action, God is in no way responsible for the horrors of the death camps – Auschwitz was the work of human beings who exercised their freedom for destruction and murder. According to Cohen such license to act against God's will raises serious doubts about the viability of the State of Israel to protect the Jewish community from future disasters. The return to a homeland may prove more threatening even than genocide for, 'in no way is the Jew allowed any longer . . . to repeat his exile amid the nations, to disperse himself in order to survive.'[15] Further, Cohen asserts that dedication to the Holy Land devoid of a belief in a transcendent Deity can become a form of paganism. The founding of a Jewish state is thus not an adequate response to the religious perplexities posed by the Holocaust.

Although Cohen's redefinition of God's nature avoids the difficulties of seeing God as responsible for the events of the Holocaust, he has eliminated a fundamental aspect of Divine activity which is presupposed by Biblical and rabbinical Judaism. Throughout Jewish sources, God is understood as both transcendent and immanent – He created the universe and continuously sustains it. The God of the Jewish faith is the Lord of History. He guided His chosen people out of Egypt, revealed Himself on Mt Sinai, delivered them up to the Promised Land, and providentially directs human history to its ultimate fulfilment in the world to come. Within this eschatological endeavour, God intervenes in history; He is a God who is present in everyday life. Conceiving God as a Divine filament in no sense corresponds with this traditional conception. Thus Cohen's solution to the problem of the Holocaust deprives the faith of a view of God which is central to the Jewish heritage. His response to the horrors of the death camps is unsatisfactory for those who seek an explanation of how a benevolent God could have permitted the slaughter of six million innocent victims.

Traditional Jewish theology

A number of theologians have been unwilling to alter the traditional understanding of God in attempting to make sense of the Holocaust. According to Eliezer Berkovits in *Faith after the Holocaust*, the modern Jewish response to the destruction of six million Jews should be modelled on Job's example. We must believe in God, he contends, because Job believed. If there is no answer to the quest for an understanding of God's silence in the face of Nazi genocide, 'it is better to be without it than in the sham of . . . the humbug of a disbelief encouraged by people who have eaten their fill at the tables of a satiated society.'[16] At Auschwitz God was hidden, yet according to Berkovits in His hiddenness He was actually present. As hidden God, He is Saviour; in the apparent void He is the redeemer of Israel. How this is to be understood is shrouded in mystery. Berkovits writes that if Jewish faith is to be meaningful in the post-Holocaust age, the Jew must make room for the impenetrable darkness of the death camps within religious belief: 'The darkness will remain, but in its "light" he will make his affirmations. The inexplicable will not be explained, yet it will become a positive influence in the formulation of that which is to be acknowledged . . . perhaps in the awful misery of man will be revealed to us the awesome mystery of God.'[17] The Holocaust is thus part of God's incomprehensible plan, defying rational justification and transcending human understanding.

Such an argument is obviously not a solution to the problem of the Holocaust; rather it is a challenge to believe in God despite overwhelming obstacles. This evasion of the theological difficulties, while leaving room for blind faith, in no way explains how God could have allowed the Holocaust to take place. Berkovits claims that in His hiddenness, the hidden God is revealed and that He was both saviour and redeemer in the death camps. But how can this be so? For some Jews such an appeal to God's inscrutable plan merely aggravates and caricatures the horrors of the Nazi régime and deprives them of any firm foundation for religious belief. Thus Berkovits offers no help for those who are unable to follow Job's example, and instead seek a visible Jewish theodicy, in which the justice and righteousness of God are defended in the face of evil and suffering.

Another attempt to provide a Biblically-based explanation for God's activity during the Nazi régime was proposed by Ignaz Maybaum in *The Face of God After Auschwitz*. In this study Maybaum argues that God has an enduring covenantal relationship with Israel, that He continues to act in history and that Israel has a Divinely sanctioned mission to enlighten other nations. According to Maybaum the Holocaust is a result of God's intervention, but not as a Divine punishment. In explaining this view, he uses the crucifixion of Jesus as a model for understanding Jewish suffering during the Holocaust. Just as Jesus was an innocent victim whose death provides a means of salvation for humanity, so the deaths of the victims of the Holocaust were sacrificial offerings. Maybaum asserts that the Jews were murdered by the Nazis because they were chosen by God for this sacrifice. In this way God's purposes can be fulfilled. 'The Golgotha of modern mankind is Auschwitz', he asserts. 'The cross, the Roman gallows, was replaced by the gas chamber.'[18]

Maybaum contends that Jewish history was scarred by three major disasters which he designates by the Hebrew word *churban* – a term referring to an event of massive destructiveness. For Maybaum each *churban* was a divine intervention which had decisive significance for the course of history. The first of these cataclysmic occurrences was the destruction of Jerusalem in 586 BC which resulted in the diaspora of the Jewish community. This uprooting of the population was a catastrophe for the nation, but it did inaugurate the Jewish mission to bring a knowledge of God and His laws to other peoples outside Israel's borders. In this respect the first *churban* was a manifestation of 'creative destructiveness'. The second *churban* was the Roman devastation of the second Temple in Jerusalem which inaugurated the establishment of the synagogue as the major focus of Jewish life where study and prayer replaced sacrifice. According to Maybaum, such activity is of a higher order than the sacrificial system of the Biblical period – this transformation of religious life was possible only through an act of destruction. Such an interpretation of the Jewish past runs counter to the traditional understanding of these events as Divine punishment for the sinfulness of the nation.

The final *churban* was the Holocaust, an event in which the Jewish people were sacrificial victims in an event of creative destructiveness. In Maybaum's view God used the Holocaust to bring about the end of the Middle Ages, and usher in a new era of modernity. The sin for which the Jews died was the retention of remnants of the medieval European feudal structure. After World War I the West could have transformed Eastern European society, but it did not act. As a result the devastation of the war served no purpose and Hitler was sent by God to bring about what the progressives failed to do. According to Maybaum, God used the Holocaust as a means to bring about the modern world. In this tragedy all that was medieval in character – including the majority of Eastern European Jews who lived in ghettos – had to perish. The murder of six million Jews was thus an act of creative destruction. With the elimination of the traditional Jewish community of Eastern Europe, world Jewry shifted to the United States, Western Europe, Russia, and Israel. In these countries Jews were able to live in an emancipated environment which celebrated rationality and progress. Jews therefore suffer in order to bring about the rule of God over the world and its peoples; their God-appointed mission is to serve the course of historical progress and bring mankind into a new era. Only a part, though admittedly a traumatically large part of the Jewish people, was exterminated. The planned genocide of the Jewish people did not succeed, and Maybaum emphasizes that the remnant that was saved has been selected by God as a perennial witness to His presence in the world and in the historical process. Of the sacrificial victims of Auschwitz he states categorically: 'Their death purged Western civilization so that it can again become a place where man can live, do justly, love mercy, and walk humbly with God.'[19]

Though this justification of the Holocaust is based on Biblical concepts, Maybaum's explanation will no doubt strike many as offensive. If God is benevolent, merciful and just in his dealings with mankind, how could He have intentionally planned the destruction of six million Jews? Surely through His omnipotence God could have brought about the redemption of the world without decimating His chosen people. Furthermore, the image of Hitler as God's instrument is a terrible and grotesque picture; to see God as a surgeon operating on the body of Israel, lacking pity for those who died in the process, is to make a mockery of God's eternal love. Unlike the ancient Israelites, whom God punished for their sins through the military intervention of Nebuchadnezzar, Jews who lost their lives in the camps were simply innocent victims of Nazi persecution. Thus Maybaum's conception of God as slayer and saviour is hardly an adequate justification for God's apparent indifference to mass death, injustice, and suffering in the concentration camps.

The Holocaust and Revelation

Another traditional approach to the Holocaust is to see in the death camps a manifestation of God's will that His chosen people survive. Such a paradoxical view is most eloquently expressed by Emil Fackenheim in a series of publications in which he contends that God revealed Himself to Israel out of the furnaces of Auschwitz. For Fackenheim the Holocaust was the most disorienting event in Jewish history – a crisis which requires from the Jewish community a reassessment of God's presence in history. Through the Holocaust, he believes, God issued the 614th commandment: Jews are forbidden to grant posthumous victories to Hitler. According to Fackenheim, Jews are here instructed to survive as Jews. They are commanded to remember in their very guts and bowels the martyrs of the Holocaust, lest their memory perish: Jews are forbidden, furthermore, to deny or despair of God, however much they may have to contend with Him or with belief in Him. They are forbidden finally to despair of the world as the place which is to become the kingdom of God lest we help make it a meaningless place. 'We help make it a meaningless place in which God is dead or irrelevant and everything is permitted; to abandon any of these imperatives, in response to Hitler's victory at Auschwitz, would be to hand him yet other posthumous victories . . . '[20] For Fackenheim, it is a betrayal of the Jewish heritage to question whether the traditional Jewish conception of God can be sustained after the Holocaust.

In his later work, Fackenheim stresses that the Holocaust represents a catastrophic rupture with previously accepted views of Judaism, Christianity and Western philosophy.[21] According to Fackenheim, the process of mending this rupture (*tikkun*) must take place in the scheme of life rather than of thought. The resistance to the destructive logic of the death camps constitutes the beginning of such repair. As Fackenheim explains: some camp inmates were unwilling to become 'muselmann', (those who were dead while still alive). Such resistance was exhibited by pregnant mothers who refused to abort their pregnancies hoping that their offspring would survive and frustrate the plans of the National Socialist Party to eliminate every Jew. Again other Jewish partisans took to the woods to fight the Nazis, and Hasidic Jews prayed even though they were forbidden to do so. Though the number of those who resisted the Nazis was small, they did exhibit that the logic of destruction could be overcome. These acts of resistance are of primary importance. It is not enough to understand the Holocaust – it must be resisted in flesh-and-blood action. In this connection, Fackenheim stresses that only as a consequence of the deed of resistance can resistive thought have any significance. The Holocaust was intended to give its victims no possibility of escaping the fate of becoming the living dead and subsequently dying in the gas chambers. The first act of resistance was the determination to survive or to die as a human being. The second step was to resist the nature of the logic of destruction. In the case of those victims who did resist, thought and action were interconnected: their recognition of the Nazi logic of destruction helped produce resistance to it – a life-and-death struggle that went on day and night.

Such resistance was more than self-protection. Since the Holocaust was a *novum* in history, this resistance was also a *novum*. As emphasized by Pelgia Levinska, a Polish Roman Catholic, 'They had condemned us to die in our own filth,' she wrote, 'to drown in mud, in our own excrement. They wished to abuse us, to destroy our human dignity. From the instant when I grasped the motivating principle . . . it was as if I had been awakened from a dream . . . I felt under orders to live and if I did die in Auschwitz, it would be as a human being, I would hold on to my dignity.'[22] Fackenheim views this statement as evidence of the ontological dimension of resistance and of a commanding voice. In the past when Jews were threatened, they bore witness to God through martyrdom but Fackenheim believes that such an act would have made no sense in the concentration camps. Such death was what the Nazis hoped to accomplish. This resistance served as a new kind of sanctification; the refusal to die was a holy act. For Fackenheim those who heard God's command during the Holocaust were the inmates of the camps who felt under an obligation to resist the logic of destruction. The rupture between the pre-Holocaust and post-Holocaust world must be mended by such resistance. Among the most significant Jewish acts of *tikkun* in the post-Holocaust world was the decision of the survivors of the Nazi period to make their homeland in Israel. Though Israel is continually endangered, the founding of a Jewish state represents a monumental attempt to overcome the Holocaust. For the first time in nearly two thousand years Jews have assumed responsibility for their own future. Furthermore, the establishment of a Jewish state is the precondition of a post-Holocaust *tikkun* of Jewish–Christian relations. Before the Holocaust Jews depended on the majority for their welfare, but after the Holocaust Jews became the majority in their own country. In Israel the Jews became independent and produced weapons with which they could defend themselves. This transformation of Jewish life offers hope for the continuation of Jewish life after the tragic events of the Holocaust.

The difficulty with Fackenheim's view is that he does not attempt to justify his claim that Auschwitz was a revelation-event bearing

Torah to twentieth century Jews. This is simply asserted, yet it is not at all clear why this should be so. On the contrary, for many Jews the Holocaust has made it impossible to believe in the traditional Jewish picture of God as a Lord of history who has revealed His will to the Jewish people. For such Jews the world is a tragic and meaningless place where human beings have no basis for hope in Divine aid or in any ultimate solution of the ills that beset them. Though they might agree that the lesson of the Holocaust is that the Jewish people must survive against all odds, this would not be because of God's revelation in the death camps. Further, it is hard to see how Fackenheim's admonition to believe in God 'lest Judaism perish' could actually sustain religious belief. Trust in God is of a different order altogether from commitment to the Jewish people, and it is regrettable that Fackenheim fails to see this distinction.

Conclusion

These varied attempts to come to terms with the Holocaust all suffer from serious defects. As we have seen, Rubenstein rejects the traditional Jewish understanding of God's nature and activity and argues for a concept of Divine reality far-removed from the Jewish heritage. For Jewish traditionalists seeking to make sense of the horrors of the Holocaust such a suggestion offers no consolation. Wiesel's theology of protest also offers no promise of hope. Cohen's conception of Deism is also so remote from mainstream Jewish thought that it cannot resolve the religious perplexities posed by the death of six million Jews in the camps. At the other end of the spectrum the views of writers who have attempted to defend the Biblical and rabbinic concept of God are beset with difficulties. Maybaum's view that God used Hitler as an instrument for the redemption of mankind is a monstrous conception. Fackenheim's assertion that God issued the 614th commandment through the ashes of the death camps will no doubt strike many as wishful thinking. Finally Berkovits' view that God was hidden during the Nazi period offers no theological solution to the problem of suffering. These major Holocaust theologians have therefore not provided satisfactory answers to the dilemmas posed by the death camps. Contemporary Jewish theology is thus in a state of crisis both deep-seated and acute: for the first time in history Jews seem unable to account for God's ways. This means that for many Jews the Holocaust is a decisive refutation of the traditional concept of a providential God who watches over his chosen people. If Judaism is to retain such a fundamental belief Jewish theologians will need to find a more adequate explanation for the events of the Nazi period. In the present eclipse of faith, this task is more urgent than ever before.

Chapter 15
New Religious Movements
Peter Clarke

The term new religions is applied in this paper to those religions that have emerged in Western Europe since 1945. The focus is on Britain with some brief comments on the situation in the rest of Western Europe. My intentions in this essay are simply to point to areas where further research might assist in deepening our understanding of the phenomenon of new religions and to attempt to assess on the basis of a limited amount of data the 'force' and 'scope' of the new religious beliefs. Following Geertz by 'force' is meant the thoroughness with which individuals who join a new religion internalize its beliefs, and by 'scope' is meant the range of social context within which these individuals regard these beliefs as having direct relevance.[1] I also extend the meaning of 'force' and 'scope' to cover such issues as the fragility and/or viability in a more general sense of the belief systems of new religions.

A great deal of research into new religions has already been carried out.[2] The area, however, is a vast one and few could deny that as far as Britain and Western Europe as a whole are concerned there is much still to be done, and that without further in-depth research, comment and observation will continue to be based on intuition rather than hard fact. What is needed first of all in the Western European context, and even in North America, is more sober, specific data which will enable the number and size, in terms of membership, of new religions to be established. Otherwise very general, unsubstantiated observations concerning the impact of new religions will continue to be made, perhaps grossly distorting the reality of the situation. Let me illustrate. In North America estimates of the size of membership of the new religions vary from 300,000 to three million.[3] Despite this one author has no difficulty in arriving at the following conclusion: 'Religion, it is plain to see, has taken a stalwart stand against the forces of secularization. This case is especially clear in contemporary America with the resurgence of neo-Eastern, neo-Pagan and neo-Christian religiosity.'[4]

Not only are careful statistics on overall membership lacking, but what statistics there are say very little about the size of the membership of specific types of new religions. If one takes neo-Paganism from the above list there is no solid data for the United States pertaining to who practises it, to what extent, and even how wide-spread the phenomenon really is.[5] Obviously the admittedly very difficult task of counting heads is not alone going to enable scholars to determine whether or not the frontiers of secularization have been pushed back, or whether secularization is a self-limiting process,[6] or whether Western Europe is an even more fertile ground for new religions than North America.[7] Even if the number of adherents turned out upon examination to be very high, this might have a shock effect and lead to various kinds of reactions, but it would not in itself be sufficient, far from it, to cause the secularization theorists to cut and run. For example, the statistical data available for the late 1970s on participation rates in new religions and para-religious movements in Montreal reveal that 25 percent of mainly unmarried, middle class, professional type people between the ages of 28 and 38 have participated in these movements.[8] This is a surprisingly high proportion of the adult population of Montreal, but from this statistic alone it is impossible to draw the conclusion that Montreal is not a secularized city. Before reaching such a conclusion one needs to know among other things more about the 'force' and 'scope' of individual commitment to the new religions, and further evidence shows that the typical participant is a 'transitory affiliate'.[9]

However, presuming that the 25 percent are 'committed members' would this necessarily indicate 'the return of the sacred'[10] to Montreal, accepting for the moment that Montreal had been undergoing a process of secularization? In order to answer this question it would be necessary to examine the content, purpose, function and general significance for the social structure of these movements.

Moreover, though many new religions claim to be able to provide dramatic proof of the spiritual dimension to all of life with a view to destroying forever the materialistic view of man allegedly predominant in the West, there is evidence to suggest that in the case of some at least of these movements the process of internal secularization sets in quite rapidly.[11] Further, with reference to the occult revival of the 1970s which on the religious–existential plane seeks to provide people with answers to the quest for the beyond, with meaning, with communal impulse, with answers to difficult existential problems there is the possibility that this will lead not to 'the return of the sacred' but to a further de-mystification of the modern world. The attempt to 'scientifically' control mystery or provide irrefutable proof of spiritual realities is, it could be argued, to introduce a form of materialism into the sphere of the 'sacred'. As one scholar has pointed out with reference to the 'scientific' methods used by some occultists 'the paradox . . . is that while the modern occultist seeks . . . the genuine supernatural experience and knowledge as a goal, the scientific means which he uses to achieve this goal would eventually render the solution useless and defeat its original purpose'.[12]

While statistical data then may tell us little in themselves about the 'spirit of the age' they are nonetheless necessary as a starting point if opinions, impressions and intuitions are not to be allowed to take precedence over hard fact when it comes to discussing the 'force' and 'scope' of new religions in Britain, Western Europe as a whole and elsewhere. Moreover, without a large number of new religions documented on the basis of comparable features, it is not only impossible to quantify and compare these movements but also very difficult to go beyond the conceptual level in writing about them.

The task of collecting sober, specific data is not made any easier, of course, by the fact that creation of a new religion, as the creation recently by schoolboys in Denmark of Aplakeltisme shows, is a relatively simple matter.[13] It is also something that happens quite frequently.

In Britain today, and this is in no sense a definitive statement on the situation but the findings to date of a piece of ongoing research, there are some 400 new religions that have emerged since *c.* 1945. Although exact enumeration is impossible it is the case that numerous other short-lived new religions arose during this same period of time but are now extinct. The 400 new religions mentioned above constitute only the tip of the iceberg. Below the surface there would appear to be a large mass of 'new' religion which is difficult to locate and measure with any precision. There is, for example, the phenomenon of neo-Paganism which according to PAN (Pagans Against Nukes) divides into 'active' and 'passive' Paganism. PAN describes itself as 'an activitist organization dedicated to the banishment of nuclear weapons and technology from our world and the re-establishment of a culture in harmony with Mother Earth'.[14] Though it distinguishes itself from other neo-Pagan religions PAN is not exclusivist for it seeks 'to unite all the pagan traditions in the world in political and magical action', to achieve its above stated aims, so that 'the Earth be greened anew'.[15]

Other neo-Pagan groups tend to define themselves more by stressing the difference between their own beliefs and those of other religions, especially the Judaeo-Christian tradition.[16] One Pagan writes 'Because of their non-dualistic concept of Godhead, pagans refuse to believe in the Christian idea that we are "born in sin" and can only be redeemed by allegiance in blind obedience to a specific code of ethics. The most striking difference this attitude brings to pagan theology is the average pagan's liberated attitude towards sexuality. Many pagans believe that the act of sex is a form of worship of the highest type and that this is a belief shared with the followers of some Eastern religions such as the Tantric sects of India and Tibet.'[17] I am not sure which Tantric sects of India and Tibet are referred to or whether or not they would agree with the comparison made.

The lack of empirical data pertaining to 'active' and 'passive' neo-Pagan movements is matched by the same lack of data on esoteric and occult movements, though some, like the Servants of Light, are well established. There has been a tendency on the part of social scientists to see these movements as lacking the 'communal impulse', thereby failing to generate what might be termed, socio-logically, social communities. However the emergence in recent times of more new 'churches' and 'denominations' of the occult and the esoteric will undoubtedly alter this tendency. One example is the Seax-Wica founded in 1973. This movement refers to itself as a 'denomination of witchcraft' and has established the Seax-Wica seminary for training its own clergy.[18]

It is possible that neo-Pagan, and related movements may simply be run down, delapidated cul de sacs of Western thought. I doubt it. There is, however, in this case also, a lack of empirical data pertaining to who practices what, to what extent and how wide-spread these phenomena are. There are, nonetheless, some interest-ing studies relating particularly to North America that advance con-clusions that might well be worth testing in the Western European context. For example, some research suggests that the occult move-ment is mainly a youth movement,[19] while other research indicates that a large number of the not so young, that is people in their thirties, are involved.[20] Further, it apparently attracts more women than men,[21] and more people in professional and/or managerial than in other occupations.[22] Moreover it appears to be more of an urban than a rural phenomenon.[23]

As far as the growth of established esoteric societies in Britain is concerned the limited amount of empirical data available presents a far from clear picture. While the Grail Foundation appears to be gaining ground, and also the Emin Foundation with its now esti-mated 700 members, the Atlanteans remain steady at 350 members, and one researcher detects a decline in the membership of Anthro-posophy since World War II.[24] In its various communities in Britain such as the Christian and Camphill Communities the Anthroposo-phical Society has an estimated 2,400 members.[25] The Christian Com-munity, for example, has 600 members in Britain, 30 of whom are priests, and of the 30 priests, 10 are women – 'the highest ratio of men to women within any of the worldwide Christian communities where women have been priests since the Church's foundation'.[26]

Anthroposophy's membership in North America is about the same as that in Britain, while the largest number of adherents, 8,000, is to be found in West Germany.[27] It would appear that the main reason for the decline in membership in Britain in recent years is not that the message has worn thin but rather due to the determination to preserve purity of doctrine. The leadership has been unwilling to adapt the organizational and administrative structures of the movement to meet the needs created by expansion. For example, as the movement spread from London northwards to Scotland, the hierarchy refused to allow members in Scotland to participate in the decision-making process by voting through the 'unspiritual' mechanism of the post, insisting instead on personal attendance at the London Headquarters. This has led to the disenfranchizement and to an extent the alienation of some members and communities in Scotland and the provinces.[28]

Many of the new religions that exist in Britain are to be found elsewhere in Western Europe. There are, however, some notable exceptions leaving aside the obvious ones such as some of the neo-Pagan movements. For example, The Analytic Action Organization (AAO), founded by a Viennese artist in Vienna, only exists, to my knowledge, in Austria and West Germany. There are others also, limited to one or two Western European countries, but not found in Britain. This is the case with the Helmholungswerk Jesu Christi, founded in West Germany in 1976 and which spreads the teachings and revelations of the 'prophet of our time', a certain Gabriel X of Wurzburg.[29] This movement also exists in France under the name Mission Rapatriement Par Jesus Christ, but nowhere else in Western Europe, at least as far as I am aware.[30]

Movements relatively strong in some Western European countries seem to have less success in others. According to reports movements that emphasize community and communal living do less well in relatively closely knit societies like Denmark and Eire than in more highly differentiated and pluralistic societies such as West Germany, France and Britain.[31] The Children of God, though it has not that large a membership, does much better in Berlin than for example in Aarhus.[32] One 'indigenous' British movement that appears to be able to take root virtually anywhere regardless of the type of society is the School of Economic Science, which has centres in Spain, Greece, Eire, Holland, Belgium and many other countries both within and beyond the confines of Western Europe.

Establishing how many new religions exist in contemporary Western Europe is one problem, but an even more intractable problem is establishing the size of membership in each case and *in toto*. Estimates for the membership of Scientology in Britain range from 2,000 to 100,000 to 360,000.[33] Are these very high estimates, estimates of actual membership or simply Scientology's mailing list? Of course what constitutes membership of one or other new religion is often a very grey area. According to the National Council of Hindu Temples (UK), being a member of Hare Krishna and being a Hindu are the same thing, for in one of its statements this body explains 'The philosophy and practices they (the Hare Krishna) follow are exactly in accord with proper Hinduism and we are proud that they are setting such a good example in this country (Britain).'[34]

It is equally difficult, but for somewhat different reasons, to determine what it means for an individual to be a 'member' of Sahaja Yoga, a movement established in Britain in 1970 by Her Holiness Mataji Shri Nirmala Devi. According to 'members' 'there is no belonging to anything, no membership'.[35] Further there is no initiation rite, in fact no ritual at all, the movement consisting simply of people 'who have experienced something', and have as a consequence become 'realized persons'.[36] An individual once 'realized' can give realization to others on a bus or an underground train or anywhere, simply by 'charging' those others, who may be totally unaware that they are being 'converted', through the medium of a look or a glance. I should add that the inward disposition of those so charged should be correct which means basically that they should be 'simple and innocent like children and strong seekers after truth'.[37] One further comment needs to be made in order to avoid giving the impression that this process of 'conversion' is totally *ad hoc* and arbitrary; 'members' of Sahaja Yoga, having achieved self-realization can 'feel the state another person is in' and on that basis decide whether or not the person has the disposition required for 'self-realization'.[38]

On initial contact not only the 'membership' but everything about Shaja Yoga appears to be unstructured, intangible and indefinable. One of its main claims is to offer a 'new category of perception' in the form of 'vibratory awareness' which is 'beyond thought, feeling or instinct', and by means of which 'all kinds of absolute questions are answered'.[39] Apart from the difficulties involved in examining a category of perception such as that one learns that the foundress, Her Holiness Mataji Shri Nirmala Devi, is not really essential to the movement. One would imagine that nothing very durable could be built on such a fragile base. However 'in reality' the foundress is a very important, charismatic figure for most of the members. Moreover despite the insistence 'that there is no membership, no belonging to anything, no initiation rite', plausibility structures, in the form of supporting therapies, legitimations, social definitions of reality and specialized language, are in the process of being developed. It is too soon to speculate on whether or not this development will save the movement from extinction.

The 'membership' of other movements, though well established, is only marginally less difficult to determine. What exactly does it mean to say, for example, that A is a member of the School of Economic Science (SES)? This movement, which has witnessed a steady growth in Britain in the past twenty years, places a great deal of emphasis on the teachings of Plato. *The Bible*, Guru Shankaracharya, known as the Archbishop of the North, accepts that Christ is the Son of God, but not the only son of God, and yet apparently has among its 'members' clergy, albeit only a few, of the established Christian Church in Britain.[40] It remains an open question whether membership of this movement is based on acceptance of certain religious beliefs and practices or on ideas about how society should be governed, or on commitment to a specific set of moral and ethical norms, including a specific type of work ethic.

How and why and what type of people become members of new religions is another area that as far as some movements at least are concerned requires further study. Leaving aside the very large and controversial area of recruitment techniques, I want simply to present a few observations on these questions based on the limited amount of evidence that I have gathered so far. With regard to 'how' and 'why', some informants, both members and ex-members of new religions, suggest that it all happened by accident, that it was a question of fate.[41] However, on further examination, it seems to have been much more than this. One ex-member of Scientology began by describing how his involvement with that particular movement was 'pure accident, bad luck', but then went on to explain how at the time he joined Scientology he was searching for something that would give direction and meaning to his life.[42]

The same or a similar story repeats itself in the case of informants who joined movements such as Silva Mind Control, Lifewaves (Ishvara) and the Divine Light Mission. A university student of physics also saw her conversion to the Divine Light Mission as an accident.[43] She then began to reveal that she had been reading books on Indian Religions since the age of 14 and felt she understood the 'language' of these books far better than 'the language of the Church (Christianity) because they do not always talk of God and because I could experience within myself what they taught'.[44] She continued 'I had no understanding of the language of the Church . . . words such as God the Father, the Holy Spirit, gifts of God, meant nothing to me.'[45]

Obviously no firm conclusions on the 'how' and 'why' of conversion can be reached on the basis of the limited amount of data collected to date, but what the data does indicate is that the conversion process may well be much more of a long, drawn-out affair than is sometimes suggested. Is it simply in the case of some new religions a question of young students coming up to university in the big city and being caught off balance by 'missionaries' or does the process begin much further back?[46]

There has been some very interesting research on the social composition of some new religions.[47] The social composition of a new religion is, however, liable to change, if not substantially at least significantly, over a relatively short period of time and this means ongoing research in this area. As movements search for new markets such as the unemployment market[48] their composition changes. The Divine Light Mission in Britain, for example, has fewer students, and fewer members from the middle class, than was the case in the 1970s.[49] And while the School of Economic Science has a sizeable proportion of professional people, some of whom are lawyers while others are musicians, sculptors and artists, it is also attracting, it would appear, more recruits from outside these professions.[50] Moreover in addition to attracting people from the established, mainstream churches, new religions draw many people from sects, and people with no religion at all.

Although enthusiasm in itself is not sufficient to ensure the persistence and growth of new religions, it is nevertheless the case that people who join new religions do demonstrate a high level of commitment.[51] In some instances, moreover, there appears to be on the part of the convert a suspension of doubt as far as the doctrinal tenets of the movement are concerned. And when doubt in this sphere exists, as it inevitably does, drills and techniques of various kinds, and counselling services, are brought into play and very often locate the source of doubt in the individual and not in the system. It is possible, however, to have doubts about doctrinal content and not to reveal these doubts, and at the same time remain in the eyes of all and sundry a fully committed member of a movement.[52] In the case of movements with strong charismatic leaders, such as the Divine Light Mission, suspension of doubt would appear to be the norm. In the Divine Light Mission, I was informed, there is no internal criticism of questioning of Maharaji's actions such as the disbandment of ashrams in Britain because 'it is believed that all changes are for the good of the disciples'.[53]

In many movements, including the Divine Light Mission and Sahaja Yoga, it is a case, as far as members are concerned, not so much of establishing the logic and consistency of the belief system but rather of 'feeling and/or seeing is believing'. For the 'member' of Sahaja Yoga the 'Kundalini (Holy Spirit) located in the lower reaches of the spinal column, rises up the spinal column to purify the chakras . . . when the chakra is opened by the Kundalini that is the point at which the individual gains self-realization. One knows that this has happened because one can feel in the palms of one's hands a cool breeze coming from Shri Mataji or a photograph of her . . . a cool breeze can also be felt coming out of the top of one's head. . . . One has a feeling of bodily peace and comfort, very joyful, very peaceful'.[54] And a disciple of the Maharaji on seeing him 'has a feeling of love for him. . . . One feels a lot of light, of intense pressure on the forehead'.[55] It is in occult movements in particular, as one would expect, that the seeing is believing syndrome is most frequently found. Moreover, in this area, for reasons that are not clear, beliefs are apparently extremely resistant to dis-confirmation. In a case study of this type of extreme resistance the researchers suggest that of the two plausible hypotheses that might account for it, reasoning deficiencies and strong prior occult beliefs, it is more likely to be the former rather than the latter that makes for the intransigence to disconfirmation.[56]

To my knowledge apart from exceptions such as 'The Way' and 'Armstrongism' members of new religions are not normally obsessed with the logic and credibility of their belief systems. Many do, however, tend to believe that they have the Truth and that others do not and use a variety of arguments to prove this. According to members of Sahaja Yoga the principle distinguishing criterion between a true and false new religion is whether or not 'it charges for God, for enlightenment', for, 'a genuine Guru never lives off his disciples'.[57] Moreover, movements that use specialized techniques, set forms of meditations, are not authentic because 'enlightenment happens from within, it is spontaneous, it evolves naturally and cannot be brought about through the use of technique'.[58] On the other hand members of the Divine Light Mission stress that there is only one path to God and that is meditation and, without being specific, speak of other religions being 'totally misguided', and of people outside the movement being 'in the mire'.[59] However, some people outside the group, such as parents, can be saved, vicariously so to speak, for example through their children who are members.[60]

Considerations of a more doctrinal nature form in some cases, as I have already suggested, the basis for a divide between new religions and old. For example, the Aladura (praying) International Church established in London in 1970 by the Rev O A Abiola states 'Aladuraism can neither be classified with the present day American Pentecostalism . . . nor has it anything in common with Western Spiritualism'.[61] The main reason given for the distinction between itself and American Pentecostalism centres on the doctrine of the Holy Spirit. The Pentecostalists allegedly believe that the Holy Spirit is a person, whereas for the Aladura the Holy Spirit is 'an energy or influence which having its source in God was felt to be in contact with man'.[62] And the Hare Krishna see as one of the main differences between themselves and other new religions the fact that while the others 'submit', in their view wrongly, to a founder or leader, Hare Krishna people 'submit', rightly, to God alone.[63]

Though further comparative research is needed in this area before any firm conclusions can be drawn, it would appear to be the case that new religious movements are neither close allies in the task of saving the world or inseparable partners in distress. Even those new religions with highly syncretistic and loosely integrated belief systems do not 'hesitate' to spell out the difference between them-selves and others. Indeed, at times, they go to very great lengths to protect their members from being contaminated by 'outsiders', whether the latter are members of new religions or no religion at all.[64]

The data, thus, on new religions, are not all that one would wish for in order to be able to arrive at sound, empirically based, general conclusions on many aspects of the phenomenon of new religions in Western Europe. Some of these aspects have been touched upon above, others, such as geographical patterns of location, have gone virtually unmentioned. A further interesting area for research, which again depends on the gathering of data on a whole cross section of new religions, concerns the impact of these new religions at the cognitive level in Western Society.

1.   NRMs: a response to secularization?

Granted the limitations imposed by the inadequacy of the data, a number of general theories have been advanced to explain the rise of new religions in recent times. According to some writers they are a response to the process of rationalization and the phenomenon of secularization which it brings in its train.[65] Following Weber, it is argued by those who take this line that instrumental rationality – the organization of life in terms of instrumental and causal considerations – is part of the essential logic of modern society, making it well nigh impossible for supernatural forces to come into play and impinge directly and in a significant way on modern consciousness and behaviour. This is a world in which recourse to the 'supernatural' has for the most part become unnecessary since in principle it is possible to master all things by calculation.

Rationality of this kind has become the 'hidden persuader', the 'silent, unobserved teacher', of those kinds of attitudes and methods of acting designated as 'modern'. The end product is a world bereft of the 'sacred', of magic and mystery, of the supernatural. Institutions central to modern society – the factory for example as well as the office – and a whole host of man-made tool kits, direct, inform and shape people's modes of thinking and ways of behaving along these lines. One writer has spoken of the 'moral economy of the factory' and many would suggest that it is there rather than in religious institutions that people are schooled in attitude and behaviour appropriate to the modern world.[66]

Modern industrial society, moreover, is splintered, fragmented and complex. There is little or no social cement in the form of a single, coherent, plausible worldview holding it together. In fact there are innumerable worldviews, competing for adherents. It is a world, moreover, in which the individual finds it well nigh impossible to relate in a 'total' and meaningful way to anyone or any one institution, since the different spheres of life – family, work, leisure and so on – have become rigidly separated from each other. Is it any wonder, one might ask, that change for an increasing number of people consists in simply 'becoming' themselves!

Modern society, it is maintained, not only makes it difficult for people to be themselves and to establish community but also to be creative in the sense of being able to claim that product X, Y, or Z is 'mine'. The structural differentiation of work processes, a fundamental of organization in the 'work place', means that most people are responsible for only a small part of a vast rationalized system of production.

New religions it has been argued are an attempt to deal with the consequences of these processes of rationalization, secularization, and centralization, offering community, self-awareness and self-improvement, and escape from the 'iron cage' of this 'de-mystified', modern, secularized, rationalized society. According to some observers the prospects of new religions rolling back the frontiers of rationalization and secularization in Western Society, including Japan, are extremely bleak, if not non-existent. In fact they see them as a further proof of the irrelevance of religion in the modern world.[67]

On the other hand there are those who claim that the new religions indicate that secularization is a self limiting phenomenon. Religion alone, it is maintained, is capable of dealing with certain matters of great consequence, which cannot be decided through direct, instrumental means, and this ensures its persistence. According to this view, religious organizations tend to lose their credibility by accommodating to the wider society and thereby undergoing a process of secularization over time. This generates revival 'within' or from without the religious organization. Thus the decline of the 'churches' using that term in a broad sense gives rise to the growth of new religions.[68] The argument here is that religion tends to oscillate between the 'supernatural' and the 'secular' and back again, and that there is in some sense a fairly constant store of it in society which, given people's desire for 'rewards' in themselves such as immortality or substitutes for such rewards, will be constantly drawn upon in one form or another.

Neither of these theories has gone unopposed. The first theory assumes, not necessarily correctly in my view, that there is a rigid dichotomy between the logic, attitudes and orientations of the modern world and those of religion. It suggests, furthermore, that attitudes and thought processes are inextricably linked to social structure. While not wanting to postulate a 'ghost in the machine' like theory of the workings of the mind, I would nevertheless suggest that the links between thought processes and attitudes and social structure are not necessarily inextricable. But more importantly, this theory, in my view, does not give sufficient consideration to the relatively high level of 'supernatural' awareness in modern society. While I do not support the view that there has been a resurgence in spiritual and mystical religion as a response to the decline of Church religion,[69] I am nevertheless impressed by the data concerning the relatively high incidence of 'religious' experience in modern society.[70] This sort of experience would obviously not come to the fore in a society such as ours where weight, consideration and esteem are given in the main to the secular, rational, scientific approach to the explanation of space–time events and processes. However, I think the mistake lies in assuming that because this approach is socially prevalent it is also culturally dominant. Such an assumption, it would seem, equates prevalence and frequency with effect. Rationalization and secularization may well be socially prevalent, but it has yet to be proved convincingly that they are culturally dominant.

I am not arguing here, as I have already pointed out, in support of the theory outlined above that secularization is a self limiting phenomenon that gives rise to new religions. My position is somewhat different. What I want to suggest is that the more complex, pluralistic, in some ways open nature of modern society has allowed not only for 'new gods' to emerge and compete in the open markets of a consumer society, but has also made it easier to express and celebrate what were until not very long ago regarded as 'embarrassing', 'irrational', 'inconsequential' beliefs, hopes and aspirations. 'Beliefs' and 'religious' insights, kept secret to avoid public embarrassment, are no longer regarded as deviant forms of knowledge in a society fed on science fiction and one in which everything can be tried and tested.

The rôle of new religions in this process of change in perspectives in the modern, industrial society in the West, has been to act as catalysts. The essentials, required to create a religion, were all there, and so also was the market. Practising, committed believers did not abandon 'churches' because the latter were in decline or had become internally secularized. This in some cases may have been the reason, but it overlooks the efficacy of the methods of recruitment used by many new religions, and a rather more fundamental reason why they appealed. Let me finish by mentioning very briefly what I believe this more fundamental reason to be.

2.   Conclusion: the appeal of the new religions

Many of the new religions that I am acquainted with seem to me to confirm Feuerbach's prediction concerning the historical trend of modern religions. The pattern unfolding, as he saw it, was of religion retreating from a concern with 'God' as 'other', to the 'god' who lives in, with, and for man, and whose real meaning is a conception of man. As a result of this trend religion has come to be interpreted as primarily moral, and as concerning more the expressive and the ritual than the intellectual and rational.

In line with this trend many new religions tend to direct their adherents to the 'god within', while at the same time making a strong assault on the intellectual, rational, 'scientific' approach to religious understanding. These religions claim to be offering a certainty and wisdom derived from 'within' in place of doubt, confusion and 'arid' intellectualism. They are seen as addressing in a direct and immediate manner the individual's personal, subjective concerns, and escaping from what is seen as the relativism and moral ambiguity of the rational, scientific, objective approach. Such relativism, regarded as a product of 'amoral' scientific thought, is not regarded as a meaningful option for living.

What the new religions claim to offer are 'spiritual' techniques that will transform the world of those who practise them. The individual will pass from the position of slave and dependant to that of master, and become in the process an active, creative agent as opposed to the passive one which he or she now is. As the Bhagwan Shree Rajneesh has expressed it: 'The real . . . is to become God . . . not to know God.' And another contemporary 'specialist', Werner Erhard, 'You are God in your universe. You made it.'

Therein, in my view, lies much of the appeal of many of the new religions, an appeal which, given the subterranean but nevertheless quite high level of religious enthusiasm and awareness in modern society, meets with an impressive response. Paradoxically, because so pre-occupied with the 'self' and so geared to the market place these new religions will probably on balance turn modern society into an even more sober, de-mystified, de-sacralized, 'iron-cage' like entity.

Chapter 16

Kingdoms of Heaven on Earth: New Religious Movements and Political Orders

Eileen Barker

In this essay I want to look at some of the ways in which new religious movements envisage the political order – what it is, what it ought to be, and how the new order ought to be achieved. Political order will be defined rather widely to refer not merely to the political apparatus or the type of rule (democracy, totalitarianism, theocracy, etc.) to be found within a society, but also the general culture and structure that encompasses a moral order and which could (in theory at least) be imposed by a ruling group. No attempt will be made to cover the whole range of ideas to be found within the new religions; nor will any attempt be made to consider the *actual* changes that the new religions might make in the political order. The essay is, in fact, part of a much wider study of the changes that new religious movements wish to implement, and some of the tensions and 'socio-illogics' that are inherent in their efforts to bring about a new world order.[1] What will be attempted here is an introduction to the diversity that is to be found between and within the movements in their accounts of (1) what is wrong with the present social order, (2) why these wrongs exist, (3) what a future order should look like, (4) how we ought to proceed if the new order is to be established – and, in conclusion, I look at some of the changes that are wrought in the Kingdom builders themselves.

1 Basic orientations to the world

There is probably no more useful introduction to the movements' general orientation towards the world and its political orders than Roy Wallis' three ideal types of new religions as world-accommodating, world-affirming and world-rejecting movements. It is with reference to these that some preliminary observations can be made.

Not all new religious movements want to change the political order. There are some that are fairly content with (or indifferent to) it as it is. These fall into what Wallis calls the 'world-accommodating' category, in which 'religion is not construed as a primarily social matter; rather, it provides solace or stimulation to personal, interior life'.[2] This is a category that is comprised chiefly of groups which fall under such general headings as neo-Pentecostalism and the Charismatic Renewal Movement, but also, Wallis suggests, of some non-Christian groups such as Subud, or the Aetherius Society. He also includes Western versions of the Soka Gakkai (Nichiren Shoshu Buddhism) in this type.

It might be assumed that movements falling into the second of Wallis' categories, 'world-affirming' new religions, would also be uninterested in changing the political order as 'the beliefs of these movements are essentially individualistic. The source of suffering, of disability, of unhappiness, lies within oneself rather than in the social structure'.[3] Movements that Wallis places in this category (such as *est*, Transcendental Meditation and the Church of Scientology) are frequently bracketed as members of the Human Potential movement, or labelled quasi- or para-religious movements. It is, however, often the socialization of the individual, itself dependent upon the moral order of social structure, that will be seen as the cause of the source of suffering etc., and, although many of Wallis' world-affirming movements make the claim that they are helping the individual to *cope* with the situation as it is, many will also claim that they either can or will transform the world. Within this category, 'producing social change is dependent upon producing individual change',[4] but, in fact, several of the movements (the Church of Scientology being an obvious example) have attempted to change at least some aspects of the political order.[5]

Wallis' third type, the 'world-rejecting' new religion, is exemplified by movements such as the Unification Church, the International Society for Krishna Consciousness (ISKCON), the Children of God (now sometimes called the Family of Love), the Manson Family and Jim Jones' People's Temple. The world-rejecting movement 'is much more *recognizably* religious than the world-affirming type':

> The world-rejecting movement expects that the millennium will shortly commence or that the movement will sweep the world, and, when all have become members or when they are in a majority, or when they have become guides and counsellors to kings and presidents, then a new world-order will begin, a simpler, more loving, more humane and more spiritual order in which the old evils and mistakes will be eradicated, and Utopia will have begun.[6]

It is, rather obviously, groups of this type that are likely to be the focus of most attention in an account of the new religions and political order.

Having performed a useful service in distinguishing these initial orientations, Wallis' types tend either to be too crude or to lead to Procrusteanism when one goes into the subject in further detail. In what follows, I have tended to abandon his categories, for they no longer seem to be helpful in accounting for the diversity that is to be found within the various types, or explaining why some movements, ostensibly belonging to different types, share certain characteristics.

II   What's the matter with what we've got?

Starting from the assumption that those who wish to change the political order believe that the existing order is not up to scratch, let us look at some accounts of what is perceived to be the matter with the present order.

World-accommodating and world-rejecting movements, but also some world-accepting movements such as the Church of Scientology, usually declare secular humanism to be one of the most evil forces in the current world. It is not, perhaps, surprising that the more fervently religious the movement, the more likely it is to decry the fact that the present order does not have God at its apex. *Which God, gods or deities ought to be running the society is, of course, dependent upon the movement – as is the means by which the Transcendental Authority will be revealed to Its subjects.*

Many of the movements pronounce against the materialism of modern society. In some cases, particularly in the Human Potential Movement or, say, Nichiren Shoshu Buddhism, this amounts to little more than a generalized way of saying that material comforts are not necessarily to be regarded as bad in and of themselves, but that there is not enough religiosity and/or spirituality. A movement like ISKCON, however, sees a concern with the material aspects not only of society, but also of oneself, to be deplorable – a sentiment summed up in the title of a book about the movement: *I Am Not My Body*.[7]

Some community-type groups (such as Findhorn or Bugbrooke) espouse a back-to-the-land ethic coupled with vegetarianism and/or a belief in 'natural' or 'organic' foods, and a prohibition on drugs or alcohol; but, for many, economic, scientific and technological advances are to be applauded – so long, that is, as they are used for the 'proper' purposes.

Some of the movements, such as the Children of God, are strongly opposed to the capitalism of modern Western society. Other movements declare that they are not necessarily against capitalism, but would prefer a fairer distribution of the wealth it produces. The Unification Church teaches that Satan, who is conceived in anthropomorphic terms, is at the root of communism, and that he is using communism in his attempt to take over the rest of the world. Although some lip service is usually paid to the desirability of democracy, many of the movements (e.g. ISKCON, Ananda Marga, the Unification Church and the Church of Scientology) have, on occasion, declared that it has become either inoperative or endangered, and that this is frequently evidenced by the persecution of religious minorities such as themselves.

Racial (and, occasionally, sexual) discrimination is a bone of contention in several of the movements. As might be expected, this is especially the case in those movements in which there is a sizeable membership of people of a disadvantaged race. In some instances the movement will have been indigenous to the disadvantaged community – the Rastafarians see the society in which they live (and which they refer to as Babylon) as, fundamentally, the exploitation of blacks by whites; in other instances (such as the People's Temple) the founder has been white but his advocacy of a society enjoying racial equality has had an appeal to poor blacks. The Unification Church, with its Korean leader, proclaims that men and women of all races must become unified, but its teachings indicate that some cultures are, at least at this point in history, in a purer 'position' than others. The Manson Family was openly racist, and 'Mo letters' (the literature of the Children of God) contain a large number of virulently anti-semitic statements.

Perhaps the areas of complaint about the present moral order concerning which there is the greatest diversity of opinion are those of sexual relations, and the rôles of women and the family. On the one hand, there are movements such as the Unification Church and ISKCON that regard lack of moral fibre as being due largely to the self-indulgent gratification of sexual desires that is to be found in the generally promiscuous behaviour of young (and older) people, and the breakdown of family life as evidenced by the high divorce rate in America and other Western countries. On the other hand, we find the Children of God, the Manson Family or the Rajneeshees declaring that part of the trouble with modern civilization is its uptight attitude towards sex; and we find the Children of God and the Raëlians viewing the family as a pernicious institution.

III Why is the world in the state it is?

For a religious movement, the question: Why is the world not as it should be? could be a question that requires some sort of theodicy for at least part of its answer. For Unificationists, their concern with pornography, promiscuity and the state of the family is explained by the Fall, which is seen as the result of Adam and Eve's misuse of the most powerful of all forces: love. Satan seduced Eve, then Eve persuaded Adam to have a sexual relationship with her before they had matured sufficiently to be blessed in marriage by God. This act of disobedience resulted in their union being centred on

Satan rather than on God, and their children and their children's children being tainted throughout history with Fallen nature (the Unificationist equivalent of original sin).[8]

The concept of original sin takes a variety of forms. Movements that are of a more fundamentalist persuasion tend to stress the wilfulness of men in denying God's laws. An example is to be found in an article in *The Plain Truth* (a publication of Herbert Armstrong's Worldwide Church of God):

> Human beings, as a whole, haven't wanted the Creator 'meddling' with their lives. He has been dismissed from the supervision of their affairs . . . God's universe runs on law. God's natural and spiritual laws are a fact of life.
>
> Violations exact fearsome penalties. But man would rather reap the consequences than submit to the way of God. Hence the carnage of the 20th century.[9]

The Soka Gakkai see the world's problems arising out of our refusal to realize the correctness of and the need for the Buddhism of Nichiren.

> The root cause for the confusion of a nation is attributed to the disturbance of Buddhist gods. Buddhist gods here signify thought. When the right way of thinking is ignored, prejudiced views and ideologies begin to be accepted by the general public. . . . When thought becomes chaotic, the people fall into disorder, and as they are disturbed, their country becomes agitated. Thus the nation goes into ruin and the race suffers misery.[10]

His Divine Grace, A C Bhaktivedanta Swami Prabhupada, the founder of ISKCON, taught his followers that men and women have lost true Krishna consciousness because the desires of their physical bodies distort their spiritual souls, which originally emanated from Lord Krishna himself. Scientologists believe that men and women have suffered many wounds, and done things that they would rather forget about, not only in this life, but also in previous incarnations. There has been a long-term, descending spiral of aberration during which harmful accretions from the past ('engrams') prevent the essential, spiritual self (the 'Thetan') from being realized.

A more secular version of this kind of explanation is given to those who undergo the *est* experience. This is not altogether surprising as Erhard went through five Scientology levels and received about 70 hours of auditing. But a not dissimilar account also comes from Bhagwan Rajneesh, who teaches that the world's problems are due to the ego which men and women acquire through social conditioning from the time of their birth; as people learn to play the rôles that society expects them to adopt in the 'appropriate' manner, they acquire false needs which conflict with their true, individual selves.

Generally speaking, religious movements are unlikely to blame structures for the state that the world is in, but some of those of a more Marxian persuasion will point to power structures or economic systems. Ananda Marga, for example, declares that

> Capitalism is directly responsible for the needless starvation of countless thousands of persons (including approximately 50 to 100 thousand children) every day.
>
> Although there are some good features of the socialist nations, we also find major failures of socialism today. In particular, the Soviet Bloc countries maintain their territory as huge prisons.[11]

IV What should the new order look like?

Theological concepts such as the millennium, apocalypse, Armageddon, and even agape are not always – perhaps not ever – easy to translate unambiguously into secular realities. Considering how fervently many of the movements want to change the society in which they find themselves, one might be forgiven for remarking that there is a disappointing paucity of blueprints for the future on offer. There are, however, enough generalizations available to indicate that the directions that the movements would take in their remedying of the world's ills are by no means identical, or even similar – even when there is a correspondence of views as to what those ills happen to be. [It is, incidentally, interesting that a movement that does go some way towards laying down plans for the political order also states that fixed policies may be unsuitable to guide the society for long: 'Trying to fix "Utopian" policies is foolishness because problems are an inherent part of life – without which development could not occur.'[12] It is, perhaps, also interesting that this movement (Ananda Marga) declares that it is *not* a religion, despite the fact that it would be considerably easier for the sociologist to classify it as such than it would be in the cases of other movements, such as the Church of Scientology, which insist that they *are* religions.]

There is a wide divergence of opinion concerning the extent to which the future order should in fact be ordered. Movements like ISKCON and the Unification Church are quite clear that some sort of hierarchical, even authoritarian, organization is necessary; other movements decry the thought of any structures. It is, however, worthy of note that many of these latter movements (Rajneeshism being an example) have developed just as strong power and communication structures within their own organizations as are to be found in movements advocating strong structural control. Ananda Marga, which has a very highly structured organization, advocates the maximum decentralization of economic power as one of its chief policies. It, like many other movements, also lays great stress on the importance of freedom: the first of the fundamental objectives proclaimed by its political arm, PROUT [PROgressive Utilization Theory] is 'Total freedom of all kinds of psychic and private expression. Opportunities for intellectual, educational, and all-round development must be freely available to all.' A second objective is that 'Financial accumulation must be limited by establishing a maximum ceiling for property ownership and annual income.'[13]

The Unification Church is quite clear that it wants to establish a theocracy – a God-centred society that will accept and live by the divine principles revealed to Sun Myung Moon. The movement's aim is to establish God's Kingdom of Heaven on earth – to restore mankind and the rest of creation to the state originally intended by God. It is not always clear exactly what the Kingdom of Heaven will look like – at least, it is not clear from the published works available to the rank-and-file membership of the movement. While I was conducting in-depth interviews with Moonies, I found no difficulty in getting them to talk to me on a wide range of questions, many of which I had, initially, been nervous of asking. There was, however, one question that seemed to stump almost all of my interviewees: 'What changes would you bring about if you were to be made Prime Minister tomorrow?' When I asked Moonies to describe what they thought the New Age would look like, most supplied rather abstract generalizations: everyone would love each other, there would be trust between people and cultures, children would be happy, crime and, in particular, pornography, would be completely eradicated. On being pressed, a few gave some more practical details – we would no longer need passports; everyone would study the movement's 'Bible', the *Divine Principle*, at school. One happy response came when, on being told that the sun would shine all day long, I had asked what would happen to the crops: 'Oh, that's all right', I was told, 'it will rain at night!'.

Some details do emerge, however. The *Divine Principle* makes it quite clear that the Kingdom of Heaven on earth involves not merely spiritual, but, just as importantly, physical restoration. The *Principle* offers a complicated interpretation of history which claims to reveal that the Messiah is on the earth at the present time. Unificationists do, in fact, believe that this is the office to which Moon has been appointed. They also believe that Jesus was appointed to that rôle, but that he was killed before he could complete his mission (of getting married and founding the ideal family), and that he was, therefore, able to offer only spiritual, not physical, salvation to the world. Moon, through his marriage to his present wife in 1960, succeeded, it is believed, in laying this crucially important foundation for the physical restoration of the Kingdom of Heaven on earth. The basic unit of the restored society will be (can now be) the ideal 'four position foundation' family that Adam and Eve (and Jesus and his wife) were meant to have founded and which will consist of a husband and his wife, joined together in a God-centred relationship, and their children, who will be born without the taint of original sin.

The ISKCON vision of the future is similar in that it is one in which life will be lived for and through a deity – in this case, Lord Krishna. Both movements believe that the time is now ripe for a great transformation, but the ISKCON vision is less concerned with physical restoration, less apocalyptic and, in some ways, less optimistic. Unlike the Moonies, who believe that, eventually, God and his followers will be able to bring about a state in which Satan is overcome and *everyone* will be able to reach a state of perfection, Krishna devotees believe that evil will always be with us. Krishna devotees believe that the world, currently in a state of turmoil and decline, is nearing the end of the materialistic age of Kali-Yuga. But the time-scale for ISKCON is infinite and changes occur only gradually, over hundreds of years; there is little of the immediacy and urgency that there is with the Unification Church and some of the other new religions, such as the Children of God which expects its apocalypse before the end of the century. For Krishna devotees, the New Age will be one of peace, love and unity – and, in this case, that means one in which Krishna consciousness is experienced by all.

The nuclear arms race has led millions of people, not just those who belong to the new religious movements, to fear that there may not actually *be* a future order – of any kind. Some movements prophesy that it is more than likely that there will be a nuclear Armageddon. (Bhagwan Rajneesh prophesied that the threat of AIDS eradicating the populations of the world is only marginally less likely than the nuclear holocaust.) Those movements that are somewhat more optimistic are likely to make a point of saying that there will be peace and security in their new order.

So far as the position of women is concerned, a few of the Human Potential, world-affirming groups take a near-feminist stance, and female sannyasins have risen higher in the Rajneeshee hierarchy than any men (except, of course, for the Bhagwan himself). Ananda Marga declares that 'women are one of the most exploited groups in the society, mentally, physically and economically'; its projects include a 'Progressive Women's Spiritual Association' and programmes are 'run by sisters for sisters' to help them to raise their consciousness. The Summit Lighthouse, the largest of the 'I Am' groups, has been led by Elizabeth Clare Prophet since her husband (Mark) died in 1973. Dada Lekhraj, the founder of the Brahma Kumaris (the daughters of Brahma), believed that women were 'intrinsically of a more religious nature and more trustworthy' and the movement sees itself primarily as a women's movement (about

900 of the 1,000 'dedicated' are women), and all the present leaders are women – not that men do not play an important role, carrying out such menial chores as shopping for food, seeing to the furnishings or dealing with problems of rent (in such matters the Sisters confess themselves 'not only helpless, but also unwilling to devote time which they feel they could more profitably spend on spiritual matters').[14]

On the whole, however, feminists who are looking for a Brave New World of equal opportunities would be ill-advised to pin their hopes on the new religions' political manoeuvrings – particularly if the movement had its origins in the East. Movements such as ISKCON have a very clear belief that women, although undoubtedly of intrinsic value in themselves, are meant to serve and look after men. The Unification Church has an 'equal but different' policy. It was Eve who was responsible for the Fall, and the *Divine Principle* explains quite clearly that it is men who are in the 'subject position' and, other things being equal, women should be expected to obey them. (In practice, however, women have held fairly high positions and had considerable power and influence within the movement; there are even a few Unificationist feminists who have questioned some of the more chauvinistic assumptions of the teachings.)

V   How is the new order to be brought about?

It is probably safe to say that the greatest leap of faith for most of the membership of the movements is the acceptance that the methods which are advocated could actually achieve the end that is promised – or, more cautiously, promised on the condition that people (especially the enlightened followers) do what is required of them. Some of the visions of the new order would seem to be well beyond the possibility of achievement by mere mortals, requiring as they do an apparent change in the laws (as we know them) of nature – including meteorology. It might be argued that some of the other changes would demand irrevocable laws of human nature and/or unnegotiable principles of social order also to be changed. What we are interested in here, however, is what the members of the new religions believe they can achieve – albeit with, on occasion, supernatural aid.

The methods that the movements advocate in order to achieve their earthly goals can be divided into two main categories: spiritual and practical. Spiritual methods include meditation and prayer; practical methods include collecting money, gaining new recruits, and, which is not quite the same thing, persuading people in positions of power to see things from the movements' point of view. Some activities (such as rituals that have a practical effect – the Unification mass weddings would be an example) might fall into either category. Another kind of distinction, which is closely connected but not entirely co-terminous with the spiritual/practical one, is that between personal changes in individual consciousness and structural and/or cultural changes. The movement may concentrate on changing individual members of the movement; it may try to produce a group with world-changing potential; it may turn its attentions outside the movement on people in general – at a grassroots level; or it may concentrate on those whom it perceives as being in positions of power or influence. Most movements will proceed on more than one of these fronts.

Some social scientists might well be of the opinion that changes in the individual are irrelevant so far as changes in the 'political order' are concerned and, therefore, irrelevant to our present concern; but this would be to ignore or to pass judgement on the belief of the membership of many of the new religions (and indeed of much of contemporary Christendom) that it is changing men (and, perhaps, women), not structures, that will bring about the *real* revolution in society – that will result in a *genuine* change in political order. Even movements such as Ananda Marga, which make quite concrete structural proposals (co-operativization, separation of economic and administrative powers, the elimination of prison punishment systems, insane asylums and lonely old people's homes, and fairly detailed plans about elections and voting), can be found laying stress primarily upon changing the individual:

> The most crucial factor for humanly harnessing the vast technological powers and giving increasingly meaningful direction to society is the development of consciousness and broad-mindedness amongst the maximum of the population.[15]

And, to some extent at least, even the social scientist must admit that, despite the fact that neither the Church of Scientology nor ISKCON advocates any particular structural changes in society, a world run by Scientologists would look very different – would be of a very different order – from one run by Krishna devotees. Both Scientologists and Krishna devotees believe in order – that is, neither advocates the anarchy one might expect from the teachings (although not the organizational practices) of, say, Bhagwan Rajneesh. And both Scientologists and Krishna devotees believe that they are on their way to creating a better, if not ideal, world in which people are able to develop their true selves – despite the fact that there is a considerable divergence between their respective concepts of the true self and the techniques required for its realization.

The Church of Scientology promises that there is, with Dianetics and Scientology, 'Hope for Survival – Hope for You; Hope for Your

Career; Hope for Your Family; Hope for This Planet.' It advertises 'The Technology of How to Change Conditions', and, upon inspection, one discovers that the technology is one which 'offers the *individual* the opportunity to become more aware, to change undesirable conditions, and to improve one's enjoyment of life'. (*Emphasis added*) For Scientologists, the underlying philosophy is that, whatever the structures, it is necessary to make sure that people in positions of authority are sane and intelligent (which the technologies of Dianetics and Scientology can make them), and that people are educated properly (through the beliefs and practices of Dianetics and Scientology). Furthermore, the Scientologists have long been active in advocating that there should be free access to all information. Once this is accomplished and their techniques are universally employed, there will be no wars because people running the world will be sane, intelligent, informed and educated enough to sort out their differences round a table; there will be no crime because the properly educated public will subscribe to decent ethical standards and will understand the futility, stupidity and wrongness of trying to get something for nothing – people will, moreover, not only be happy to produce goods that are of value but they will also be more concerned with the higher, spiritual, aspects of life.

For the ISKCON membership, what is necessary is that the devotees should develop, not their intelligence or mental capacities, but their spiritual awareness of Krishna and Krishna's central role in the total order of things. This is to be achieved, at least in part, by not indulging the physical body in sensual satisfactions, and through correct devotion to Krishna. Devotees are expected to abstain from meat and all intoxicants such as drugs and alcohol, and to lead celibate lives (except for the procreation of children within marriage).

While Krishna devotees, Moonies and Margiis are enjoined to lead strictly ascetic lives, and while Scientologists and Divine Light Mission Premies lead fairly unremarkable lives in so far as their personal habits are concerned, the Rajneesh sannyasins are encouraged to be completely uninhibited and to enjoy sexual relationships with anyone at any time should they feel so inclined (so long, that is, as careful precautions are taken to prevent the spread of sexually transmitted diseases), members of Synanon have been encouraged to swap partners at regular intervals, and the Children of God are inveigled into becoming 'Hookers for Jesus' and indulging in 'flirty fishing' (using sex for proselytization).

From a sociological perspective, some of the techniques for self-improvement can be seen as having a postive consequence for 'getting things done'; most obviously, the fostering of concepts such as duty, responsibility and, above all, obedience to one's leader can ensure that a controllable workforce may be mobilized. The Unificationists are explicit about the practical functions of obedience: over and above the fact that learning to be obedient is good for the development of the individual, it is also pointed out that if everyone were to do just what he or she thought was right, then we would never get anywhere; if, however, we obey our leader's commands, we can get somewhere – and should the leader, on occasion, happen to be wrong, we should still follow him because eventually it will be obvious that he was wrong (God will show him his mistake), and, the group, having learned its lesson, will be able to progress, still united, from strength to strength. The *Divine Principle* provides a further concept that has usefully practical consequences for the movement: indemnity. The teachings explain that if a bad action has been carried out in the past, then a good action can, as it were, cancel out the bad one. The more unpleasant and difficult the task, the more indemnity is involved, and the more the performer has contributed to the restoration process.

Throughout the ages, and throughout contemporary Christendom, millions of people have believed, and still do believe, in the efficacy of prayer in changing and/or influencing natural, personal and/or political events. Members of the new religions are no exception; many spend hours in prayer every day in the hope of bringing about a better world. Members of the Unification Church are given, or give themselves, 'prayer conditions' that can last for days or even weeks (praying in relays). These may be for very specific purposes (such as the attempt to influence the outcome of Moon's appeal against his prison sentence).

Other 'techniques', such as chanting and meditation, may be less familiar within a Western context, yet will have long been employed in Eastern religions. Perhaps the best-known chant to have come from the East in recent years is that of the ISKCON mantra:

> Hare Krishna, Hare Krishna,
> Krishna Krishna, Hare Hare,
> Hare Rama, Hare Rama,
> Rama Rama, Hare Hare.

Devotees believe that through their continuous repetition of the name of the deity, not only does the chanter become more Krishna conscious, but Krishna himself is incarnated through the very utterance of his name. The Ananda Marga has been less visible than ISKCON in its chanting, but twice a day the margii will repeat the mantra, 'Baba Nam Kevalam', which was given to them by their leader, Srii Srii Anandamurti. The daily practice of chanting 'Nammyoho-renge-kyo' is at the very heart of the belief system of Nichiren Shoshu Buddhism. Performing the chant has, it is claimed, well-nigh miraculous effects; testimony upon testimony proclaims not only how the chanter is spiritually uplifted, but also how he or she consequently succeeds in business, has better health and enjoys more satisfying relationships with the rest of the world. It is, more-over, believed that benefit in Buddhism is not a selfish concept:

> It spreads outwards to one's family and society as supported by the concept that man is in no way separate from his environment.[16]

Yogic practices vary according to the full range bequeathed by Eastern cultures and, correspondingly, the effects that they have, or are believed to have, cover a wide span of interests. Techniques of meditation range from the quiet concentration observed by the Brahma Kumaris to the vigorously physical exercises of Dynamic or Kundalini meditation practised by the Rajneeshees. Some of the movements believe that changes will come about through the effect of a 'critical mass' meditating, as in the case of the Science of Creative Intelligence (Transcendental Meditation) or World Goodwill (which is an off-shoot of the Arcane School); others commit themselves to a particular endeavour – as in the case of *est*'s Hunger Project, which collects large amounts of money not to feed the hungry, but in order to raise people's consciousness that starvation and malnutrition must be eliminated. Yet other techniques used by movements in the hope of influencing the world – and, indeed, the cosmos – include those of an esoteric nature, such as are practised by the Emin Foundation and numerous occultist, pagan and magic groups. 'It is the destiny of man to build the Heavenly Jerusalem on Earth. . . . It is the aim of the occultist, in consort with all men of good will, to bring about this heavenly fact into earthly reality.'[17] The rituals performed by modern witches and magicians are believed to invoke very real and powerful forces to this end. Cleansing rituals of a more familiar kind are also assumed by many groups to have a greater effect than merely purifying the individual concerned. Raëlians believe that, after publicizing the Elohim's revolutionary message of love, we have to learn the practice of 'Sensual Meditation' so as to elevate humanity's level of consciousness, responsibilty and harmony. We shall then be ready for the Elohim (our Fathers from Space) to come to this planet, and so we must build a temple/embassy, ready to receive them and as near Jerusalem as possible. In short, whatever the technique, there can be no doubt that the age of science has not created a population immune to the belief that society and the world order could be significantly altered by practices that have not, as yet, appeared susceptible to empirical investigation, let alone to any kind of objective proof that they could lead to the results which are claimed for them.

Not all the methods employed by the new movements in their efforts to bring about a new social order are as person-centred as those that have just been mentioned. Some of the movements have started to create the new order *within* the existing order by living in ashrams, or, more adventurously, in quasi-self-sufficient communes:

Findhorn and Bugbrooke have already been mentioned, and, of course, Jonestown would be another example. Less tragically, but none the less dramatically, there was the creation then downfall of Rajneeshpuram, the ranch in Oregon to which the Rajneeshees moved when they left their earlier commune in Poona. Another community that has been the subject of public scrutiny is New Vrindaban, in West Virginia, where devotees have already constructed a considerable part of a vast complex of temples and other buildings that were destined to serve as the centre of pilgrimage for the worship of Krishna in the West. Following the exposure of a number of scandals, ISKCON's Governing Body Commission has expelled the New Vrindaban guru, not least because the means that he appears to have been prepared to employ in the furtherance of raising Krishna consciousness were pronounced to be in flagrant violation of Krishna conscious values.

Another kind of social practice that is internal to the movements concerned, but which is seen as a positive move in the direction of overcoming racial and class barriers, consists of the cross-cultural marriages within the Unification Church and inter-caste marriages within the Ananda Marga.

Turning attention to those outside the movements, efforts have been made to alleviate hunger and poverty by programmes such as AMURT (the Ananda Marga University Relief Team), the Unification Church's International Relief Friendship Foundation or ISKCON's provision of free vegetarian meals for the needy. Nearly all such ventures have, however, tended to be limited in their scope. At a slightly different grassroots level, members of the Unification Church also work in what is known as their 'Home Church' area; in addition to their specific 'mission', fund raising and 'witnessing' for new members, the Unificationists have (in principle) a 'parish' of three hundred and sixty people whom they visit, offering to help around the house, to shop, to baby-sit or to mow the lawn.

Generally speaking, the new religions seem to be unlikely to hold out any hope of achieving any radical transformation – at least in the required direction – through democratic government; many of the movements make a point of distancing themselves from party politics. The erstwhile ISKCON guru in charge of South Africa was quoted as saying 'We are not necessarily in favour of one man one vote in South Africa and we're not necessarily not in favour.'[18] It is not uncommon to hear members of the movements explain that nothing can be done 'through the normal channels' as politicians are impotent or corrupt. The movement that has achieved the most successful 'conventional' position in politics is undoubtedly the Soka Gakkai which controls (although it is officially separate from) the third largest political party in Japan: Komeito (the Clean Government Party). In the West, perhaps the most direct involvement in party politics by a member of a new religion was the election, in 1986, of a member of the Unification Church to the French Parliament as a representative of the *Rassemblement National*, a coalition of right-wing groups led by Le Pen, the leader of *Le Front National*.

More frequently, campaigns are fought on specific issues. The Soka Gakkai has, for example, been responsible for numerous campaigns to foster world peace, the Church of Scientology is constantly campaigning for freedom of information and the ending of certain psychiatric practices, and the Unification Church has campaigned against pornography and in support of President Nixon.

It is the Unification Chuch that has received the greatest amount of publicity and scrutiny of its attempts to transform the existing order. There is no space to list all the methods that it has employed to this end but, as an all-out attack on the social scene from a comparatively small organization (the number of full-time Moonies in the West has never exceeded four figures), the movement has made an impressive impact – its actual achievement in terms of its stated goals is, of course, another matter. The most striking strategy of the movement is the number and range of fronts on which it has proceeded. It has founded and funded organizations (such as the Freedom Leadership Foundation and CAUSA) that are specifically devoted to attacking communism, but many other projects, such as the publication of a number of daily newspapers around the world, including *The Washington Times*, have helped the movement to disseminate its views on world affairs. The movement has also established a network of like-minded people in various fields, who, while not necessarily having much (or any) sympathy with Sun Myung Moon or his followers, have got to know each other and, should the need arise, are now able to work together on various projects that happen to be in accord with the political aspirations of the movement. Much of this 'networking' has been accomplished through the hospitality that the Unification Church has extended to notables at dinners, at receptions and, most importantly, at conferences. Conferences have been sponsored by the movement for scientists and other academics (including sociologists of religion), theologians, ministers of religion, lawyers, journalists, the military, and both local and national politicians.

Sometimes it does, indeed, seem that conferences are among the most popular methods that the new religions employ in their attempts to bring about a new world order. The Church of Scientology has organized a series of conferences, concerned especially with religious freedom; the Foundation of Universal Unity (the Divine Light Emissaries) has held several conferences on the subject of science and spirituality; the Soka Gakkai (as already intimated) is continually sponsoring meetings, lectures and publications – mainly on the topic of peace; and the Brahma Kumaris have held numerous conferences around the world, again, often on the subject of peace. In January 1986, the Bhaktivedanta Institute (founded, like ISKCON, by Prabupadha) sponsored a World Congress on the Synthesis of Science and Religion. The list could be continued, but what can be noticed is that recurrent themes at such meetings have been peace, moral and spiritual awareness, the importance of absolute values and absolute truth, and the desire to unify or to create some kind of synthesis between science and religion. It is also the case that the conferences are usually well-publicized, that Nobel Laureates and other public figures are 'honoured guests', and that, even if the rest of the world is unimpressed with the outcome of such meetings, many of the members themselves seem to find a confirmation that they really are achieving something when their conferences manage to draw the apparent support of such eminent people to promote the Kingdom-building efforts of their movement.

VI What happens to the Kingdom builders?

It would be a mistake to think that all the members of any one new religion have exactly the same understanding of what the content of a future order will be, or how it is to be achieved. Furthermore, the movements themselves have changed over the past two decades or so – in some cases, quite dramatically. Most of the early American members of the Unification Church were expecting an apocalyptic event to take place in 1967.[19] With the passage of the years, imminent dates of immanence have continued to have a crucial significance, but the understanding of the changes to be expected by each successive date, although still dramatic, seems, at least to an outsider, to have become progressively less apocalyptic.

At the beginning of the last section, I suggested that the real crunch of faith for much of the membership of the new religions lies in accepting the connection between a visionary (but as yet invisible goal) and the means advocated for achieving that goal. Thus far, I have been generalizing in order to paint a broad picture that indicated variety *between* the movements. In this final section, I draw primarily from my study of the Unification Church in an attempt to distinguish between four different types of 'Kingdom builders' that can be found *within* a single movement. Less intensive research into some of the other movements suggests that the types are not peculiar to the Unification Church but are also to be found in other movements, especially, but not exclusively, other world-rejecting movements. Naturally, not every individual will fit neatly into one or other of the types – some straddle two adjacent views, and others sometimes appear to vacillate between apparently contradictory positions. Several Kingdom builders have 'progressed' from one type to another – there was, for example, the Moonie who told me

> When I first joined, I thought that if I stuck around long enough I would be there among the chosen when God waved His magic wand. Now I realize that if anyone is going to build the Kingdom of Heaven on earth it's got to be people like me.

And there was the Divine Light Mission Premie who said

> I think you'll find a lot of Premies have changed. I feel that – well, it's difficult to express, but I feel that I've 'taken my own power back' – if you can understand: I'm no longer waiting for Maharaj Ji to perform a miracle – I realize that I've just got to do what's right in my own life and get on with it.

The first of the ideal types of Kingdom builders, which has a large (but possibly diminishing) membership at the rank and file level, consists of those whom I shall call 'magic-wanders'. They accept unquestioningly that whatever they are doing is making a direct contribution to the restoration of the Kingdom of Heaven. Unification magic-wanders believe that their Messiah knows exactly what has to be done, and that all the magic-wander has to do is to have faith, and to fund-raise, witness, indemnify, or whatever he or she is instructed to do to the utmost of his or her ability. If the Kingdom of Heaven were not to materialize, it would not be because there was anything the matter with the vision or the method, but because people had not had sufficient faith or been sufficiently diligent in following Moon's instructions. People's faith and obedience may falter, but the truths revealed by the *Principle* and the Messiah are absolute. Within this category, there can be found a wide range of sophistication. For some, the beliefs are worked out as a systematic and practical theology; for others, there seems to be little but a superstitious acceptance. People of this type are unlikely to be affected by set-backs; apparently contrary evidence is more likely to reinforce their convictions by being interpreted as a sign that Satan is getting worried. But magic-wanders can also 'snap' suddenly out of their faith – possibly as a result of deprogramming.

The second type is one that has become increasingly common with the passage of time, and the passing of dates that were expected to herald changes which have not obviously materialized. Members of this type believe that Moon is indeed the Messiah, but that there is not going to be an apocalyptic change so much as a gradual development towards the new order. The Unification Church is thought to be moving in the right direction (that is, according to the *Divine Principle*), but it is accepted that the members, including perhaps Moon, do not have a precise blueprint for the Kingdom of Heaven. It is suspected that a certain amount of trial and error is inevitable in the restoration process; mistakes may be made on occasion but, so long as the members stick together and try to stay within the guide-lines laid down by the *Principle*, progress will be made and the Kingdom will eventually be established – or at least, we shall have got a lot nearer to the restoration than we are at the moment. For members in this category, personal responsibility extends to checking that the methods employed appear to be moving society in the *direction* of the Kingdom of Heaven. If it appears that the connection is too tenuous, then this type of Moonie might, after a period of doubt, deliberation and soul searching, decide to leave the movement.

Members of the third type of Kingdom builders have quite severe reservations about the efficacy of the means. On the one hand, they may believe that the New Age could be realized, but they are uncertain about the methods being used – all that they can do is just to hope and pray that there is some connection, because the Unification Church seems to them to be the only movement making a really serious attempt. They may, on the other hand, be sceptical about the possibility of there ever being a Kingdom of Heaven, but they find more to admire and like within the movement than they find in the outside society, and they feel that the standards of the movement are higher and more desirable than any to be found elsewhere. Members of this type tend to be those in positions of some responsibility, or else, possibly, employed in a mission that can be seen to be of a positive (non-materialistic) value in and of itself.

The final type does not, strictly speaking, contain Kingdom builders. It consists of a group of apostates who have ceased to remain committed to life in the movement. They may still accept the truth of the *Divine Principle*, but they have become unconvinced that Unificationists are truly living up to the *Principle* – they may even believe that the practices employed by the movement are contrary to its avowed principles. It may be that the consequences of attempting to build the Kingdom of Heaven are seen as counter-productive – that the means do not justify the end, or, perhaps, that the leaders can no longer command their respect. Or they may feel that the means that the movement is employing are not getting anywhere – that, despite the remarkable accomplishments of the movement since its inauguration thirty years ago, the Kingdom of Heaven does not seem to be coming any closer. A further possibility is that the *Principle* itself is rejected.

Defection is, of course, worrying for any movement; but, to movements that aspire to build the Kingdom of Heaven on earth, it presents a far more threatening situation than the loss of a few Kingdom builders. The fundamental problem for the Unification movement is that there are those who have had the opportunity of hearing the revelations contained in the *Divine Principle*, and yet are not willing to follow its call. Unification theology does stress that there are certain key figures who play (or have played) crucially important roles in the restoration process, and members have tended to think of themselves as being in a special position as Kingdom builders; but the theology also teaches that the Messiah's mission can fail if he is not accepted and followed by members of society as a whole (as happened in the case of Jesus). The Kingdom cannot be truly established unless everyone, not just the chosen few, turns to a God-centred life – as defined by the Messiah. There are those in the movement who remain convinced that if only everyone could hear the *Principle* and see the Church in action, they would become convinced of the truth of its message. The plain fact is, however, that not only do 90 percent of those who have attended Unification workshops not join the movement,[20] there is also a high voluntary defection rate among members who have spent some time in the movement but who have, for one reason or another, decided that they no longer want to be Kingdom builders in obedience to Moon.[21] It is hard to see how the movement can overcome such disillusionment and/or scepticism, especially when it states that it is fighting against totalitarian régimes such as those of atheistic socialism in order to establish a God-centred, democratic theocracy (assuming this not to be a contradiction in terms) in which everyone is free and responsible for his or her own decisions. And, of course, even if the new order were to be established, there must always be a question about just how stable it could be, as even children born without the taint of original sin can, according to the *Divine Principle*, still 'fall' before reaching a stage of perfection – as the original Fall, which presumably occurred in the best of all possible orders, would bear witness.

'How would you control anti-social dissidents?' is, indeed, one of the questions that might well be asked of all those who believe that they have the techniques, truths, insights or what-have-you that will change people's hearts and minds as a means to achieving a new political order. There tends to be little in the movements' literature that addresses such a question; it is, moreover, a question that most of the movements would prefer to define as irrelevant, in so far as they believe that proper knowledge/education/socialization would obviate the need for mental institutions or prisons (except, perhaps, for the pathologically violent). I have, however, been told by a Scientologist that if, in the new order, someone insists on not behaving in a social manner, they would need to be 'rehabilitated', and I have been told by more than one Unificationist that if people were to persist in not accepting the truth of the *Divine Principle*, then they would have to be put in a mental hospital – because they could not be really sane if they were to reject what is, so obviously, the truth. It should, however, be stressed that there are other Scientologists and other Unificationists who would strongly disagree with such diagnoses. Several Unificationists now insist that it is by no means required that everyone should be a Unificationist and that, just so long as a 'critical mass' is established, it will not have disastrous effects if some people do fall. It has, furthermore, been argued that once the world is really God-centred, there will no longer be any need for the Unification Church to exist.

It is not clear that such apparent accommodations are quite as accommodating as they may at first appear; but there can be no doubt that, during recent years, there have been several noticeable changes in the interpretation of the degree of exclusivity and absolutism involved in the visionary new orders and the means of achieving these. There is no space to examine the content of and reasons for such revisions in this paper, but it might be suggested that such an analysis could provide some of the (many) reasons why visions of new political orders frequently undergo radical revisions as the religions become less new.[22] Hopes of establishing the Kingdom of Heaven on earth may be appealing in the short run, but would appear to be far less easy to maintain in the long term than is the hope of a Kingdom of Heaven – in Heaven.

Chapter 17
Old Laws and New Religions
Bryan Wilson

'Discrimination' is a word that, in recent decades, has acquired distinctly pejorative connotations, and modern societies, at least in the West, have made laws to prohibit discrimination in various departments of social life. It might be supposed, particularly in light of recurrent international expression at the very highest political levels that even in matters of religion, formal discrimination had finally become a thing of the past. If men have the right, as these international tribunals proclaim, freely to believe, practise, and teach whatever religion that each of them chooses, it may well be supposed that complete religious equality has been attained. Citizens may claim equal rights regardless of their religion, and different religions are said to be equal before the law with respect to the facilities that they may enjoy and the rights that they may exercise.

The empirical evidence, however, is that in few countries, if any, is such equality the reality. It is perhaps most nearly approached in societies that are formally secular – secular, that is, in the sense of being committed to official neutrality in religious matters, as is the United States of America. It is perhaps furthest from attainment in societies that are constitutionally secularist – that is, anti-religious, as in the Soviet Union, or in societies that are constitutionally committed to the support of one religion, as is Pakistan. The consciously-created state – such as the United States – may, after all, order its affairs in accord with abstract, rational principles, but most modern states – those of Western Europe, for instance – are what may be designated as continuing societies, not consciously created so much as merely evolving from pre-political systems. These societies inherit a customary commitment to a particular tradition of religious faith which is identified with the political, social and cultural patterns of the people's way of life. That religion may have acquired formal legal status and – often by a process of the accretion of custom, as well as by legal enactment – may have accumulated a wide variety of privileges and assumed, unchallenged, even automatic rights. Such religions, understandably enough, are preferred religions, enjoying advantages not available to other faiths, or, if available, then available only as concessions. The rational principle of religious equality is almost everywhere qualified by the actual historically determined practices, procedures and dispositions of each society and of its people. The law in any country is not quickly responsive, and perhaps not at all responsive to those bland and unexceptionable pronouncements, somewhat facilely promulgated by international organizations, which commend religious freedom on the basis of abstract, general, rational and liberal assumptions about what a society might be like.

Beyond this disparity between the exhortative formal resolutions of international bodies, on the one hand, and social actuality, on the other, lies the question of just what constitutes a proper religion. To propose the general principle of religious non-discrimination presupposes that we all agree what religion is, what it requires, and what constitutes religious belief, practice and organization. Obviously, in all modern democratic societies there is an acknowledged measure of religious diversity. The range of variation of what is often called religious pluralism is considerable in countries like the United States, Australia, and Britain, but much more marginal in countries such as Belgium or Sweden. But even states which accept in principle the idea of religious pluralism may define it within parameters limited by historical considerations from which the contemporary situation is relatively remote. Beyond these parameters lie the penumbral areas of alien religion and quasi-religion.

The issues bring liberal, albeit abstract principles into direct contention with concrete, historical and traditional cases. In some measure, this confrontation occurs in all societies, even those in which political revolution has facilitated total constitutional revision and the endeavour to formulate state laws in accordance with rational principles. But these issues are particularly acute in societies in which evolution rather than revolution has been the pattern of social development – and perhaps nowhere are they more apparent than in Britain, where old laws and new religions today experience an uneasy co-existence. The diversification of religious expression and belief is ill-accommodated by the existing laws, but there is little likelihood – pressure on parliamentary time being what it is – that new legislation will be enacted. England is a society torn between the egalitarian principles that proceed on assumptions of formal rationality that all religions are to be treated equally, and the actual received tradition of one entrenched and privileged religion, in relation to which all other faiths are, in a sense, merely tolerated and implicitly regarded as misguided, wayward, inferior, or errant forms of faith. The English law courts, today, regularly affirm that the law does not discriminate among religions, but deals with each impartially. In fact, as I shall seek to show, impartiality is quite impossible, given the historical context of the assumptions on which much English law relating to religion was – and continues to be – based. Those assumptions are implicit where they are not explicit,

both in statute law and in the body of case law and interpretation
of statutes which constitute so large a part of the English legal
tradition.

The religion described as 'by law established' in England is that
of the Church of England, of which the reigning monarch is the
temporal head. Twenty-four bishops and two archbishops of the
Church have seats in the House of Lords, the upper house of the
legislature, and the State is involved (albeit less so than formerly)
in the appointment of bishops in the Church. Although not supported by taxation or by financial assistance from the State, the
Church of England enjoys special status and the prestige of its
historical pre-eminence and association with the monarchy as the
official church of the nation. Over three centuries since the first
Toleration Act of 1688, many of the provisions which, for the Church
of England, were presumptive rights, have been accorded by formal
legal enactment, as privileges and concessions to other religious
bodies. Among these privileges are the protection of the law from
interference with religious services; the right to conduct marriages
on their own premises according to their own rituals; exemption
from local taxes on their property, for which properties of the
Church of England are automatically exempt; and, by registering
their trusts as religious, and hence as charitable, to escape most
forms of national taxation. To qualify for these concessions, all self-
styled religions, which historically, and in the legislation still, are
alluded to as 'nonconformist' or 'dissenting', must be able to establish their credentials as *bona fide* religious organizations.

My essay focuses on a limited range of concessions for which
religious bodies in England might qualify which are, however, automatically conferred as rights to that church which is by law established. Although the issues themselves may appear to be of very
limited consequence – may indeed, when set in the wider context
of religious and political liberty, appear as trivial – none the less,
they constitute a prism through which the spectrum of issues of
vital importance to religion in modern society may be perceived.
Clearly, in a liberal, democratic society the laws do not prescribe
what people shall or shall not believe. In this sense, there is religious
freedom and equality. Within the limits of the common criminal
law, people are free to engage in activities in pursuance of their
beliefs and in the open attempt to persuade others to believe and
to act similarly. The law becomes involved only in respect of the
extension to each religious body of the privileges that various enactments have made available for religions which establish their
eligibility.

The situation, and the problems which arise, are similar to those
of other countries: the law becomes involved either in defining
religion or in according recognition to associations which claim to

be religious. That this type of concessionary law is open to abuse is evident, as became apparent in post-war Japan, where liberal laws permitted a large number of organizations to register as religions, even though they were in fact businesses, laundries or restaurants using 'religion' as a front in order to obtain tax concessions. Japanese law was subsequently changed to eliminate these bogus organizations. However, even while putting aside such flagrant abuse of law, the determination of what is legitimately religious remains a serious issue. Commercial activities *per se* certainly do not necessarily establish a case against an organization, since many churches engage in commercial and even financial activities of one kind or another: the issue turns on quite different, less directly forensic, and more explicitly sociological considerations.

What an English court of law must do in determining the application of these laws is to apply the formulations of legal statutes by interpreting the actual intentions of the legislators with due regard to the ways in which those intentions have been interpreted in earlier litigation. In the case of religion, however, it is apparent that what English lawmakers often had in mind was a provision of far narrower application than the range of instances to which the law is now applied. At the time when the various statutes affecting religion were passed, the diversity among religious bodies in England was much less than it is today. Those laws assumed that, although there were various forms of 'dissent' and 'nonconformity', virtually all of them were, none the less, confined within the Christian tradition, and that Christian precepts and concepts were applicable. The terminology was Christian, or at least monotheistic. The courts have not infrequently said that it is not their business to define religion, and they have at times openly acknowledged their lack of competence to do so, and yet judges must apply laws which assume that courts know what constitutes religion and its attendant phenomena. Again and again, the courts find themselves seeking expert advice about particular 'self-styled' religious movements, with a view to determining whether they are religious and whether the principle implicit in particular laws – laws which quite clearly conceived of religion much more narrowly – can be said to apply to them.

The privileges for which religious organizations are eligible in England are:

a) Charitable status, which allows the organization to operate without being subject to most forms of national direct taxation;
b) exemption for their religious buildings from payment of local taxes (known as 'rates');
c) the licensing of buildings to permit the performance therein of

marriages in accordance with the religious rites of that particular religious organization;

d) registration of buildings as 'places of religious worship' which is in itself a *prima facie* claim to other privileges.

To extend these privileges to a particular organization the appropriate authorities must be satisfied on various points. The authorities concerned, however, are not one centralized department of state: they are discrete and separate agencies which do not work in conjunction with each other. Registration is a matter for the director of Population Censuses and Surveys, the Registrar-General, who must be satisfied that the organization is religious, and that its buildings are used for activities that he regards as 'religious worship', before he will register a building. Dependent on such registration is the facility for the organization to employ its own officials to conduct legally-binding marriage ceremonies for its members. Registration will influence (but not dictate) the decision of local government officers with respect to granting exemption from payment of local rates. Those local government agencies enjoy a certain autonomy in rating decisions, although they may be influenced by general policies pronounced by the Government through its Department of Environment. Charitable status is granted by yet another agency – the Charity Commissioners, a separate, quasi-legal body, which is independent of government control. Charitable status is granted to a trust set up by a religious body providing that it promotes religious instruction. Charitable status secures the major tax concessions that are available to religious organizations.

Many of the cases that have been brought before the courts have been brought by organizations seeking to be declared 'religious' and to have their religious services recognized as worship. Thus courts have to settle how 'religion' is defined and what is conceived to constitute 'public religious worship'. When charitable status is disputed, the courts apply various criteria, which have grown up over the course of hundreds of years. They are not logically set forth; they overlap and are interdependent, and lack suitable external and objective points of reference. If charitable status is to be conferred, it must be possible first to declare a movement to be a religion: but no exhaustive or definitive indicia of religion are incorporated in the law itself. In general, the case has been satisfied by showing that the beliefs of a movement may be said to be 'monotheistic'. Whatever else may constitute religion (and the courts are hesitant about all else) the courts accept that monotheism is religion. The second criterion is that the movement's beliefs and practices should not be 'subversive of all religion and morality'. Disregarding the contradiction between a positive finding for the first desideratum and the possibility of applying neutrally the whole of the second, it is clear

that if the courts consider that a movement subverts morality (however that may be defined) then they will declare that it cannot
qualify for charitable status. Thus, to obtain charitable privileges, the
activities of the organization must be ruled to be for the public
benefit, and the law assumes that whatever conduces to advancing
religion is, indeed, for the public benefit.

The question of what constitutes 'public worship' is handled in a
way which is also beset with difficulties. Worship is held to consist
in attitudes of submission, reverence, adoration, and actions which
manifest these dispositions, as well as acts of propitiation and
prayer. The law dictates that certain privileges are accorded only if
what is undertaken is *public* worship, however, and what, in effect,
has been disputed before the courts has been whether this phrase
means 'for the public', 'by the public', 'in public', or by a group 'of
the public' who, however, are self-selected. The points of contention
in all these various issues have been brought to the attention of
academic advisers to the courts – comparative religionists and sociologists of religion. The courts have heard them but, inevitably, since
there is much to dispute, they have not always heeded them.

The definition of 'religion' by the courts

Judges have at various times acknowledged their incompetence to
settle the matter of what constitutes religion: none the less, they
must come to some sort of decision in order to settle each specific
case. They have laboured with various biases, particularly that of
strong religious conviction: there is no doubt that the original legislators, in extending privileges that were once the monopolistic pre-
rogative of the Church of England, also had very limited ideas of
how far a religion could deviate from that of the Anglican church if
it was to be counted as a religion at all. Although charitable trusts
include the advancement of religion as one of the legitimate and
eligible goals of a charity, in effect at times that goal has been so
narrowly interpreted that 'religion' has been taken to mean 'Christianity', and Christianity has at times been taken to mean Anglicanism. Thus in 1754, Lord Hardwicke ruled that the teaching of Judaism was not a charitable object, and applied the funds which the
testator had left to provide instruction in Judaism instead to the
provision of instruction in Christianity [De Costa v De Paz]. Commenting on this decision in a subsequent case [Re Bedford Charity,
1819] Lord Eldon concluded that 'it is the duty of every single judge
presiding in an English Court of Justice, when he is told that there
is no difference between worshipping the Supreme Being in Chapel,
Church or Synagogue, to recollect that Christianity is part of the law
of England.' That that spirit is not entirely dead became apparent

in the way Lord Comyn commented in the libel action brought by the Moonies against the *Daily Mail* in 1981, but judges have reduced this bias steadily over the years. Yet the 'bias' (I use the word neutrally) is legitimate in the sense that it is often evident in the legislation itself – and was built into the intentions of legislators. In Bowman v Secular Society, [1917, AC 406, 429, 443], the House of Lords ruled that it was not criminal or unlawful to deny Christianity, and allowed a gift to the Secular Society to be valid, but, in appraising the general situation, one of the *obiter dicta* of Lord Parker was that 'a trust for the purpose of any kind of monotheistic theism would be a good charitable trust'. In so saying, he echoed the principles advanced by Lord Macnaghten for charitable trusts; the law had come to recognize that 'any form of monotheistic theism is a religion'.

Monotheism however is not regarded by comparative religionists or sociologists of religion as an exhaustive definition of religion, and the English courts have as yet failed to recognize non-theistic (or polytheistic) faiths to be religions. Although religious bodies of these persuasions may actually enjoy privileges granted to religions, whether they would be confirmed in these privileges if they were challenged at law is unclear. When pressed, the courts return to formulae which apply to Christianity, Judaism, and Islam, but not to the other great world religions. They say, as said Dillon J [Re South Place Ethical Society: Barralet v Attorney-General 1980 IWLR 1565] 'It seems to me that two of the essential attributes of religion are faith and worship: faith in god and worship of that god' – to which he added the definition given in the *Oxford English Dictionary*, 'A particular system of faith and worship . . . Recognition on the part of man of some higher unseen power as having control of his destiny, and as being entitled to obedience, reverence and worship.' The inclusion of 'worship' and the references to 'a god' indicate that cultural bias, and historical bias, still persist in judicial thinking. Of course, it could certainly be said that such bias was also in the minds of the legislators who have framed the various laws, so that judges, wittingly or otherwise, endorse the intention and the specific meaning of those who made the law, as they are obliged to do. Yet, they continue to affirm the principles of impartiality of the law as among various religions. They affirm, and regularly re-affirm in these cases the principle that 'As between different religions, the law stands neutral' [Lord Reid: Gilmour v Coats 1949 AC 426, 458] and 'The Court does not favour one religion more than another. The court is not a tribunal equipped to determine whether the doctrines of any branch of the Christian Church, or any Christian denomination or sect, or any non-Christian religion are true or false and does not attempt to decide that question.'

The law in England affects and may also be affected by legal decisions in those other countries which have similar legal systems, and decisions elsewhere respecting the charitable status of religion have been settled on very much broader principles of interpretation of the law than have cases in England. Thus, in Australia [High Court of Australia: Church of the New Faith and Commissioner for Payroll Tax, October 1983] the High Court sought to come to grips with the issues in a spirit manifestly more liberal than any judgement that has as yet come from English courts. In that case, Mason ACJ, and Brennen J acknowledged that minority religions had to be protected. They declared:

> The chief function in the law of a definition of religion is to mark out an area within which a person subject to the law is free to believe and to act in accordance with his belief without legal restraint . . . Religion is . . . a concept of fundamental importance to the law. A definition cannot be adopted merely because it would satisfy the majority of the community or because it corresponds with a concept currently accepted by that majority . . . The freedom of religion being equally conferred on all, the variety of religious beliefs which are within the area of legal immunity is not restricted.

They held that

> for the purposes of the law, the criteria of religion are twofold: first, belief in a supernatural Being, Thing, or Principle; and second, the acceptance of canons of conduct in order to give effect to that belief [though canons of conduct which offend against ordinary laws are outside the area of any immunity, privilege, or right conferred on the grounds of religion].

They further maintained that even if a religious leader were a sham and a charlatan this would not invalidate the fact that his followers had a religion:

> charlatanism is a necessary price of religious freedom, and if a self-proclaimed teacher persuades others to believe in a religion which he propounds, lack of sincerity or integrity on his part is not incompatible with the religious character of the beliefs, practices, and observances accepted by his followers.

In the same case, two other judges, Wilson and Deane JJ set out several indicia of religion, after having rejected that idea that a supernatural Being was an essential element of religion. They declared that the indicia of religion must be discovered from 'empirical observation of accepted religions' and said,

> One of the more important indicia of 'a religion' is that the particular collection of ideas and/or practices involves belief in the supernatural, that is to say, belief that reality extends beyond that which is capable of perception by the senses. If that be absent, it is unlikely that one has 'a religion'. Another is that the ideas relate to man's nature and place in

the universe and his relation to things supernatural. A third is that the ideas are accepted by adherents as requiring or encouraging them to observe particular standards or codes of conduct or to participate in specific practices having supernatural significance. A fourth is that, however loosely knit and varying in beliefs and practices adherents may be, they constitute an identifiable group or identifiable groups. A fifth . . . is that the adherents themselves see the collection of ideas and/or practices as constituting a religion. All of these indicia are satisfied by most or all of the leading religions: it is unlikely that a collection of ideas and/or practices would properly be characterized as a religion if it lacked all or most of them . . .

It is clear that the thinking of these judges reflects both an awareness of the existence in society of a much wider range of religious commitment and belief (than was acknowledged in legislation), and also that the way in which to interpret the law must have regard both to sociological evidence and to sociological methods of enquiry (empirical observation of social phenomena). Yet it is also clear, in the English case, that if the function of judges is to interpret law in accordance with the intentions of legislators, then in England, a much narrower conception of religion might be said to be appropriate, until such time as laws themselves are repealed and new ones made.

Definitions of 'Worship' by the courts

Two issues have arisen for different religious groups in recent years which have involved the courts in definitions of 'worship'. Organizations may obtain privileges by having their buildings registered as places of religious worship, and by being recognized as places of 'public worship' by local government authorities. In 1970, the Church of Scientology brought a court action to cause the Registrar-General to register as a place of 'religious worship' one of their chapels, which he had refused to register. The court ruled that the Registrar-General was certainly not bound to accept the word of those seeking registration that their organization did indeed constitute a religion. In that case [Regina v Registrar-General Ex p. Segerdal 2 QB 697 1970] Lord Denning said:

> We have had much discussion on the meaning of the word 'religion' and of the word 'worship' taken separately, but I think we should take the combined phrase 'place of meeting for religious worship' as used in the statute of 1855. It connotes to my mind a place of which the principal use is as a place where people come together as a congregation or assembly to do reverence to God. It need not be the God which the Christians worship. It may be another God, or an unknown God, but it must be reverence to a deity. There may be exceptions. For instance, Buddhist temples are not properly described as places of meeting for

religious worship. But apart from exceptional cases of that kind it seems to me the governing idea behind the words 'place of meeting for religious worship' is that it should be a place for the worship of God. I am sure that would be the meaning attached by those who framed this legislation in 1855.

And Lord Justice Buckley opined:

> Worship I take to be something which must have some at least of the following characteristics: submission to the object worshipped, veneration of that object, praise, thanksgiving, prayer, or intercession . . . I do not say that you would need to find every element in every act which could properly be described as worship, but when you find an act which contains none of these elements it cannot, in my judgment, answer to the description of an act of worship.

The partiality of the law in this instance is clear: it conceives that 'worship' must imply an object of worship. Yet 'worship' is not an unchanging phenomenon in society. As conceptions of deity change, so do conceptions of worship, and in movements which do not proclaim a supreme Being – Buddhism for example – what is done at religious gatherings is clearly not 'worship' in this narrow sense of the term. The language in which the term 'worship' is current is language of a particular culture and particular time-period. The term is built into various laws, but religious activities come to take on a different nature, no longer encompassed by the term worship as traditionally understood. Concepts change: worship once involved sacrifice, but were any religious group today to seek to re-institute sacrificial forms of worship, they would assuredly fall foul not only of the law relating to the registration of religious buildings, but of the criminal law itself. Yet, our laws relating to what constitutes religious practice are stuck with a time-bound and culture-bound set of assumptions about the necessary character of religious activities.

Lord Denning acknowledges that Buddhism may be an exception, and Buddhist temples *are* registered and exempted from rates in England. But why should there be exceptions: if one exception be granted, does this not open the way for others? Or does it imply that the very basis of assumption on which the law rests has become, with the passage of time, unduly narrow? Again, it must be evident that not all Christian groups undertake worship in the form postulated by Lord Justice Buckley and yet they enjoy the privileges of registration and rating exemption. Quakers provide a cogent example of a sect which does not meet to supplicate, praise, give thanks, or manifest submission to a deity. Christian Scientists provide an example of a movement in which the idea of deity is considerably de-anthropomorphized, as Mind, Principle, Spirit, to which older conceptions of ritualized worship are clearly inappropriate. Contemporary Protestant theologians re-define God in impersonal terms, as an ultimate concern, a ground of being, and explicitly reject the idea of a personal God 'out there': with such changed conceptions, traditional notions of worship become anachronistic. The term 'worship' implies a personal relationship – a sense of personal commitment and obligation. It characterizes personal dispositions and becomes inappropriate when the personal element disappears from the prevailing conception of the supernatural. Even the general public, when its reactions can be assessed (for instance, however inadequately, by opinion polls) steadily abandons ideas of a personal god in favour of conceptions of a more abstract kind. In the recent survey of European Values, covering ten European countries, it was shown that although 75 percent of people professed belief in God, only 32 percent professed belief in a personal God: the majority of believers conceived of God as some type of abstract agency. Abstractions do not require worship: is there not something incongruous about worshipful acts to an impersonal force?

The other recent case affecting worship relates to the Exclusive Brethren. One local government authority in England disputed in the early 1980s whether Brethren meeting halls were in fact places of public worship, on the grounds that outsiders were given no indication that the halls were used for worship – there was no sign, no notice-board, or other indication: they held that these halls were, in effect, places of private worship and hence, ineligible for exemption. Whereas older legislation affecting dissenters gives the impression that any such self-designated congregation might in itself constitute a sufficient 'public', recent legislation (perhaps influenced by the laws on charities which, however, were not specifically at issue in this case) implies that 'public' means open to the public, in some sense providing a public benefit. In earlier cases, it had already been established that the rituals of an enclosed order are not charitable since they fail to amount to public benefit [Gilmour v Coats 1949 AC 426, 458, and also Cocks v Manners 1871 12 Equity p. 574], and that the rituals of such an order do not constitute public worship [Association of Franciscan Order of Friars Minor v City of Kew (Australia) Victoria Law Reports 1944 199]. It was established in the Mormon Temple case [Henning v Church of Jesus Christ of Latter-Day Saints 1964 AC 420] that 'public worship' must be something more than the congregational worship of an existing community. The Temple was ineligible for rating exemption because it 'was not open to the public at large but only to a selected class of the Mormon sect known as "Mormons of good standing".' Lord Reid said:

> In my view, the conception of public religious worship involves the coming together for corporate worship of a congregation or meeting or assembly of people, but I think that it further involves that the worship

is in a place which is open to all properly disposed persons who wish to be present.

The Brethren, however, were not enclosed, did admit members of the public who turned up, even though they certainly did not issue a general invitation nor especially encourage outsiders to attend. The Court ruled that there must be some form of invitation for religious worship to constitute 'public religious worship'. Lord Justice Stevenson said:

> worship must be made public . . . there must be signs to indicate at least the place is a place of religious worship . . . and that the public would not be trespassing if they entered but have permission, expressed or implied, to go there. Such signs may be given by the building itself. . . . Many, if not most, churches, and chapels, indicate their nature and the nature of what goes on inside them by their style of architecture or religious symbols or the ringing of a bell, as well as by notices of services on a notice board, or in leaflets or a newspaper, or by speakers preaching and appealing to the public in the open air or by house to house calls.

As will be evident, many of the 'signs' are indeed specific to the Christian religion: and yet, Britain is now a multi-religious society in which the meeting places of many faiths do not at all resemble a church, nor are in the habit of announcing their activities either by bell or printed notice.

Other groups could be affected by this Appeal Court decision respecting the Brethren. Ultra-orthodox Jews would not welcome the 'unclean' into their synagogues, yet those synagogues are exempted from the rates. On the basis of this decision, they have no claim for exemption – although no doubt they will continue to receive it since local government is unlikely to take action, particularly since these Jews are highly concentrated in particular districts. Similarly, Zoroastrians, of whom there is a community in London, would have no claim to exemption, since their movement is entirely closed – outsiders cannot join, and no one can be converted to a faith where all participants are of necessity inborn.

Thus, although the law claims not to distinguish between one sect and another, it is apparent from these cases that there is a historical inbuilt bias. The Acts by which privileges were conferred were concessions, extending little by little to other religious groups the privileges once enjoyed by the Church of England alone. But the ecclesiastical principles on which the Church of England was formed differ radically from those on which sects came into being (or which are implicit in the Asian religions which now flourish in England). The polity of the Church of England was Erastian: it was assumed that everyone belonged or 'ought to belong'. Sects, on the contrary, were self-selected dissenters. The Church of England conceived of itself as having a 'public service' commitment in its activities – the Church prayed for the nation. Sects, in contrast, provided for those who deliberately stood apart: they never regarded themselves as committed to provide for everyone. Even those sects which were anxious to recruit – and this is not a universal feature of sects – did not expect to recruit everyone. They conceived of themselves as standing apart from the wider society; they had an implicit minority consciousness as a 'gathered remnant'. It is evident that the law actually prefers certain types of sect because of the assumptions it makes about the public nature of worship – assumptions rooted in Anglicanism. If a sect is concerned to convert the public, it is shown greater favour at law: sects which are not interested in converting outsiders are the ones likely to fall foul of the law relating to exemption from rates, and to have more difficulty in claiming charitable status. Oddly, although the law prefers proselytizing sects, this can scarcely have been the preference of the Church of England or of the legislators (most of them undoubtedly members of that Church): the intention of the legislators can hardly have been to provide preferential privileges specifically for those sects most actively working in competition with the Church of England. One other contradiction may be noticed in passing: the Law Courts have recognized the Exclusive Brethren as a body entitled to charitable status, because their religious work is counted as for the public benefit, and so exempted from national taxation: but the Appeal Court dealing with the separate issue of exemption from local rating, rejected the idea that worship in Brethren meeting halls was 'public' and denied them local exemption from rates. Thus whilst the High Court dealing with the charitable status of the Brethren regarded their activity as for the public benefit, the Appeal Court hearing the entirely separate case respecting their places of public worship regarded their worship as being insufficiently for the public benefit to qualify for exemption from local taxes. (For the record, it may be noted that subsequently the Brethren modified their practice, and erected notice boards indicating that their meeting-rooms were places of public worship.)

In conclusion

The cases that have tested the laws pertaining to religion in England have not all arisen from religions that are very new. Some continue to arise from older and more traditional sects, but the new religious movements are likely to present a more radical challenge to the various laws that pertain to religion – laws so randomly scattered and so lacking in consistency that they cannot remotely be designated as a 'legal framework', much less a 'legal system'. Religious choice can be expected to widen as modern populations become increasingly detached from specific geographical locations and distinctive historical roots. That detachment from indigenous culture has many causes, not least among them the processes of migration from one country and one culture to another, and the rapid acceleration of social, geographic and diurnal mobility within a given country. The idea that a given people inherit a common culture and a common religious tradition becomes more and more of a fiction, yet it is a fiction embodied within the law. The radical contemporaneity of modern mass media of communications, the decline in the general influence of the past over the present, and the future-orientation of modern institutions make ever more questionable the concepts entrenched in legal enactments and promote an inevitable process of legal obsolescence. The law becomes less and less relevant to actual social phenomena, but it remains remarkably durable.

We may perceive two simultaneous processes at work. Rational principles are increasingly advocated and, since they confirm the patterns of social organization that are everywhere advancing, these precepts are taken as normative. At the same time, there are persistent demands that innovative systems of belief and practice that define themselves as religious should be banned, restricted or disprivileged. (We need only to recall such cases as the restrictions imposed on Scientology in Victoria, South and Western Australia, England, and the United States; or the recent history of the Rajneeshis in India and America; the police raids on Moonie premises in France; the curious indictment of the Rev Moon on tax charges in America; and the sustained efforts to preclude unpopular movements from the concessionary privileges that are notionally available to all religions.) Attitudes and episodes such as these will no doubt recur, but, given the current processes of social change, they rest on the basis of cultural assumptions that are increasingly dubious.

One facet of this problem which is refracted through the prism which the law holds up to social phenomena, is that the bodies which, in any normal sociological usage, conform to the designation 'religious', fall outside the reference of those rather limited, culturally-determined concepts that are built into the law (and to some extent into everyday usage). The law tends to have a limited view, requiring that all religions be necessarily recognizable by reference to established or received traditions: thus, the law in England maintains its distinct monotheistic bias with its attendant assumptions about the necessary styles and forms of religious activities, entrenched in the law as 'worship'. Only with the employment of more abstract categories, capable of subsuming a range of intrinsically somewhat divergent, but in principle functionally similar phenomena, will parity before the law be achieved for different religious groups. If equality before the law is what is sought – and the judges themselves have regularly endorsed the idea that the law is neutral with respect to religion – then, culturally specific terms like 'deity'; 'worship' and all the connotations of anthropomorphism will need to be replaced by more encompassing abstract concepts.

One might, however, raise one further question. Is absolute equality before the law – whatever the lip-service to the concept – always what is wanted in respect to religion? One can envisage two radically divergent positions: the formally rational position adopted by high level (but remote) international agencies: that as all men are to be regarded as equal, so their religions should be so regarded. The simplest solution for the legal approach to religion for those of this persuasion would be for all religious privileges to be swept away, permitting the law to abandon the attempts to decide on concessions by defining what qualified as 'religion' or as 'worship'. The alternative, conservative contention is to suggest that it is appropriate that the law of any country should seek to reinforce historical cultural values, the spiritual inheritance of the people, and to protect these in the face of the mounting pluralism of what might be held to be morally disruptive phenomena which bring uncertainty, contradiction and unrest in the religious and cultural sphere. In *continuing*, as distinct from *created* societies (in Europe as distinct from the United States) there is a persisting cultural tradition rooted in a religious past and sustained by a variety of normative attitudes: although equality before the law may have become a desideratum in the modern shape of those societies, there are certain received assumptions about the lengths to which that principle might be applied. For those who take this position, the crucial question is whether the law can divest itself of substantive normative conceptions of religion without undermining the sense of social cohesion and identity. For those of this persuasion, there is, and has to be, a social *parti-pris* with respect to the extent to which it is desirable – by way of the extension of privileges – to encourage new and various systems of belief and practice. The presumption is that morality and religion are not merely a matter of observing what people do and then bringing law into conformity with these patterns of actual behaviour – the position advocated by Justices Wilson and Dean in the Australian High Court 1983 – but rather of sustaining a received system of norms which direct the shape of social life. In short, in this view the law is seen as an agency which embodies a historical and continuing sense of the general will: it requires that citizens (who in England, at least, are also seen as 'subjects') should in their various dispositions, including the spiritual, be supportive of the society. In the English law, as it now stands, both strands can be detected – the strong affirmation of principles of showing no favour to one religion rather than another, and the actual cases in which preference for the integrity of historical culture continues to be manifest. One may yet ask how long the spirit of the old laws will resist the challenge of the new faiths.

Notes

Chapter 3   The Politics of Religion in Broadcasting

1 Andrew Boyle, *Only the Wind Will Listen*, London, 1972, Chapter 5.
2 Reith to Temple, 23.6.30.
3 See 'In the Chair', Barrington-Wand of *The Times*, Donald MachLachlan, London, 1971, p.81.
4 To G K Bell, 7.10.26
5 Reith, *Broadcast Over Britain*, 1924, p.200.
6 Ibid.
7 See A. Briggs, *Governing the BBC*, 1979.
8 See Michael Tracey, *Whitehouse*, London, 1979.
9 *St Martin's-in-the-Fields Calling*, Athenaeum Press, 1932.
10 Gerard Mansell, *Let Truth be Told*, London, 1982.
11 See Currie, Gilbert & Rorsley, *Churches and Churchgoing*, Oxford, 1977, p.167.
12 *Christianity and the Social Order*, Penguin Books, 1942.
13 *The Greatest Drama Ever Staged*, Hodder, 1938.
14 V. Gollancz, 1943.
15 *Who was Jesus?*, BBC, 1977.
16 Penguin Books, 1970.
17 Wm Haley to BBC, *Moral Values in Broadcasting*, 1948.
18 See Michael Tracey, op. cit.
19 *Religious Broadcasting & the Public*, BBC, 1955

Chapter 5   The Church's Debate on Social Affairs

1 Digby C Anderson (ed.) *The Kindness that Kills: the Churches' Simplistic Response to Complex Social Issues*, London 1984.
2 Jonathan Sacks, *Wealth and Poverty: A Jewish Analysis*, Social Affairs Unit, 1985.
3 Irving Hexham, *The Bible, Justice and the Culture of Poverty: Emotive Calls to Action versus Rational Analysis*, Social Affairs Unit, 1985.
4 James Sadowsky, *The Christian Response to Poverty: Working with God's Economic Laws*, Social Affairs Unit, 1986.
5 Antony Flew, *The Philosophy of Poverty: Good Samaritans or Procrusteans?* Social Affairs Unit, 1985.
6 Report of the Archbishop of Canterbury's Commission on Urban Priority Areas, *Faith in the City*, London, 1985.

7 Unpublished MS, *From Doom to Hope*, a response by the Chief Rabbi to *Faith in the City*.

8 *Catholic Social Teaching in the US Economy* a Pastoral Letter from the Bishops; for a detailed discussion see Walter Block, *The American Bishops and Their Critics*, Fraser Institute, 1986.

9 Digby Anderson, *The Kindness that Kills*, op. cit.

10 Quoted by Malcolm Deas, 'Catholics and Marxists', *London Review of Books*, 19 March 1981.

11 Peter Bauer, 'Ecclesiastical Economics of the Third World: Envy Legitimised' in Digby Anderson, *The Kindness that Kills*, op. cit.

12 Anthony Flew, *The Philosophy of Poverty*, op. cit.

13 David Sheppard, *Bias to the Poor*, London, 1983; and Digby Anderson, 'Eating Sheppard's Pie: Hints on Reading the Sociological Gospel' in Digby Anderson, *The Kindness that Kills*, op. cit.

14 *Faith in the City*, op. cit.

15 J M Bonino, *Christians and Marxists*, London, 1976, p. 114.

16 David Sheppard, *Bias to the Poor*, op. cit.

17 Ans J Van der Bent, *Christians and Communists*, World Council of Churches, 1980, p. 33.

18 Discussed in Bertie Everard, 'Unchristian Critiques of Multinationals: the Case of South Africa' in Digby Anderson, *The Kindness that Kills*, op. cit.

19 Ibid.

20 Ibid., p. 122, note 5.

21 Discussed by John Greenwood, 'The Closed Shop and the Closed Conscience: The Churches' Failure to Argue the Moral Case', in Digby Anderson, *The Kindness that Kills*, op. cit.

22 *The Cuts and the Wounds*, Report of the Internal Economy Group of the Thames North Province Church and Society Panel, 1982.

23 Discussed by Graham Dawson, 'God's Creation, Wealth Creation and the Idle Redistributors', in Digby Anderson, *The Kindness that Kills*, op. cit.

24 Discussed by Robert Miller, 'Unemployment: Putting Faith in the New Princes', in Digby Anderson, *The Kindness that Kills*, op. cit.

25 'Ecclesiastical Economics of the Third World', op. cit.

26 Discussed by Caroline Cox and John Marks, 'Complaining about Education Cuts: Materialist Diversions from Proper Concerns', in Digby Anderson, *The Kindness that Kills*, op. cit.

27 Discussed by Dennis O'Keefe, 'Racism: Neither a Sin Apart nor an Excuse for Hysteria', in Digby Anderson, *The Kindness that Kills*, op. cit.

28 Discussed by P A J Waddington, 'Black Crime, the "Racist" Police and Fashionable Compassion', in Digby Anderson, *The Kindness that Kills*, op. cit.

29 The Chief Rabbi, *From Doom to Hope*, op cit.

30 Jonathan Sacks, *Wealth and Poverty: A Jewish Analysis*, op. cit.

31 Alejandro A Chafuen, *Christians for Freedom; Late Scholastic Economics*, Ignatius Press, 1986.

Chapter 7   Religion and Utopia

1 Martin Buber, *Paths in Utopia* (Boston, 1958), p. XXV.

2 For the *pansophias*, see Frank E Manuel and Fritzie P Manuel, *Utopian Thought in the Western World* (Cambridge, The Belknap Press of Harvard University Press, 1979), pp. 205 ff.

3 Gershom Scholem, 'Toward an Understanding of the Messianic Idea in Judaism', in his *The Messianic Idea in Judaism and Other Essays in Jewish Spirituality* (London, 1971), pp. 1–36.

4 On Joachim and his influence, see Marjorie Reeves, *The Influence of Prophecy in the Later Middle Ages: A Study in Joachimism* (Oxford, 1969); also her *Joachim of Fiore and the Prophetic Future* (London, 1976).

5 See on this Karl Löwith, *Meaning in History* (Chicago, 1959), pp. 145 ff.

6 David Lodge, 'Utopia and Criticism: The Radical Longing for Paradise', *Encounter*, Vol. 32, April 1969, p. 71.

7 The whole of Max Weber's religious sociology is relevant here – e.g. *The Protestant Ethic and the Spirit of Capitalism*. See also R K Merton, *Science, Technology, and Society in Seventeenth-Century England* (1938; New Jersey, 1978).

   The subject is a vast one, and I acknowledge my lack of competence. I should at least state that something like an authentic Utopian tradition has been claimed for China – in such concepts as *ta-t'ung*, the Golden Age of 'Great Unity', *t'ai-p'ping*, the 'Great Harmony', as well as in various anarchist and Communist traditions prevalent among the peasantry. See Jean Chesneaux, 'Egalitarian and Utopian Traditions in the East', *Diogenes*, Vol. 62, 1968, pp. 76–102. But to my mind the important thing is that, as Chesneaux admits, despite the existence of these Utopian 'elements' they did not cohere into a true Utopia, unlike the West with its very similar history of Utopian 'pre-figurations' (classical and Christian). The Chinese did not, in other words, establish a *tradition*, a *genre*, of Utopian thinking and writing. The parallel with science is instructive: for here too, as Joseph Needham has amply shown, the Chinese reached high levels of scientific and technical development without 'breaking-through' to a *scientific revolution* – i.e. a tradition of scientific theory and practice.

   In the discussion following the talk, Dr Peter Moore, in defending the idea of Chinese Utopianism, made the interesting point that both Christianity and Buddhism, as compared with other world-religions, are markedly 'open', 'non-legalistic', religions and so liable to dispose their adherents to Utopian conceptions.

8 Christopher Hill, *The World Turned Upside Down* (New York, 1972), p. 147.

9 See Thomas Molnar, *Utopia – The Perennial Heresy* (London, 1972).

10 H G Wells, 'The So-Called Science of Sociology', in Wells, *An Englishman Looks at the World* (London, 1914), pp. 192–206.

11 H G Wells, *A Modern Utopia* (1905; Lincoln, USA, 1967), p. 299.

12 G K Chesterton, 'Mr H G Wells and the Giants', in his *Heretics* (London, 1905), pp. 62–85.

13 For a remarkable Utopian vision spanning the entire universe, see J D Bernal, *The World, The Flesh, and the Devil* (1929; London, 1970). A good deal of science-fiction, of the Utopian kind, has also covered a similar

area – e.g. Olaf Stapledon, *Last and First Men* (1930), and many of Arthur C Clarke's novels, such as *Childhood's End* (1953).

Chapter 8 Was Marx a Religious Thinker?

1 K Popper, *The Open Society and Its Enemies*, London, 1962, Vol. 2, p. 1.
2 N Berdiaeff, *Les sources et le sens du communisma russe*, Paris, 1963, p. 316.
3 V Pareto, *Mind and Society*, New York, 1935, Vol. 4, p. 1292.
4 J Schumpeter, *Capitalism, Socialism, and Democracy*, London, 1943, p. 5.
5 E Wilson, *To the Finland Station*, London, 1968, p. 115.
6 I Deutscher, *The Non-Jewish Jew*, London, 1968, p. 26.
7 A Toynbee, *A Study of History*, London, 1960, p. 400.
8 K Marx, *Selected Writings*, ed. D McLellan, Oxford, 1977, pp. 508f.
9 K Marx, *Selected Writings*, p. 45.
10 F Engels, *Anti-Duhring*, Moscow, 1954, pp. 65f.
11 K Marx and F Engels, *Selected Works*, London, 1968, p. 435.
12 K Kautsky, *Ethik und materialistische Geschichtsauffassung*, Stuttgart, 1906, p. 141.
13 F Engels, *Ludwig Feuerbach*, Moscow, 1946, p. 60.
14 A good example of Lenin's views on God are contained in his two letters to Gorki of 1913: see V Lenin, *On Religion*, London, n.d., pp. 49ff.

Chapter 10 Nicaragua: the Theology and Political Economy of Liberation

Some of the Nicaraguan viewpoints expressed in this essay are drawn from the papers and discussions which proceeded during the seminar, attended by the writer, held at the Centro de Convenciones, Managua, 8–10 October 1986, on religion, revolution and social change, arranged by the International League of Religious Socialists (ILRS) and the Nicaraguan Ministry of Housing.

1 M E Vijil-Icaza, ILRS Seminar, opening remarks.
2 For example, A Bradstock, *Saints and Sandinistas. The Catholic Church in Nicaragua and its Response to the Revolution*, 1987; D Haslam, *Faith in Struggle. The Protestant Churches in Nicaragua and their Response to the Revolution*, 1987; T Beeson and J Pearce, *A Vision of Hope. The Churches and Change in Latin America*, 1984.
3 P Berryman, *The Religious Roots of Rebellion, Christians in the Central American Revolutions*, 1984, p. 29.
4 G Gutierrez, *A Theology of Liberation*, 1974 (first published 1971 as *Teologiá de la liberación, Perspectivas*), p. 18, note 33.
5 The strongest criticisms have come from the 'Christians for Socialism' movement; see, for example, J Osorio, 'The Church, Christians and the People's Movement in Latin America', n.d., Chilean Christian Group.
6 D McLellan, *Religion and Marxism*, 1987, p. 148.

7 C Jerez, 'Christian Commitment to Social and Political Change in Central America', ILRS Seminar paper.

8 C Jerez, 'Central America and the Church', *The Month*, November 1987, p. 401.

9 H Jung, 'Behind the Nicaraguan Revolution', *New Left Review*, (117) 1979, pp. 69–89.

10 Conor Cruise O'Brien, 'God and Man in Nicaragua', *The Atlantic Monthly*, August 1986, p. 64.

11 L H Serra, 'Ideology, Religion and Class Struggle in the Nicaraguan Revolution', in R Harris and C M Vilas, *Nicaragua: A Revolution under Siege*, 1985, p. 152.

12 J A Booth, *The End of the Beginning. The Nicaraguan Revolution*, 1982, p. 135–6.

13 L Hechanova, 'Toward a Moral Theology of Violence', *Christian Worker*, (3) 1986; and *The Gospel and Struggle*, CIIR, 1986.

14 Serra, 'Ideology, religion and Class Struggle', p. 153.

15 Jerez, 'Christian Commitment to Social and Political Change'.

16 Personal interview with Fr Uriel Molina at the Centro Antonio Valdivieso, 1 October 1986.

17 Serra, 'Ideology, religion and Class Struggle', p. 158; L N O'Shaughnessy and L H Serra, *The Church and Revolution in Nicaragua*, 1986, p. 6.

18 C Jerez, *The Church and the Nicaraguan Revolution*, CIIR Justice Papers No. 5, 1984, p. 17.

19 O'Brien, 'God and Man in Nicaragua', p. 55.

20 See the excellent survey in R Munck, *Politics and Dependency in the Third World the Case of Latin America*, 1984.

21 Perhaps the most comprehensive exposition now available is that provided in the writings of Immanuel Wallerstein, following the approach of Andre Gunder Frank. For the most condensed statement, see *Historical Capitalism*, 1983.

22 Vijil-Icaza, opening remarks, ILRS seminar.

23 C Jerez, 'Christian Commitment to Social and Political Change'.

24 Gutierrez, *A Theology of Liberation*, chapters 6 and 7.

25 R Stahler-Sholk, 'Economic Relations between the North and the South, with particular reference to Central America', ILRS Seminar paper.

26 R L Harris, 'The Economic Transformation and Industrial Development of Nicaragua', in Harris and Vilas, *Nicaragua: A Revolution under Siege*, pp. 37–8.

27 Centro de Publicaciones 'Los Muchachos', *Juventud Sandinista*, April 1986.

28 Vijil-Icaza, opening remarks, ILRS Seminar.

29 For a historical survey, see D Kraft (ed.), *Voices for Disarmament: Twenty-five Years of the Christian Peace Conference*, Prague, 1983.

30 D J Ormrod and A Race, 'Building a Theology of Disarmament in the USSR', *Theology*, LXXXVIII, May 1985 (723), pp. 192–3.

31 R Rufino Dri, 'Liberation Theology Against Neo-Conservatism Masked as Theology', *CPC Quarterly*, 82 (II), 1985; P Richard, 'The church of the poor in Nicaragua, *CPC Quarterly*, 86–88 (II–IV), 1986.

32 Information Department of the Christian Peace Conference, Prague, Bulletin no. 374, November 5 1986, p. 23.

33 F Betto, *Fidel y la Religion. Conversaciones con Frei Betto*, La Habana, 1985,

and translated as *Fidel and Religion. Castro talks on Revolution and Religion with Frei Betto*, New York, 1987 (with an introduction by Harvey Cox).

34 R M Croose-Parry, review article of the above, *Afkar Inquiry*, April 1987.

35 O'Brien, 'God and Man in Nicaragua', p. 55.

Chapter 11   The Contribution of Religion to the Conflict in Northern Ireland

1 Brian Mawhinney and Ronald Wells, *Conflict and Christianity in Northern Ireland*, Lion Publishing, 1975, p. 73.

2 *The Times*, August 30th, 1969.

3 Padraig O'Malley (Ed.), *The Uncivil Wars: Ireland Today*, The Blackstaff Press, 1983, p. 11.

4 Michael Macdonald, *Children of Wrath: Political Violence in Northern Ireland*, Polity Press, 1986, p. 4.

5 Macdonald, *Children of Wrath*, p. 4.

6 John Hickey, *Religion and the Northern Ireland Problem*, Dublin, 1984, pp. 67 and 72.

7 Frank Wright, 'Protestant Ideology and Politics in Ulster' in *European Journal of Sociology*, Vol. 14, 1973, p. 247.

8 Eric Gallagher and Stanley Worrall, *Christians in Ulster 1968–1980*, Oxford, 1982, pp. 5–7.

9 John Darby (Ed.), *Northern Ireland: The Background to the Conflict*, Appletree Press, 1983, pp. 21ff.

10 Macdonald, *Children of Wrath*, p. 7.

11 Macdonald, *Children of Wrath*, p. 6.

12 Macdonald, *Children of Wrath*, p. 8.

13 Macdonald, *Children of Wrath*, p. 11.

14 Conor Cruise O'Brien, *States of Ireland*, London, 1972, p. 38.

15 Dominic Murray, *Worlds Apart: Segregated Schools in Northern Ireland*, Appletree Press, 1985, pp. 22 and 26.

16 Murray, *Worlds Apart*, p.27.

17 Murray, *Worlds Apart*, pp. 21 and 23.

18 John Darby (Ed.), *Education and Community in Northern Ireland: Schools Apart?*, New University of Ulster, 1977, p. 26.

19 Murray, *Worlds Apart*, pp. 55–57.

20 Murray, *Worlds Apart*, pp. 44–45.

21 Murray, *Worlds Apart*, pp. 91–105.

22 Murray, *Worlds Apart*, p. 30.

23 Murray, *Worlds Apart*, p. 133.

24 Bill McSweeney, 'The religious dimension of the troubles in Northern Ireland' in Paul Badham (Ed.), *Religion, State and Society in Modern Britain*, Paragon, chapter 5.

25 Edward Moxon-Browne, *Nation, Class and Creed in Northern Ireland*, London, 1983, p. 38.

26 *Declaration on Religious Liberty*, Vatican II, 7th December, 1965.

27 Steve Bruce, *God Save Ulster: The Religion and Politics of Paisleyism*, Oxford, 1986, p. 121.

28 Bruce, *God Save Ulster*, p. 122.

29 Bruce, *God Save Ulster*, pp. 69–73.

30 Keith Jeffery (Ed.), *The Divided Province: The Troubles in Northern Ireland 1969–1985*, London, 1985, p. 40.
31 Bruce, *God Save Ulster*, p. 77.
32 Michael Dewar, *The British Army in Northern Ireland*, Guild Publishing, 1985, p. 28.
33 In justification of this claim consider the dramatic personal victory won by Ian Paisley in the 1979 elections to the European Community, where he established himself as manifestly the most popular politician in Northern Ireland. The same is not true of his party, but the Official Unionists have succeeded in holding the DUP at bay only by becoming increasingly like it. For further discussion cf. McSweeney, *The Religious Dimension* and Bruce, *God Save Ulster*, pp. 116–120.
34 Bruce, *God Save Ulster*, p. 214.
35 McSweeney, *The Religious Dimension* and Bruce, *God Save Ulster* p. 227 citing Ian Paisley, *The EEC and the Vatican*, Belfast, 1984.
36 Bruce, *God Save Ulster*, pp. 89 and 29.
37 McSweeney, *The Religious Dimension*.
38 Gallagher and Worrall, *Christians in Ulster*, p. 193.
39 McSweeney, *The Religious Dimension*.
40 Bruce, *God Save Ulster*, p. 237.
41 Moxon-Browne, *Nation, Class and Creed in Northern Ireland*, p. 125.
42 Gallagher and Worrall, *Christians in Ulster*, pp. 130–152, 190–213.

Chapter 12   Christianity and Religious Pluralism: the Ethics of Interfaith Relations

1 According to one estimate some 31 percent of the world is in some sense Christian. By the turn of the century it will, it is estimated, be only 25 percent!
2 Since there is no question about religious affiliation in the UK census all figures for religious communities are extremely unreliable. But at a consevative estimate members of other faith communities number more than two and a half million.
3 In *Considering Dialogue*, London, 1981.
4 Cf. the statement of the Council of Florence (1438–45): The Holy Roman Church believes firmly, professes and proclaims that none of those who are outside the Catholics church – not only pagans, but Jews also, heretics and schismatics – can have part in eternal life, but will go into eternal fire . . . unless they are gathered into that Church before the end of life.
5 See *Considering Dialogue*, pp. 2–3.
6 Martin Luther, Weimar Collected Works 40, 1, p. 609.
7 In *Considering Dialogue*, and in my *Towards A New Relationship: Christians and People of Other Faith*. The most recent brief survey of the whole 'open' tradition is in the Booklet prepared for the General Synod of the Church of England, July 1984, entitled *Towards a Theology for Interfaith Dialogue*, London, 1984.
8 See Alan Race, *Christians and Religious Pluralism: Patterns in the Christian Theology of Religions*, London, 1983.
9 I would be most grateful for any information there may be about this being done.

10 Five that are: *The Unknown Christ of Hinduism*, London, 1964, 2nd Edition, 1981. *The Trinity and the Religious Experience of Man*, London, 1973. *Worship and Secular Man*, London, 1972, and *The Intrareligious Dialogue*, New York, 1978, and *Myth, Faith and Hermeneutic*, New York, 1979.

11 There is a good deal of highly condensed but extremely suggestive material on the theological significance of people of other faiths and ideologies and on the concept of ideology especially in relation to 'syncretism'.

12 As the member churches of the WCC consider, test and evaluate these guidelines they will need to work out for themselves and with their specific partners in dialogue statements and guidelines for their own use in specific situations. WCC *Guidelines*, p. 21.

13 The General Synod of the Church of England, for example, adopted the BCC *Guidelines* by some 300 votes to 2 against.

14 A man will not really be intelligible to you, if, instead of listening to him, you determine to classify him. F D Maurice *The Religions of the World*, Sixth Edition, London, 1886, p. 96.

15 Cf. the Qur'anic statement: '(the Jews) . . . slew him not nor crucified, but it appeared so unto them: and lo! those who disagree concerning it are in doubt thereof: they have no knowledge thereof save pursuit of a conjecture, they slew him not for certain. But Allah took him up unto himself . . . ' (Surah, 4.157–158).

16 'The Rules of the Game' are reprinted conveniently in *Mission Trends No. 5: Faith Meets Faith* eds. Anderson and Stransky, New York and Grand Rapids, 1981, pp. 11–122.

17 P. 99 and pp. 24–5. Cf. p. 69, 'Faith is not *a* religion but stands at the basis of *all* religions.'

18 P. 101.

19 P. 102.

20 P. 102.

21 *Faith and Belief*, Princeton, N.J., 1979, p. 4.

22 I have a vivid recollection of my first meeting with Dr Smith on the back seat of a bus showing members of a conference around Richmond, Virginia. I gave him my card on which were printed the name of the Committee I serve: The Committee for Relations with People of Other Faiths. Dr Smith put his finger on the 's' and raised his eyebrows. If up to this time I have not managed to get the 's' removed it is not because I do not assent wholeheartedly to Dr Smith's proposition, I do. But in a fallen world there is a certain convenience in using words as other people use them, and we have to call the 'cumulative religious traditions of humankind' by some shorter term!

23 *Questions of Religious Truth*, London, 1967, p. 71.

24 P. 74.

25 P. 76.

26 P. 76.

27 *Between Man and Man*, trans. R Gregor Smith, London, 1947 and reissued 1961, p. 24.

28 *Courage for Dialogue*, Geneva, 1981, p. 57.

29 D T Niles 'Karl Barth – a Personal Memory' *The S.E. Asia Journal of Theology*, No. 11 (Autumn 1969), pp. 10–11. I retell the story as it is in the notes to Gerald H Anderson's 'Religion and Christian Mission' in *Christian Faith in a Religiously Plural World*, ed. D G Dawe and J B Carman

(Maryknoll, N.Y., 1978). Actually Karl Barth has more to contribute to our theme than the stereotype (based solely on the *Church Dogmatics* 2/1, 17) of this thinking might suggest. It is his disciples who have spoken of 'Biblical realism' and 'Radical discontinuity'. There is an intriguing paper by Arvind Nirmal, the Indian theologian, 'Some Theological Issues connected with Inter Faith Dialogue and the Implication for Theological Education in India' in the *Bangalore Theological Forum*, Vol. XII, No. 2, 1980, which takes up Barthian themes in interreligious relationships.

30 It is not, I think, a problem at all if Brian Hebblethwaite's position is adopted: 'the prime task of theology is that of understanding. What makes a man or a woman a theologian is first and foremost a desire to know the truth about his or her religion or that of other people. To that end the theologian has to set aside both pietistic and apologetic motives. He is not primarily concerned, qua theologian, to deepen faith or to defend a gospel'. *The Problem of Theology*, Cambridge, 1980, pp. 20–21.

31 *Towards a World Theology*, p. 74. Compare this with the fascinating formulation which occurs on page 101 of the same book: 'Several years ago I had occasion to characterize the study of comparative religion as moving from the talk of an 'it' to talk of a 'they'; which became a 'we' talking of a 'they', and presently a 'we' talking of 'you'; and finally – the goal – a 'we all' talking together about 'us'. Smith is referring to a paper 'Comparative Religion: Whither and Why?' in *The History of Religions: Essays in Methodology*, ed. Mircea Eliade and Joseph M. Kitagawa, Chicago, 1959, pp. 31–58.

32 *The Self as Agent*, London, 1957, re-issued 1969, p 15.

33 *The Contradiction of Christianity*, London, 1976, p. 15.

34 *Church Dogmatics*, Edinburgh, 1962, Vol. IV, part 3, p. 773. Note the comment of a contemporary German missiologist: 'Anderseits wirkte sich die kerugmatische Antithese gegen alles Religiose in dieser theologischen Epoche als ein bis heute spurbares Handicap fur die missionarische Begegnung mit den anderen Religionen aus.' Horst Burkle *Missionstheologie*, Stuttgart, 1978, p. 19.

35 P. 773.

36 'Mission and Humanization', in the *International Review of Mission*, Vol. LX No. 237, Jan., 1971, p. 21.

37 As, e.g., discussed by David F Wells, *The Search for Salvation*, Leicester, 1978, pp. 34 ff.

38 The sensitivity to issues like this in WCC circles is indicated by the title of a book by the Librarian of the Ecumenical Centre in Geneva: *The Utopia of a World Community*, A J van der Bent, Geneva, 1974.

39 'Our purpose in dialogue should not be to eliminate differences, but to appreciate each other's faith, and co-operate with one another in overcoming violence, war, injustice and irreligion in the world . . . There are many devils to be cast out. World religions should come together to vanquish them, before they destroy human community completely.' K L Sheshagiri Rao speaking at a conference in the USA in 1976, see *Christian Faith in a Religiously Plural World*, p. 58.

40 Cf. Klaus Klostermaier: 'By dialogue I do not mean . . . the exchange of views between theologians of different religions. Interesting and necessary as it is, it is not "dialogue" but "comparative religion". The real dialogue is an ultimate personal depth – it need not even be a talking

about religious or theological topics. Real dialogues . . . challenge both partners, making them aware of the presence of God, calling them to a metanoia from an unknown depth.' Art., 'Dialogue – the words of God', in *Inter-Religious Dialogue*, ed. Herbert Jai Singh, Bangalore, 1967. Quoted in D K Swearer *Dialogue – The Key to Understanding Other Religions*, p. 35.

41 See the comments of the BCC *Guidelines*, p. 6.

42 Cf. Hendrik Kraemer on the aims of interreligious relationships: 'There may be two aims: a pragmatic or a fundamental one. The pragmatic has to aim first and foremost at removing mutual misunderstandings and serving common human responsibilities. This may lead to a deeper exchange of witness and experience, but, if so, it is a by-product. The fundamental aim directly involves this open exchange of witness, experience, cross-questioning and listening. The seriousness of true religion demands that one shall be one's true religious self . . . ' *World Cultures and World Religions*, p. 356. Panikkar and Kraemer would agree that one 'preconceived solution' would be that all religions say fundamentally the same thing.

43 *Courage for Dialogue*, p. 9.

44 In *Jesus Through Other Eyes: Christology in Multi-Faith Context*, Oxford, 1981, p. 30.

45 In 'Negations: an article on dialogue among religions' in *Religion and Society*, Bangalore, XX (4), p. 74.

46 *The Open Secret*, London, 1979. Newbigin adds: 'The Christian will go into dialogue believing that the power of the Spirit can use the occasion for the radical conversion of his partner as well as of himself.'

47 Pp. 12 and 7.

48 *Courage for Dialogue*, p. 43.

49 It is often easier for Christians of the so-called Third World to express themselves clearly about that. I remember a conversation about this with Dr Lamin Sanneh, now of Harvard, in which he gave thanks that he was not handicapped by guilt for Western imperialism in his dialogue with Muslims.

50 The *Pirke Aboth* (Ethics of the Fathers) 2.12, slightly modified. The original reads 'and drawing them nearer the Torah.'

Chapter 13   The Multi-Faith Dimensions of Sanctuary in the United Kingdom

Some of the general background material on sanctuary in this essay draws upon a paper by the author: 'Sanctuary as Concealment and Exposure: The Practice of Sanctuary in Britain as Part of the Struggle for Refugee Rights', presented at the Symposium on *The Refugee Crisis: British and Canadian Responses*, held at Keble College and Rhodes House, Oxford, on 4–7 January 1989, under the sponsorship of the Refugee Studies Programme, Oxford University.

1 *The Observer*, 'Revealed: Safe House Network for Refugees', 8.1.89.

2 For background to the Refugee Forum see *The Migrants and Refugees European Manifesto 1989*, available from the Refugee Forum, 54 Tavistock Place, London WC1.

3 See *The Guardian*, 'Mendis Seized in Church', 19.1.89; *The Independent*, 'The Police Came With Hammers at Dawn', 19.1.89.

4 See *Report of the Findings of the Independent Inquiry into Whether Viraj Mendis has a Well-Founded Fear of Persecution in the Event of his Removal to Sri Lanka*, Viraj Mendis Independent Inquiry, 1988; *Viraj Mendis – Life or Death: The Evidence Supporting a Full Review of the Case*, Viraj Mendis Defence Campaign, 1988.

5 E.g. *The Independent*, 'Mendis Arrest Sparks Furious Political Row', 19.1.89; *The Guardian*, 'A Case and a Symbol', 19.1.89.

6 Joshua chapter 20 v. 1–6 & v. 9.

7 M Siebold, 'Sanctuary', in *Encyclopaedia of the Social Sciences*, 1934, p. 534.

8 Ibid., p. 536.

9 L Grant and I Martin, *Immigration Law and Practice*, The Cobden Trust, London, 1982.

10 For background see R Golden and M McConnell, *Sanctuary: The New Underground Railroad*, New York, 1986: G MacEoin, *Sanctuary: A Resource Guide for Understanding and Participating in the Central American Refugees' Struggle*, New York, 1985.

11 For details see Hanneke Garver's report in D Mattijsen, *Sanctuary: the Congregation as Refuge*, Kerk in Wereld Centrum, Driebergen, the Netherlands, 1986, p. 6.

12 For details see Inge Tranholm-Mikkelson's report in ibid., p. 6.

13 'Sanctuary in Sweden', in *Searchlight*, November 1987, p. 18.

14 M McConnell, 'The Swiss Sanctuary Movement', in *Refugees*, September 1986, pp. 22–26.

15 See D Mattijsen and H Glimmerveen, *Asylum and Sanctuary: A Bird's Eye View of the Situation in the Netherlands*, Kerk en Wereld Centrum, de Hoorst 1, Postbus 19, 3970AA Driebergen-Rijsenburg, the Netherlands, 1986.

16 A leaflet about the Charter and the International Network of Local Initiatives on Asylum can be obtained from INLIA Foundation, Guldenstraat 20 (4th Floor), P.O. Box 2513, 9704 CM Groningen, the Netherlands.

17 Groningen Charter leaflet.

18 Ibid.

19 P Weller, *Sanctuary – The Beginning of a Movement?*, The Runnymede Trust, London, 1987.

20 See ibid., p. 10.

21 See P Weller 'Sanctuary Fast: Local Baptist Church Fights Deportation Order', in *Grassroots*, March–April, 1984, pp. 26–27.

22 For the whole story of the campaign see P Weller, *Legalised Abduction: The Struggle of Vinod Chauhan*, Vinod Chauhan Defence Campaign, 1984.

23 The background to the Nicola sanctuary can be found in *The Refugee Challenge: A Rejection of the Home Affairs Committee Report on Refugees and Asylum Seekers*, Refugee Forum, 1985.

24 *Viraj Mendis Must Stay*, Larkin Publications, London, 1986; *Viraj Mendis – Life or Death*, Larkin Publications, London, 1988.

25 *Birmingham Post*, 'Family in Sanctuary Attempt at Mosque', 4.1.89.

26 For an overview of the case see S Conlan, 'Guilty Until Proven Innocent', in *Racial Justice*, Spring 1989.

27 Rt Hon Douglas Hurd, CBE, MP, 'Race Relations and the Rule of Law', Home Office News Release, 24.2.89.
28 Quoted in P Weller, 'Muslims, Deportation and Sanctuary', in *Islam in Europe*.
29 Quoted in ibid., p. 4–5.
30 See 'Renoukaben's Sanctuary in Leicester', in op. cit., *Sanctuary: Manchester Perspectives*, p. 33.
31 Quoted in op. cit., *Why Sanctuary?*, pp. 30–31.
32 See 'Rajwinder in Sanctuary', op. cit., *Sanctuary: Manchester Perspectives*, p. 34.
33 In op. cit., *Why Sanctuary?*, pp. 31–32.
34 Rabbi D Saperstein, (ed.), *Providing Sanctuary, the Jewish Role: A Practical Guide for Congregations and Individuals*, Union of American Hebrew Congregations, 838 Fifth Avenue, New York, NY 10021.
35 S Cohen, 'A Place of Safety', in *The Jewish Socialist*, Autumn 1988, p. 14.
36 See op. cit., *Why Sanctuary?*, pp. 2–12 for the cases of the Adedimeji family, Dora Oppong, the Donkoh family, the 'X' family, the Oziki family, and others already referred to in this essay.
37 D Haslam and K Phillips, *Rainbow Gospel: Report of a Churches' Conference on Challenging Racism in Britain*, The British Council of Churches, London, 1988, p. 47.
38 *Towards a Statement of the Rights of Migrants and Settlers*, report of a Working Group of the Catholic Bishops' Conference of England and Wales, 1988.
39 Community and Race Relations Unit, *Issues Paper No. 3, A Statement on Sanctuary*.
40 In op. cit., *Why Sanctuary?*, pp. 33–36.
41 P Weller and R Patel, (eds.) *Why Sanctuary?* pack, £4.50 per copy including p & p, from CRRU, British Council of Churches, Inter Church House, 35–41 Lower Marsh, London, SE1 7RL.
42 Ibid., pp. 34–35.
43 Ibid., p. 36.
44 See C Stastny's discussion of a translated manuscript of the last chapter H Bianchi's *Justice and Culture*, on 'Asylum and Sanctuary', in 'The Roots of Sanctuary', in *Refugee Issues*, Vol. II, August 1985, pp. 28–29.
45 Draft of the East London Sanctuary Group Newsletter No. 2 (unpublished).
46 C Disbrey, 'Sanctuary: God's Safe House', in *Third Way*, February 1988, p. 12.
47 *The Times*, 'Sinhalese Refugee and Sanctuary', 13.5.88.
48 In op. cit., *Why Sanctuary?*, pp. 22–24.
49 World Council of Churches, *Guidelines on Dialogue*, Geneva.
50 S Cherry, 'Myth, Symbol and Sacrament: The Viraj Mendis Story', in *Christian*, January–February 1989.
51 Ibid., p. 8.
52 J Watkins, 'Foreword' in *Sanctuary: Manchester Perspectives*, p. 4.
53 'Sanctuary . . . at the Heart of Christianity', in *Racial Justice*, Winter 1987–88, p. 9.
54 See 'Europe 1992', a special issue of *Refugees*, World Council of Churches, Geneva, Switzerland, March 1989.

Chapter 14   Jewish Faith and the Holocaust

1 E Wiesel, *Nights*, Bantam Books, 1982. As quoted by R Rubenstein and J Roth *Approaches to Auschwitz*, London, 1987, p. 283.
2 Ibid., p. 285.
3 E Wiesel, *The Trial of God*, New York, 1979, p. 129.
4 Ibid., p. 133.
5 R Rubenstein and J Roth, *op.cit.*, p. 287.
6 E Wiesel, *A Jew Today*, New York, 1978, p. 136.
7 Ibid., p. 164.
8 R Rubenstein, *After Auschwitz*, Bobbs Merrill, 1966, p. 153.
9 R Rubenstein and J Roth, *Approaches to Auschwitz*, London, 1987.
10 R Rubenstein *After Auschwitz* as quoted by R Rubenstein and J Roth *op.cit.*, pp. 312–313.
11 Ibid., p. 315.
12 A Cohen, *Tremendum*, Crossroad Publishing Company, 1981. As quoted by R Rubenstein and J Roth, *op.cit.*, p. 330.
13 Ibid., p. 331.
14 Ibid., p. 332.
15 Ibid., p. 333.
16 E Berkovits, *Faith After the Holocaust*, Ktav Publishing House Inc., 1973, pp. 5–6.
17 Ibid., p. 70.
18 I Maybaum, *The Face of God After the Auschwitz*, Polak and Van Gennep, 1965, p. 36.
19 Ibid., p. 84.
20 E Fackenheim, *Judaism 16*, Summer, 1967 pp. 272–273.
21 E Fackenheim, *To Mend the World*, Schoken Books, 1982.
22 Ibid., 250.

Chapter 15   New Religious Movements

1 C Geertz, *Islam Observed*, Chicago/London, 1968, pp. 111–113.
2 For an overview see, for example, E Barker (ed.) *New Religious Movements: A Perspective for Understanding Society*, New York and Toronto 1982, and B R Wilson (ed.) *The Social Impact of New Religions*, New York, 1981.
3 This estimate was attributed to Professor M T Singer by G Collins in *The New York Times STYLE*, 15.3.82.
4 J D Hunter, Subjectivisation and Evangelicalism in *Journal for the Scientific Study of Religions* (henceforth JSSR), Vol. 21, No. 1, March 1982, p. 39.
5 N Ben-Yehuda, 'A Quest for the Beyond: The Revival of the Occult, Science Fiction and Modern Myths: Towards an Explanatory Scheme.' (Unpublished paper in the author's possession.)
6 R Stark and W S Bainbridge, 'Secularization and Cult Formation in the Jazz Age', in *JSSR*, Vol. 20, No. 4, 1981, pp. 360–373.
7 Ibid., p. 371.
8 F Bird and R Reimer, 'Participation Rates in New Religious and Para-Religious Movements' in *JSSR*, Vol. 21, No. 1, 1982, pp. 1–14.
9 Ibid., pp. 4ff.

10 B R Wilson, 'The Return of the Sacred' in *JSSR*, Vol. 18, No. 3, 1979, pp. 268–280.
11 F R Lynch, '"Occult Establishment" or "Deviant Religion"? The Rise and Fall of a Modern Church of Magic' in *JSSR*, Vol. 18, No. 3, 1979, pp. 281–298.
12 Ben-Yehuda, p. 38.
13 This religion was created by secondary school students in Aarhus in October 1982.
14 *Pipes of Pan*, No. 10, Imbolc 1983, p. 1.
15 Ibid.
16 *The Cauldron*, No. 26, Beltane 1982.
17 Ibid.
18 Data from a written communication from R Buckland DD, Seax-Wica Seminary, Charlottesville, 9.2.83.
19 E A Tiryakian, 'Toward the Sociology of Esoteric Culture' in *American Journal of Sociology*, 78, 1972, pp. 391–412. See also P Hartman 'Social Dimensions of Occult Participation' in *British Journal of Sociology*, 27, 1970, pp. 169–183.
20 M Marty, 'The Occult Establishment', *Social Research*, 37, 1970, pp. 212–230. See also Lynch, op.cit.
21 Hartman, op.cit.
22 Ibid and Tiryakian op.cit.
23 Ibid.
24 G Ahern, 'Five Karmas, or Anthroposophy in Great Britain', in *Update*, Vol. 6, No. 4, Dec. 1982, pp. 68–78.
25 Ibid., p. 75.
26 Ibid., p. 73.
27 Ibid., p. 69.
28 Ibid., p. 76.
29 Data from *Movements Religieux*, No. 33, January 1983, p. 5.
30 Ibid.
31 Data from interviews Aarhus, Dec. 1982.
32 Ibid.
33 Interviews, March 1983.
34 Statement by National Council of Hindu Temples (UK) 14.3.83 pl.
35 Interview material – Sahaja Yoga – March 1983.
36 Ibid.
37 Ibid.
38 Ibid.
39 *Sahaja Yoga, Book One*, by Her Holiness Mataji Shri Nirmala Devi, Delhi, 1982.
40 Interview material SES – March 1983.
41 Interview material – Scientology – March 1983.
42 Interview material – the Divine Light Mission – February 1983.
43 Interview material – Scientology, op.cit.
44 Interview material – Divine Light Mission, op.cit.
45 Ibid.
46 J V Downton, Jr 'Spiritual Conversions and Commitment: The Case of the Divine Light Mission', *JSSR*, Vol. 14, No. 4, 1980.
47 For examples see E Barker (ed.), op.cit.; Bird and Reimer, op.cit. and R Wallis, *The Road to Total Freedom*, London, 1976.
48 Interview material – Aarhus, December 1982.

49 Interview material – Divine Light Mission – op.cit.
50 Interview material – School of Economic Science – op.cit.
51 Interview material from 20 different movements in Britain collected between April 1982–March 1983.
52 Interview material – Sahaja Yoga – op.cit.
53 Interview material – Divine Light Mission – op.cit.
54 Interview material – Sahaja Yoga – op.cit.
55 Ibid.
56 V A Benassi, B Singer and C B Reynolds 'Occult Belief: Seeing is Believing', *JSSR*, Vol. 19, No. 4, pp. 337–349.
57 Interview material – Sahaja Yoga – op.cit.
58 Ibid.
59 Interview material – Divine Light Mission – op.cit.
60 Ibid.
61 *Introductory Publication of the Aladura International Church, United Kingdom and Overseas* by Olu Abiola, General Superintendent (n.d.) pl.
62 Ibid.
63 Interview material – Hare Krishna – March 1983.
64 This point was made from interviews by members and ex-members of Scientology, Divine Light Mission, and other movements.
65 For example see Notes, B R Wilson, *Contemporary Transformations of Religion*, OUP/London 1976, pp. 104.
66 A Inkeles, Making Men Modern, *American Journal of Sociology*, 75, 2, 1969, p. 213.
67 Wilson, *Contemporary Transformations of Religion*, op.cit., p. 96.
68 R Stark and W S Bainbridge, op.cit., and 'Towards a Theory of Religion: Religious Commitment', *Journal for the Scientific Study of Religion*, 19.2.80, pp. 114–128. And R Stark, 'Must all Religions be Supernatural?', in B R Wilson (ed.) *The Social Impact of New Religious Movements*, New York, 1981.
69 C Campbell, The Secret Religion of the Educated Classes, *Sociological Analysis*, 39, 2, pp. 146–156.
70 D Hay and A Morisey, 'Reports of Ecstatic, Paranormal or Religious Experience in Great Britain and the United States: A Comparison of Current Trends', *Journal for the Scientific Study of Religion*, Vol. 17, 3, 1978, pp. 255–268.

Chapter 16 Kingdoms of Heaven on Earth:
New Religious Movements and Political Orders

1 I would like to thank the Nuffield Foundation of Great Britain for a grant to help with the research from which this essay is drawn. The more general analysis is to be found in Eileen Barker, *Armageddon and Aquarius: New Religions in Contemporary Christendom*, Manchester University Press, 1988.
2 Roy Wallis, *The Elementary Forms of the New Religious Life*, London: Routledge & Kegan Paul, 1984: 34.
3 Ibid., p. 24.
4 Ibid., p. 24.
5 Frances Westley, *The Complex Forms of the Religious Life*, Chico, Ca: Scholars Press, 1983.

6 Wallis, op.cit., p. 9.
7 Angela Burr, *I Am Not My Body: A Study of the International Hare Krishna Sect*, New Delhi: Vikas, 1984.
8 *Divine Principle*, Washington DC: Holy Spirit Association for the Unification of World Christianity, 1973.
9 John Ross Schroeder, 'Why Doesn't God Do Something?' *The Plain Truth*, June 1986, p. 8.
10 Daisaku Ikeda, *Lectures on Buddhism*, 2 Vols.s, Tokyo: Seikyo Press, 1962: 279, quoted in Daniel A Metraux, 'The Soka Gakkai's Search for the Realization of the World of *Rissho Ankokuron'*, *Japanese Journal of Religious Studies*, 1986 13/1: 38–9.
11 *A New Ideology for a New Era*, PROUT leaflet, p. 2.
12 Ibid.,
13 Ibid., p. 4.
14 Vieda Skultans, 'The Brahma Kumaris and the Role of Women', p. 3 mimeographed paper, n.d. See also *Brahma – The Father of Humanity*, a booklet produced by the Brahma Kumaris, n.d.
15 PROUT op.cit., p. 3.
16 *UK Express: An Introduction to Nichiren Shoshu Buddhism*, NSUK, 1982, p. 11.
17 T M Luhrmann, 'Witchcraft, Morality and Magic in Contemporary London', *International Journal of Moral and Social Studies*, Vol. 1, No. 1, Spring 1986, p. 84.
18 *The London Standard*, 12 May 1986.
19 See John Lofland, *Doomsday Cult: A Study of Conversion, Proselytization, and Maintainance of Faith*, New York: Irvington, Enlarged edition 1977.
20 See Eileen Barker, *The Making of a Moonie: Brainwashing or Choice?*, Oxford, 1984.
21 For an elaboration of this point see Eileen Barker, 'Defection from the Unification Church: Rates of Membership, Turnover and their Consequences' in David G Bromley (ed.) *Falling from the Faith: The Causes, Course and Consequences of Religious Disaffiliation*, Beverley Hills, Ca. & London: 1988 in press.
22 Not that 'old religions' may not be involved in attempts to establish new political orders, Liberation theology and the Jihad pointing to but two obvious examples.

Contributors

Dr Robert Runcie is the Archbishop of Canterbury.

Professor Colin Seymour-Ure is Professor of Government at the University of Kent at Canterbury.

Dr Kenneth Wolfe is Senior Leverhulme Research Fellow at the Centre for the Study of Religion and Society at the University of Kent at Canterbury.

The Rev Professor David Martin was formerly Professor of Sociology at the London School of Economics.

Dr Digby Anderson is Director of the Social Affairs Unit.

The Rev Robert Van de Weyer lectures in Economics in Cambridge and is leader of the Little Gidding community.

Professor Krishan Kumar is Professor of Sociology at the University of Kent at Canterbury.

Professor David McLellan is Professor of Political Theory at the University of Kent at Canterbury.

Sir John Lawrence Bt has written numerous books on Christianity and is an expert on Christianity in communist countries.

Dr David Ormrod is a Lecturer in Economic History at the University of Kent at Canterbury.

The Rev Dr Paul Badham is Reader in Theology and Religious Studies and Chairman of Religion and Ethics at St David's University College, University of Wales.

The Rev Kenneth Cracknell is Senior Tutor at Wesley House, Cambridge.

Mr Paul Weller is a Senior Lecturer and Head of the Religious Resource and Research Centre of the Derbyshire College of Higher Education.

Rabbi Dr Dan Cohn-Sherbok lectures in Theology at the University of Kent at Canterbury.

Dr Peter Clarke is Research Fellow, Centre for the Study of New Religious Movements, Kings College, London.

Dr Eileen Barker is Senior Lecturer in Sociology at the London School of Economics.

Dr Bryan Wilson is Reader in Sociology at the University of Oxford and a Fellow of All Souls.